Rick Steves'
Spanish
Phrase Book & Dictionary
First Edition

D0595893

**AVALON
TRAVEL**

Avalon Travel Publishing, 1400 65th Street, Suite 250, Emeryville, CA 94608, USA

Avalon Travel Publishing is a division of Avalon Publishing Group, Inc.

Printed in the United States of America by Worzalla.
First edition. Second printing March 2004.

ISBN 1-56691-524-4

Europe Through the Back Door Managing Editor:
  Risa Laib
Europe Through the Back Door Editors:
  Cameron Hewitt, Jill Hodges
Avalon Travel Publishing Editor: Matt Orendorff
Translation: Gloria Villaraviz Weeden, Inma Raneda
Phonetics: Risa Laib, Cameron Hewitt
Production & Typesetting: Matt Orendorff
Cover Design: Kari Gim
Maps & Graphics: David C. Hoerlein, Zoey Platt
Photography: Rick Steves, Dominic Bonuccelli
Front cover photos:
  foreground– © Getty Images, Inc.
  background–Palacia de Communicaciones, Madrid;
  © Krzysztof Dydynski

Distributed to the book trade by Publishers Group West, Berkeley, California

Other ATP travel guidebooks by Rick Steves

Rick Steves' Best of Europe
Rick Steves' Europe 101: History and Art for the Traveler
  (with Gene Openshaw)
Rick Steves' Europe Through the Back Door
Rick Steves' Mona Winks (with Gene Openshaw)
Rick Steves' Postcards from Europe
Rick Steves' France (with Steve Smith)
Rick Steves' Germany, Austria & Switzerland
Rick Steves' Great Britain
Rick Steves' Ireland (with Pat O'Connor)
Rick Steves' Italy
Rick Steves' Scandinavia
Rick Steves' Spain & Portugal
Rick Steves' Amsterdam, Bruges & Brussels
  (with Gene Openshaw)
Rick Steves' Florence (with Gene Openshaw)
Rick Steves' London (with Gene Openshaw)
Rick Steves' Paris (with Steve Smith and Gene Openshaw)
Rick Steves' Rome (with Gene Openshaw)
Rick Steves' Venice (with Gene Openshaw)
Rick Steves' Phrase Books: French, German, Italian,
Portuguese, and French/Italian/German

For the latest on Rick's lectures, guidebooks, tours, and public
television series, contact Europe Through the Back Door, Box
2009, Edmonds, WA 98020, tel. 425/771-8303, fax 425/771-
0833, www.ricksteves.com, or e-mail: rick@ricksteves.com.

CONTENTS

TABLE OF CONTENTS

TABLE OF CONTENTS

Illustrations

Maps

Hi, I'm Rick Steves.

I'm the only monolingual speaker I know who's had the nerve to design a series of European phrase books. But that's one of the things that makes them better.

You see, after 25 summers of travel through Europe, I've learned first-hand: (1) what's essential for communication in another country, and (2) what's not. I've assembled the most important words and phrases in a logical, no-frills format, and I've worked with native Europeans and seasoned travelers to give you the simplest, clearest translations possible.

But this book is more than just a pocket translator. The words and phrases have been carefully selected to help you have a smarter, smoother trip in Spain without going broke. Spain used to be cheap and chaotic. These days it's neither. It's better organized than ever—and often as expensive as France or Germany. The key to getting more out of every travel dollar is to get closer to the local people, and to rely less on entertainment, restaurants, and hotels that cater only to foreign tourists. This book will not only help you order a meal at a locals-only Sevilla restaurant—it will help you talk with the family who runs the place . . . about their kids, social issues, travel dreams, and favorite *música*. Long after your memories of museums have faded, you'll still treasure the personal encounters you had with your new Iberian friends.

A good phrase book should help you enjoy your Iberian experience—not just survive it—so I've added a healthy dose of humor. A few phrases are just for fun and aren't meant to be used at all. Most of the phrases are for real and should be used with "please" *(por favor)*. I know you can tell the difference.

To get the most out of this book, take the time to internalize and put into practice my Spanish pronunciation tips. Don't worry too much about memorizing grammatical rules, like the gender of a noun—the important thing is to communicate!

This book has a handy dictionary and a nifty menu decoder. You'll also find tongue twisters, international words, telephone tips, and a handy tear-out "cheat sheet." Tear it out and keep it in your pocket, so you can easily memorize key phrases during otherwise idle moments. As you prepare for your trip, you may want to read this year's edition of my *Rick Steves' Spain & Portugal* guidebook.

The Spanish speak less English than their European neighbors. But while the language barrier may seem a little higher, the locals are happy to give an extra boost to any traveler who makes an effort to communicate.

My goal is to help you become a more confident, extroverted traveler. If this phrase book helps make that happen, or if you have suggestions for making it better, I'd love to hear from you. I personally read and value all feedback. My address is Europe Through the Back Door, P.O. Box 2009, Edmonds, WA 98020, tel. 425/771-8303, fax 425/771-0833, e-mail: rick@ricksteves.com.

Happy travels,

GETTING
STARTED

Spanish opens the door to the land of siestas and fiestas, fun and flamenco. Imported from the Old World throughout the New, Spanish is the most widely spoken Romance language in the world. With its straightforward pronunciation, Spanish is also one of the simplest languages to learn.

Here are some tips for pronouncing Spanish words:

C usually sounds like C in cat.
>But C followed by E or I sounds like TH in think.

D sounds like the soft D in soda.
G usually sounds like G in go.
>But G followed by E or I sounds like the guttural
>J in Baja.

H is silent.
J sounds like the guttural J in Baja.
LL sounds like Y in yes.
Ñ sounds like NI in onion.
R is trrrilled.
V sounds like B in bit.
Z sounds like TH in think.

1

Spanish vowels:

A sounds like A in father.
E can sound like E in get or AY in play.
I sounds like EE in seed.
O sounds like O in note.
U sounds like OO in moon.

Spanish has a few unusual signs and sounds. The Spanish add extra punctuation to questions and exclamations, like this: *¿Cómo está?* (How are you?) *¡Fantástico!* (Fantastic!) You've probably seen and heard the Spanish *ñ*: think of *señor* and *mañana*. Spanish has a guttural sound similar to the J in Baja California. In the phonetics, the symbol for this clearing-your-throat sound is the italicized *h*.

Spanish words that end in a consonant are stressed on the last syllable, as in *Madrid*. Words ending in a vowel are generally stressed on the second-to-last syllable, as in *amigo*. To override these rules, the Spanish sometimes add an accent mark to the syllable that should be stressed, like this: *rápido* (fast) is pronounced **rah**-pee-doh.

When you're speaking a Romance language, sex is unavoidable. Even the words are masculine or feminine, and word endings can change depending on gender. A man is *simpático* (friendly), a woman is *simpática*. In this book, we show gender-bender words like this: *simpático[a]*. If you're speaking of a woman (which includes women speaking about themselves), use the *a* ending. It's always pronounced "ah." Words ending in *r*, such as *doctor*, will appear like this: *doctor[a]*. A *doctora* is a female doctor. Words ending in *e*, such as *amable* (kind), apply to either sex.

The endings of Spanish nouns and adjectives agree. Cold weather is *tiempo frío*, and a cold shower is a *ducha fría*.

Plurals are a snap. Add *s* to a word that ends in a vowel, like *pueblo* (village) and *es* to a word that ends in a consonant, like *ciudad* (city). Visit a mix of *pueblos* and *ciudades* to get the full flavor of Spain.

In northern and central Spain, Spanish sounds as if it's spoken with a lisp. *Gracias* (thank you) sounds like **grah**-thee-ahs. As you head farther south, you'll notice a difference in pronunciation. In southern Spain, along the coast, people thpeak without the lisp: *Gracias* sounds like **grah**-see-ahs. Listen to and imitate the Spanish people around you.

You'll often hear the Spanish say, *"Por favor"* (Please). The Spanish are friendly, polite people. Use *por favor* whenever you can.

¡Buen viaje! Have a good trip!

Here's a quick guide to the phonetics used in this book:

ah	like A in father.
ay	like AY in play.
ee	like EE in seed.
eh	like E in get.
ehr	sounds like "air."
g	like G in go.
h	like the guttural J in Baja.
ī	like I in light.
oh	like O in note.
or	like OR in core.
oo	like OO in moon.
ow	like OW in now.
oy	like OY in toy.
s	like S in sun.

SPANISH
BASICS

Meeting and Greeting

Hello.	Hola.	**oh**-lah
Good morning.	Buenos días.	**bway**-nohs **dee**-ahs
Good afternoon.	Buenas tardes.	**bway**-nahs **tar**-days
Good evening.	Buenas tardes.	**bway**-nahs **tar**-days
Good night.	Buenas noches.	**bway**-nahs **noh**-chays
Hi. (informal)	¿Qué tal?	kay tahl
Welcome!	¡Bienvenido!	bee-yehn-vay-**nee**-doh
Mr.	Señor	sayn-**yor**
Mrs.	Señora	sayn-**yoh**-rah
Miss	Señorita	sayn-yoh-**ree**-tah
How are you?	¿Cómo está?	**koh**-moh ay-**stah**
Very well,	Muy bien,	**moo**-ee bee-**yehn**
thank you.	gracias.	**grah**-thee-ahs
And you?	¿Y usted?	ee oo-**stehd**
My name is ___.	Me llamo ___.	may **yah**-moh
What's your name?	¿Cómo se llama?	**koh**-moh say **yah**-mah
Pleased to	Mucho gusto.	**moo**-choh **goo**-stoh
meet you.		
Where are	¿De dónde es	day **dohn**-day ays
you from?	usted?	oo-**stehd**
I am / We are /	Estoy / Estamos /	ay-**stoy** / ay-**stah**-mohs /
Are you...?	Está usted...?	ay-**stah** oo-**stehd**

4

...on vacation	*...de vacaciones*	day vah-kah-thee-**oh**-nays
...on business	*...de negocios*	day nay-**goh**-thee-ohs
See you later.	*Hasta luego.*	**ah**-stah loo-**ay**-goh
Goodbye.	*Adiós.*	ah-dee-**ohs**
Good luck!	*¡Buena suerte!*	**bway**-nah **swehr**-tay
Have a good trip!	*¡Buen viaje!*	bwayn bee-**ah**-hay

You'll hear people say *"Buenas tardes"* (Good afternoon/evening) starting about 2:00 p.m. You won't hear *"Buenas noches"* (Good night) until around 10 p.m.

Essentials

Hello.	*Hola.*	**oh**-lah
Do you speak English?	*¿Habla usted inglés?*	**ah**-blah oo-**stehd** een-**glays**
Yes. / No.	*Sí. / No.*	see / noh
I don't speak Spanish.	*No hablo español.*	noh **ah**-bloh ay-spahn-**yohl**
I'm sorry.	*Lo siento.*	loh see-**ehn**-toh
Please.	*Por favor.*	por fah-**bor**
Thank you.	*Gracias.*	**grah**-thee-ahs
It's (not) a problem.	*(No) hay problema.*	(noh) ī proh-**blay**-mah
Good. / Very good. / Excellent.	*Bien. / Muy bien. Excelente.*	bee-**yehn** / **moo**-ee bee-**yehn** ayk-seh-**lehn**-tay
You are very kind.	*Usted es muy amable.*	oo-**stehd** ays **moo**-ee ah-**mah**-blay
Excuse me. (to pass)	*Discúlpeme.*	dee-**skool**-pay-may
Excuse me. (to get attention)	*Perdone.*	pehr-**doh**-nay
It doesn't matter.	*No importa.*	noh eem-**por**-tah
You're welcome.	*De nada.*	day **nah**-dah
Sure.	*Por supuesto.*	por soo-**pway**-stoh
O.K.	*De acuerdo.*	day ah-**kwehr**-doh
Let's go.	*¡Vamos!*	**bah**-mohs
Goodbye.	*Adiós.*	ah-dee-**ohs**

Where?

Where is the...?	¿Dónde está la...?	**dohn**-day ay-**stah** lah
...tourist information office	...Oficina de Turismo	oh-fee-**thee**-nah day too-**rees**-moh
...train station	...estación de trenes	ay-stah-thee-**ohn** day **tray**-nays
...bus station	...estación de autobuses	ay-stah-thee-**ohn** day **ow**-toh-boo-says
Where is a cash machine?	¿Dónde hay un cajero automático?	**dohn**-day ī oon kah-**hehr**-oh ow-toh-**mah**-tee-koh
Where are the toilets?	¿Dónde están los servicios?	**dohn**-day ay-**stahn** lohs sehr-**bee**-thee-ohs
men	hombres, caballeros	**ohm**-brays, kah-bah-**yay**-rohs
women	mujeres, damas	moo-**hehr**-ays, **dah**-mahs

Spanish makes it easy if you're looking for a *banco, farmacia, hotel, restaurante,* or *supermercado.*

How Much?

How much is it?	¿Cuánto cuesta?	**kwahn**-toh **kway**-stah
Write it?	¿Me lo escribe?	may loh ay-**skree**-bay
Is it free?	¿Es gratis?	ays **grah**-tees
Is it included?	¿Está incluido?	ay-**stah** een-kloo-**ee**-doh
Do you have...?	¿Tiene...?	tee-**ehn**-ay
Where can I buy...?	¿Dónde puedo comprar...?	**dohn**-day **pway**-doh kohm-**prar**
I / We would like...	Me / Nos gustaría...	may / nohs goo-stah-**ree**-ah
...this.	...esto.	**ay**-stoh
...just a little.	...un poquito.	oon poh-**kee**-toh
...more.	...más.	mahs
...a ticket.	...un billete.	oon bee-**yeh**-tay
...a room.	...una habitación.	**oo**-nah ah-bee-tah-thee-**ohn**
...the bill.	...la cuenta.	lah **kwayn**-tah

How Many?

one	*uno*	**oo**-noh
two	*dos*	dohs
three	*tres*	trehs
four	*cuatro*	**kwah**-troh
five	*cinco*	**theen**-koh
six	*seis*	says
seven	*siete*	see-**eh**-tay
eight	*ocho*	**oh**-choh
nine	*nueve*	**nway**-bay
ten	*diez*	dee-**ayth**

You'll find more to count on in the Counting section beginning on page 14.

When?

At what time?	*¿A qué hora?*	ah kay **oh**-rah
open / closed	*abierto / cerrado*	ah-bee-**yehr**-toh / thehr-**rah**-doh
Just a moment.	*Un momento.*	oon moh-**mehn**-toh
Now.	*Ahora.*	ah-**oh**-rah
Soon.	*Pronto.*	**prohn**-toh
Later.	*Más tarde.*	mahs **tar**-day
Today.	*Hoy.*	oy
Tomorrow.	*Mañana.*	mahn-**yah**-nah

Be creative! You can combine these phrases to say: "Two, please," or "No, thank you," or "Open tomorrow?" or "Please, where can I buy a ticket?" Please is a magic word in any language. If you want to buy something and you don't know the word for it, just point and say, *"Por favor"* (Please). If you know the word for what you want, such as the bill, simply say, *"La cuenta, por favor"* (The bill, please).

Struggling with Spanish

Do you speak English?	¿Habla usted inglés?	**ah**-blah oo-**stehd** een-**glays**
A teeny weeny bit?	¿Ni un poquito?	nee oon poh-**kee**-toh
Please speak English.	Hable en inglés, por favor.	**ah**-blay ayn een-**glays** por fah-**bor**
You speak English well.	Usted habla bien el inglés.	oo-**stehd** ah-blah bee-**yehn** ehl een-**glays**
I don't speak Spanish.	No hablo español.	noh **ah**-bloh ay-spahn-**yohl**
We don't speak Spanish.	No hablamos español.	noh ah-**blah**-mohs ay-spahn-**yohl**
I speak a little Spanish.	Hablo un poco de español.	**ah**-bloh oon **poh**-koh day ay-spahn-**yohl**
Sorry, I speak only English.	Lo siento, sólo hablo inglés.	loh see-**ehn**-toh **soh**-loh **ah**-bloh een-**glays**
Sorry, we speak only English.	Lo siento, sólo hablamos inglés.	loh see-**ehn**-toh **soh**-loh ah-**blah**-mohs een-**glays**
Does somebody nearby speak English?	¿Hay alguien por aquí que hable inglés?	ī **ahl**-gee-ehn por ah-**kee** kay **ah**-blay een-**glays**
Who speaks English?	¿Quién habla inglés?	kee-**ehn ah**-blah een-**glays**
What does this mean?	¿Qué significa esto?	kay sig-**nee**-fee-kah **ay**-stoh
What is this in Spanish / English?	¿Cómo se dice esto en español / inglés?	**koh**-moh say **dee**-thay **ay**-stoh ayn ay-spahn-**yohl** / een-**glays**
Repeat?	¿Repita?	ray-**pee**-tah
Please speak slowly.	Por favor hable despacio.	por fah-**bor** ah-blay day-**spah**-thee-oh
Slower.	Más despacio.	mahs day-**spah**-thee-oh
I understand.	Comprendo.	kohm-**prehn**-doh
I don't understand.	No comprendo.	noh kohm-**prehn**-doh
Do you understand?	¿Comprende?	kohm-**prehn**-day
Write it?	¿Me lo escribe?	may loh ay-**skree**-bay

Handy Questions

English	Spanish	Pronunciation
How much?	¿Cuánto?	**kwahn**-toh
How many?	¿Cuántos?	**kwahn**-tohs
How long...?	¿Cuánto tiempo...?	**kwahn**-toh tee-**ehm**-poh
...is the trip	...es el viaje	ays ehl bee-**ah**-hay
How many minutes / hours?	¿Cuántos minutos / horas?	**kwahn**-tohs mee-**noo**-tohs / **oh**-rahs
How far?	¿A qué distancia?	ah kay dees-**tahn**-thee-ah
How?	¿Cómo?	**koh**-moh
Can you help me?	¿Puede ayudarme?	**pway**-day ah-yoo-**dar**-may
Can you help us?	¿Puede ayudarnos?	**pway**-day ah-yoo-**dar**-nohs
Can I / Can we...?	¿Puedo / Podemos...?	**pway**-doh / poh-**day**-mohs
...have one	...tener uno	tay-**nehr oo**-noh
...go free	...ir gratis	eer **grah**-tees
...borrow that for a moment / an hour	...tomar prestado eso por un momento / una hora	toh-**mar** pray-**stah**-doh **ay**-soh por oon moh-**mehn**-toh / **oo**-nah **oh**-rah
...use the toilet	...usar el baño	**oo**-sar ehl **bahn**-yoh
What?	¿Qué?	kay
What? (didn't hear)	¿Cómo?	**koh**-moh
What is this / that?	¿Qué es esto / eso?	kay ays **ay**-stoh / **ay**-soh
What is better?	¿Qué es mejor?	kay ays may-**hor**
What's going on?	¿Qué pasa?	kay **pah**-sah
When?	¿Cuándo?	**kwahn**-doh
What time is it?	¿Qué hora es?	kay **oh**-rah ays
At what time?	¿A qué hora?	ah kay **oh**-rah
On time?	¿Puntual?	poon-too-**ahl**
Late?	¿Tarde?	**tar**-day
How long will it take?	¿Cuánto tiempo lleva?	**kwahn**-toh tee-**ehm**-poh **yay**-bah
What time does this open / close?	¿A qué hora abren / cierran?	ah kay **oh**-rah **ah**-brehn / thee-**ay**-rahn

Is this open daily?	¿Abren a diario?	**ah**-brehn ah dee-**ah**-ree-oh
What day is this closed?	¿Qué día está cerrado?	kay **dee**-ah ay-**stah** thay-**rah**-doh
Do you have...?	¿Tiene...?	tee-**ehn**-ay
Where is...?	¿Dónde está...?	**dohn**-day ay-**stah**
Where are...?	¿Dónde están...?	**dohn**-day ay-**stahn**
Where can I find...?	¿Dónde puedo encontrar...?	**dohn**-day **pway**-doh ayn-kohn-**trar**
Where can we find...?	¿Dónde podemos encontrar...?	**dohn**-day poh-**day**-mohs ayn-kohn-**trar**
Where can I buy...?	¿Dónde puedo comprar...?	**dohn**-day **pway**-doh kohm-**prar**
Where can we buy...?	¿Dónde podemos comprar...?	**dohn**-day poh-**day**-mohs kohm-**prar**
Is it necessary?	¿Es necesario?	ays nay-thay-**sah**-ree-oh
Is it possible...?	¿Es possible...?	ays poh-**see**-blay
...to enter	...entrar	ayn-**trar**
...to picnic here	...hacer un picnic aquí	ah-**thehr** oon peek-**neek** ah-**kee**
...to sit here	...sentarse aquí	sehn-**tar**-say ah-**kee**
...to look	...mirar	mee-**rar**
...to take a photo	...sacar una foto	sah-**kar** **oo**-nah **foh**-toh
...to see a room	...ver una habitación	behr **oo**-nah ah-bee-tah-thee-**ohn**
Who?	¿Quién?	kee-**ehn**
Why?	¿Por qué?	por kay
Why not?	¿Por qué no?	por kay noh
Yes or no?	¿Sí o no?	see oh noh

To prompt a simple answer, ask, *"¿Sí o no?"* (Yes or no?). To turn a word or sentence into a question, ask it in a questioning tone. A simple way to ask, "Where are the toilets?" is to say, *"¿Servicios?"*

El Yin y Yang

English	Spanish	Pronunciation
cheap / expensive	*barato / caro*	bah-**rah**-toh / **kah**-roh
big / small	*grande / pequeño*	**grahn**-day / pay-**kayn**-yoh
hot / cold	*caliente / frío*	kahl-**yehn**-tay / **free**-oh
cool / warm	*fresco / cálido*	**fray**-skoh / **kah**-lee-doh
open / closed	*abierto / cerrado*	ah-bee-**yehr**-toh / thehr-**rah**-doh
push / pull	*empuje / tire*	aym-**poo**-hay / **tee**-ray
entrance / exit	*entrada / salida*	ayn-**trah**-dah / sah-**lee** dah
arrive / depart	*llegar / salir*	yay-**gar** / sah-**leer**
early / late	*temprano / tarde*	tehm-**prah**-noh / **tar**-day
soon / later	*pronto / más tarde*	**prohn**-toh / mahs **tar**-day
fast / slow	*rápido / despacio*	**rah**-pee-doh / day-**spah**-thee-oh
here / there	*aquí / allí*	ah-**kee** / ah-**yee**
near / far	*cerca / lejos*	**thehr**-kah / **lay**-hohs
indoors / outdoors	*dentro / afuera*	**dayn**-troh / ah-**fwehr**-ah
good / bad	*bueno / malo*	**bway**-noh / **mah**-loh
best / worst	*mejor / peor*	may-**hor** / pay-**or**
a little / lots	*un poco / mucho*	oon **poh**-koh / **moo**-choh
more / less	*más / menos*	mahs / **may**-nohs
mine / yours	*mío / suyo*	**mee**-oh / **soo**-yoh
this / that	*esto / eso*	**ay**-stoh / **ay**-soh
everybody / nobody	*todos / nadie*	**toh**-dohs / **nah**-dee-ay
easy / difficult	*fácil / difícil*	**fah**-theel / dee-**fee**-theel
left / right	*izquierda / derecha*	eeth-kee-**ehr**-dah / day-**ray**-chah
up / down	*arriba / abajo*	ah-**ree**-bah / ah-**bah**-hoh
above / below	*encima / debajo*	en-**thee**-mah / day-**bah**-hoh
young / old	*joven / viejo*	**hoh**-behn / bee-ay-**hoh**
new / old	*nuevo / viejo*	noo-**ay**-boh / bee-**ay**-hoh
heavy / light	*pesado / ligero*	pay-**sah**-doh / lee-**hehr** oh
dark / light	*oscuro / claro*	oh-**skoo**-roh / **klah**-roh

BASICS

happy / sad	feliz / triste	fay-**leeth** / **tree**-stay
beautiful / ugly	bonito / feo	boh-**nee**-toh / **fay**-oh
nice / mean	simpático[a] / antipático[a]	seem-**pah**-tee-koh / ahn-tee-**pah**-tee-koh
smart / stupid	listo / estúpido	**lee**-stoh / ay-**stoo**-pee-doh
vacant / occupied	libre / ocupado	**lee**-bray / oh-koo-**pah**-doh
with / without	con / sin	kohn / seen

Big Little Words

I	yo	yoh
you (formal)	usted	oo-**stehd**
you (informal)	tú	too
we	nosotros	noh-**soh**-trohs
he	él	ehl
she	ella	**ay**-yah
they (m / f)	ellos / ellas	**ay**-yohs / **ay**-yahs
and	y	ee
at	a	ah
because	porque	por-**kay**
but	pero	**pay**-roh
by (via)	por	por
for	para	**pah**-rah
from	de	day
here	aquí	ah-**kee**
if	si	see
in	en	ayn
it	ello	**ay**-yoh
not	no	noh
now	ahora	ah-**oh**-rah
only	solo	**soh**-loh
or	o	oh
that	eso	**ay**-soh
this	esto	**ay**-stoh
to	a	ah
very	muy	**moo**-ee

Very Spanish Expressions

Vale.	**bah**-lay	O.K. / That's good. / I understand. / Uh-huh.
Diga(me). (literally "Talk to me")	**dee**-gah (-may)	Hello (answering phone) / **Can I help you?**
Mira.	**mee**-rah	Look.
¿De veras? / ¿De verdad?	day **behr**-ahs / day behr-**dahd**	Really?
¡Caray!	kah-rī	Wow!
De nada. (literally "It's nothing")	day **nah**-dah	You're welcome.
¡Salud!	sah-**lood**	Cheers! / Bless you! (after sneeze)
marchar	mar-**char**	to go out and cruise / party
La última?	lah **ool**-tee-mah	ask in a busy market to find out who is next in line (literally "The last?")
Próxima?	**prohk**-see-mah	Next (in line)?
No hay problema.	noh ī proh-**blay**-mah	No problem.
De acuerdo.	day ah-**kwehr**-doh	O.K.
¡Qué lástima!	kay **lah**-stee-mah	What a pity!
Así es la vida.	ah-**see** ays lah **bee**-dah	That's life.
Que será, será.	kay say-**rah** say-**rah**	What will be, will be.
¡Buena suerte!	**bway**-nah **swehr**-tay	Good luck!
¡Vamos!	**bah**-mohs	Let's go!
¡Luego!	loo-**ay**-goh	Bye!

COUNTING

Numbers

0	*cero*	**theh**-roh
1	*uno*	**oo**-noh
2	*dos*	dohs
3	*tres*	trehs
4	*cuatro*	**kwah**-troh
5	*cinco*	**theen**-koh
6	*seis*	says
7	*siete*	see-**eh**-tay
8	*ocho*	**oh**-choh
9	*nueve*	**nway**-bay
10	*diez*	dee-**ayth**
11	*once*	**ohn**-thay
12	*doce*	**doh**-thay
13	*trece*	**tray**-thay
14	*catorce*	kah-**tor**-thay
15	*quince*	**keen**-thay
16	*dieciséis*	dee-ay-thee-**says**
17	*diecisiete*	dee-ay-thee-see-**eh**-tay
18	*dieciocho*	dee-ay-thee-**oh**-choh
19	*diecinueve*	dee-ay-thee-**nway**-bay
20	*veinte*	**bayn**-tay

14

21	*veintiuno*	bayn-tee-**oo**-noh
22	*veintidós*	bayn-tee-**dohs**
23	*veintitrés*	bayn-tee-**trehs**
30	*treinta*	**trayn**-tah
31	*treinta y uno*	**trayn**-tah ee **oo**-noh
40	*cuarenta*	kwah-**rehn**-tah
41	*cuarenta y uno*	kwah-**rehn**-tah ee **oo**-noh
50	*cincuenta*	theen-**kwehn**-tah
60	*sesenta*	say-**sehn**-tah
70	*setenta*	say-**tehn**-tah
80	*ochenta*	oh-**chehn**-tah
90	*noventa*	noh-**behn**-tah
100	*cien*	thee-**ehn**
101	*ciento uno*	thee-**ehn**-toh **oo**-noh
102	*ciento dos*	thee-**ehn**-toh dohs
200	*doscientos*	dohs-thee-**ehn**-tohs
1000	*mil*	meel
2000	*dos mil*	dohs meel
2001	*dos mil uno*	dohs meel **oo**-noh
2002	*dos mil dos*	dohs meel dohs
2003	*dos mil tres*	dohs meel trehs
2004	*dos mil cuatro*	dohs meel **kwah**-troh
2005	*dos mil cinco*	dohs meel **theen**-koh
2006	*dos mil seis*	dohs meel says
2007	*dos mil siete*	dohs meel see-**eh**-tay
2008	*dos mil ocho*	dohs meel **oh**-choh
2009	*dos mil nueve*	dohs meel **nway**-bay
2010	*dos mil diez*	dohs meel dee-**ayth**
million	*millón*	mee-**yohn**
billion	*mil millones*	meel mee-**yoh**-nays
number one	*número uno*	**noo**-may-roh **oo**-noh
first	*primero*	pree-**may**-roh
second	*segundo*	say-**goon**-doh
third	*tercero*	tehr-**thehr**-oh
once / twice	*una vez /*	**oo**-nah bayth /
	dos veces	dohs **bay**-thays
a quarter	*un cuarto*	oon **kwar**-toh

a third	*un tercio*	oon **tehr**-thee-oh
half	*mitad*	mee-**tahd**
this much	*esta cantidad*	**ay**-stah kahn-tee-**dahd**
a dozen	*una docena*	**oo**-nah doh-**thay**-nah
some	*algo*	**ahl**-goh
enough	*bastante*	bah-**stahn**-tay
a handful	*un puñado*	oon poon-**yah**-doh
50%	*cincuenta*	theen-**kwehn**-tah
	por cien	por thee-**ehn**
100%	*cien por cien*	thee-**ehn** por thee-**ehn**

Once (eleven) is considered a lucky number in Spain. It's the word you'll see on booths that sell tickets for the national lottery, run by and for the blind.

Money

Where is a cash machine?	*¿Dónde hay un cajero automático?*	**dohn**-day ī oon kah-**hay**-roh ow-toh-**mah**-tee-koh
My ATM card has been...	*Mi tarjeta del cajero automático ha sido...*	mee tar-**hay**-tah dayl kah-**hay**-roh ow-toh-**mah**-tee-koh ah **see**-doh
...demagnetized.	*...desmagneti-zada.*	days-mahg-nay-tee **thah**-dah
...stolen.	*...robada.*	roh-**bah**-dah
...eaten by the machine.	*...tragada por el cajero.*	trah-**gah**-dah por ehl kah-**hay**-roh
Do you accept credit cards?	*¿Aceptan tarjetas de crédito?*	ah-**thayp**-tahn tar-**hay**-tahs day **kray**-dee-toh
Can you change dollars?	*¿Me puede cambiar dólares?*	may **pway**-day kahm-bee-**ar doh**-lah-rays

What is your exchange rate for dollars...?	¿A cuanto pagan el dólar...?	ah **kwahn**-toh **pah**-gahn ehl **doh**-lar
...in traveler's checks	...en cheques de viajero	ayn **chay**-kays day bee-ah-**hay**-roh
What is the commission?	¿Cuánto es la comisión?	**kwahn**-toh ays lah koh-mee-see-**ohn**
Any extra fee?	¿Tienen alguna cuota extra?	tee-**ehn**-ehn ahl-**goo**-nah **kwoh**-tah **ayk**-strah
Can you break this? (big bill into smaller ones)	¿Me puede dar cambio más pequeño?	may **pway**-day dar **kahm**-bee-oh mahs pay-**kayn**-yoh
I would like...	Me gustaría...	may goo-stah-**ree**-ah
...small bills.	...billetes pequeños.	bee-**yeh**-tays pay-**kayn**-yohs
...large bills.	...billetes grandes.	bee-**yeh**-tays **grahn**-days
...coins.	...monedas.	moh-**nay**-dahs
€50	cincuenta euros	theen-**kwehn**-tah **yoo**-rohs
Is this a mistake?	¿Es esto un error?	ays **ay**-stoh oon ehr-**ror**
This is incorrect.	Es incorrecto.	ays een-koh-**rehk**-toh
Did you print these today?	¿Imprimió esto hoy?	eem-pree-mee-**oh ay**-stoh oy
I have no money.	No tengo dinero.	noh **tayn**-goh dee-**nay**-roh
I'm poor.	Soy pobre.	soy **poh**-bray
I'm rich.	Soy rico[a].	soy **ree**-koh
I'm Bill Gates.	Soy Bill Gates.	soy "Bill Gates"
Where is the nearest casino?	¿Dónde está el casino más cercano?	**dohn**-day ay-**stah** ehl kah-**see**-noh mahs thehr-**kah**-noh

COUNTING

Spain uses the euro currency. Euros (€) are divided into 100 cents. Use your common cents—cents are like pennies, and the euro has coins like nickels, dimes, and quarters.

KEY PHRASES: MONEY

euro (€)	*euro*	**yoo**-roh
money	*dinero*	dee-**nay**-roh
cash	*efectivo*	ay-fehk-**tee**-voh
credit card	*tarjeta de crédito*	tar-**hay**-tah day **kray**-dee-toh
bank	*banco*	**bahn**-koh
cash machine	*cajero automático*	kah-**hay**-roh ow-toh-**mah**-tee-koh
Where is a cash machine?	*¿Dónde hay un cajero automático?*	**dohn**-day ī oon kah-**hay**-roh ow-toh-**mah**-tee-koh
Do you accept credit cards?	*¿Aceptan tarjetas de crédito?*	ah-**thayp**-tahn tar-**hay**-tahs day **kray**-dee-toh

Money Words

euro (€)	*euro*	**yoo**-roh
cents	*céntimos*	**thehn**-tee-mohs
money	*dinero*	dee-**nay**-roh
cash	*efectivo*	ay-fehk-**tee**-voh
cash machine	*cajero automático*	kah-**hay**-roh ow-toh-**mah**-tee-koh
bank	*banco*	**bahn**-koh
credit card	*tarjeta de crédito*	tar-**hay**-tah day **kray**-dee-toh
change money	*cambio de moneda*	**kahm**-bee-oh day moh-**nay**-dah
exchange	*cambio*	**kahm**-bee-oh
buy / sell	*comprar / vender*	kohm-**prar** / bayn-**dehr**
commission	*comisión*	koh-mee-see-**ohn**
traveler's check	*cheque de viajero*	**chay**-kay day bee-ah-**hay**-roh
cash advance	*adelanto de dinero*	ah-day-**lahn**-toh day dee-**nay**-roh
cashier	*cajero*	kah-**hehr**-oh

bills	*billetes*	bee-**yeh**-tays
coins	*monedas*	moh-**nay**-dahs
receipt	*recibo*	ray-**thee**-boh

You'll get the best rates by using an ATM or debit card to withdraw money from cash machines. Every cash machine (*cajero automático*) should be multilingual, but if you encounter one that speaks only Spanish you'll probably see these words: *anotación* (enter), *continuar* (enter), *retirar* (withdraw), *confirmar* (confirm), *corregir* (correct), *borrar* (erase), and *cancelar* (cancel). Your PIN number is a *número clave*.

Banks are open from 9:00 a.m. until 2:00 p.m. Monday through Friday. Traveler's checks are widely accepted, but commissions are steep (starting around $5). Big department stores like *El Corte Inglés* in Madrid exchange money at decent rates during their business hours. *Casas de cambio* (exchange offices) are open long hours, but you'll pay for the convenience with a lousy rate or sky-high commission.

COUNTING

Time

What time is it?	*¿Qué hora es?*	kay **oh**-rah ays
It's...	*Son las...*	sohn lahs
...8:00 in the morning.	*...ocho de la mañana.*	**oh**-choh day lah mahn-**yah**-nah
...16:00.	*...dieciséis.*	dee-ay-thee-**says**
...4:00 in the afternoon.	*...cuatro de la tarde.*	**kwah**-troh day lah **tar**-day
...10:30 (in the evening).	*...diez y media (de la noche).*	dee-**ayth** ee **may**-dee-ah (day lah **noh**-chay)
...a quarter past nine	*...nueve y cuarto.*	**nway**-bay ee **kwar**-toh
...a quarter to eleven.	*...once menos cuarto.*	**ohn**-thay **may**-nohs **kwar**-toh
noon	*doce, mediodía*	**doh**-thay, may-dee-oh-**dee**-ah

midnight	*doce de la noche, medianoche*	**doh**-thay day lah **noh**-chay, may-dee-ah-**noh**-chay
It's...	*Es...*	ays
...early / late.	*...temprano / tarde.*	tehm-**prah**-noh / **tar**-day
...on time.	*...puntual.*	poon-too-**ahl**
...sunrise.	*...amanecer.*	ah-mah-nay-**thehr**
...sunset.	*...puesta de sol.*	**pway**-stah day sohl
It's my bedtime.	*Es la hora de acostarme.*	ays lah **oh**-rah day ah-koh-**star**-may

COUNTING

Timely Expressions

I will return / We will return at 11:20.	*Volveré / Volveremos a las once y veinte.*	vohl-vay-**ray** / vohl-vay-**ray**-mohs ah lahs **ohn**-thay ee **bayn**-tay
I will arrive / We will arrive by 18:00.	*Llegaré / Llegaremos a las dieciocho.*	yay-gah-**ray** / yay-gah-**ray**-mohs ah lahs dee-ay-thee-**oh**-choh
When is checkout time?	*¿Cuál es la hora de salida?*	kwahl ays lah **oh**-rah day sah-**lee**-dah
At what time does...?	*¿A qué hora...?*	ah kay **oh**-rah
...this open / close	*...abren / cierran*	**ah**-brehn / thee-**ay**-rahn
...this train / bus leave for ___	*...sale el tren / autobús para ___*	**sah**-lay ehl trayn / ow-toh-**boos pah**-rah
...the next train / bus leave for ___	*...sale el próximo tren / autobús para ___*	**sah**-lay ehl **prohk**-see-moh trayn / ow-toh-**boos pah**-rah
...the train / bus arrive in ___	*...llega el tren / autobús a ___*	**yay**-gah ehl trayn / ow-toh-**boos** ah
I / We would like to take the 16:30 train.	*Me / Nos gustaría tomar el tren de las cuatro y media.*	may / nohs goo-stah-**ree**-ah toh-**mar** ehl trayn day lahs **kwah**-troh ee **may**-dee-ah
Is the train...?	*¿Va el tren...?*	bah ehl trayn
Is the bus...?	*¿Va el autobús...?*	bah ehl ow-toh-**boos**
...early / late	*...adelantado / con retraso*	ah-day-lahn-**tah**-doh / kohn ray-**trah**-soh
...on time	*...a tiempo*	ah tee-**ehm**-poh

In Spain, the 24-hour clock (military time) is used mainly for train, bus, and ferry schedules. Friends use the same "clock" we do. You'd meet a friend at 3:00 *de la tarde* (in the afternoon) to catch a train at 15:15.

More Time

minute	*minuto*	mee-**noo**-toh
hour	*hora*	**oh**-rah
in the morning	*por la mañana*	por lah mahn-**yah**-nah
in the afternoon	*por la tarde*	por lah **tar**-day
in the evening	*por la noche*	por lah **noh**-chay
night	*noche*	**noh**-chay
at 6:00 sharp	*a las seis en punto*	ah lahs says ayn **poon**-toh
from 8:00 to 10:00	*de ocho a diez*	day **oh**-choh ah dee-**ayth**
in half an hour	*en media hora*	ayn **may**-dee-ah **oh**-rah
in one hour	*dentro de una hora*	**dehn**-troh day **oo**-nah **oh**-rah
in three hours	*en tres horas*	ayn trehs **oh**-rahs
anytime	*a cualquier hora*	ah kwahl-kee-**ehr oh**-rah
immediately	*inmediata-mente*	een-may-dee-ah-tah-**mehn**-tay
every hour	*cada hora*	**kah**-dah **oh**-rah
every day	*cada día*	**kah**-dah **dee**-ah
last	*último*	**ool**-tee-moh
this	*este*	**ay**-stay
next	*próximo*	**prohk**-see-moh
May 15	*quince de mayo*	**keen**-thay day **mah**-yoh
high season	*temporada alta*	taym-poh-**rah**-dah **ahl**-tah
low season	*temporada baja*	taym-poh-**rah**-dah **bah**-hah
in the future	*en el futuro*	ayn ehl foo-**too**-roh
in the past	*en el pasado*	ayn ehl pah-**sah**-doh

COUNTING

KEY PHRASES: TIME

minute	*minuto*	mee-**noo**-toh
hour	*hora*	**oh**-rah
day	*día*	**dee**-ah
week	*semana*	say-**mah**-nah
What time is it?	*¿Qué hora es?*	kay **oh**-rah ays
It's...	*Son las...*	sohn lahs
...8:00.	*...ocho.*	**oh**-choh
...16:00.	*...dieciséis.*	dee-ay-thee-**says**
At what time does this open / close?	*¿A qué hora abren / cierran?*	ah kay **oh**-rah **ah**-brehn / thee-**ay**-rahn

The Day

day	*día*	**dee**-ah
today	*hoy*	oy
yesterday	*ayer*	ah-**yehr**
tomorrow	*mañana*	mahn-**yah**-nah
tomorrow morning	*mañana por la mañana*	mahn-**yah**-nah por lah mahn-**yah**-nah
day after tomorrow	*pasado mañana*	pah-**sah**-doh mahn-**yah**-nah

The Week

week	*semana*	say-**mah**-nah
last week	*la semana última*	lah say-**mah**-nah **ool**-tee-mah
this week	*esta semana*	**ay**-stah say-**mah**-nah
next week	*la semana próxima*	lah say-**mah**-nah **prohk**-see-mah
Monday	*lunes*	**loo**-nays
Tuesday	*martes*	**mar**-tays
Wednesday	*miércoles*	mee-**ehr**-koh-lays
Thursday	*jueves*	**hway**-bays
Friday	*viernes*	bee-**ehr**-nays
Saturday	*sábado*	**sah**-bah-doh
Sunday	*domingo*	doh-**meen**-goh

The Month

month	*mes*	mays
January	*enero*	ay-**nay**-roh
February	*febrero*	fay-**bray**-roh
March	*marzo*	**mar**-thoh
April	*abril*	ah-**breel**
May	*mayo*	**mah**-yoh
June	*junio*	*h*oon-yoh
July	*julio*	*h*ool-yoh
August	*agosto*	ah-**goh**-stoh
September	*septiembre*	sehp-tee-**ehm**-bray
October	*octubre*	ohk-**too**-bray
November	*noviembre*	noh-bee-**ehm**-bray
December	*diciembre*	dee-thee-**ehm**-bray

The Year

year	*año*	**ahn**-yoh
spring	*primavera*	pree-mah-**bay**-rah
summer	*verano*	bay-**rah**-noh
fall	*otoño*	oh-**tohn**-yoh
winter	*invierno*	een-bee-**ehr**-noh

Holidays and Happy Days

holiday	*festivo*	fay-**stee**-boh
national holiday	*festivo nacional*	fay-**stee**-boh nah-thee-oh-**nahl**
religious holiday	*día religioso*	**dee**-ah ray-lee-*h*ee-**oh**-soh
Is today / tomorrow a holiday?	*¿Es hoy / mañana un día festivo?*	ehs oy / mahn-**yah**-nah oon **dee**-ah fay-**stee**-boh
Is a holiday coming up soon? When?	*¿Hay alguna fiesta pronto? ¿Cuándo?*	ī ahl-**goo**-nah fee-**eh**-stah **prohn**-toh **kwahn**-doh
What is the holiday?	*¿Qué fiesta es?*	kay fee-**eh**-stah ehs

Merry Christmas!	*¡Feliz Navidad!*	fay-**leeth** nah-bee-**dahd**
Happy new year!	*¡Feliz Año Nuevo!*	fay-**leeth ahn**-yoh **nway**-boh
Easter	*Pascuas*	**pahs**-kwahs
Happy anniversary!	*¡Feliz aniversario!*	fay-**leeth** ah-nee-behr-**sah**-ree-oh
Happy birthday!	*¡Feliz cumpleaños!*	fay-**leeth** koom-play-**ahn**-yohs

The Spanish sing "Happy birthday" to the same tune we do, but they don't fill in the person's name. Here are the words: *Cumpleaños feliz, cumpleaños feliz, te deseamos todos cumpleaños, cumpleaños feliz.*

Other happy days in Spain include *Semana Santa* (Holy Week), leading up to Easter. It's a festive time throughout Iberia, especially in Sevilla. *Corpus Christi* comes early in June, *Ascensión de Maria* on August 15th, and *Día de la Hispanidad,* Spain's national holiday, is on October 12.

TRAVELING

Flights

All airports have bilingual signage with the local language and always English. Also, nearly all airport service personnel and travel agents speak English these days. Still, these words and phrases could conceivably come in handy.

Making a Reservation

I'd like to... my reservation / ticket.	*Me gustaría... mi reserva / billete.*	may goo-stah-**ree**-ah... mee ray-**sehr**-bah / bee-**yeh**-tay
We'd like to... our reservation / ticket.	*Nos gustaría... nuestra reserva / nuestros billetes.*	nohs goo-stah-**ree**-ah... **nway**-strah ray-**sehr**-bah / **nway**-strohs bee-**yeh**-tays
...confirm	*...confirmar*	kohn-feer-**mar**
...change	*...cambiar*	kahm-bee-**ar**
...cancel	*...cancelar*	kahn-thay-**lar**
seat by the aisle / window	*asiento de pasillo / ventana*	ah-see-**ehn**-toh day pah-**see**-yoh / vayn-**tah**-nah

25

At the Airport

Which terminal?	¿Qué terminal?	kay tehr-mee-**nahl**
international flights	vuelos interna-cionales	**bway**-lohs een-tehr-nah-thee-oh-**nah**-lays
domestic flights	vuelos domésticos	**bway**-lohs doh-**may**-stee-kohs
arrivals	llegadas	yay-**gah**-dahs
departures	salidas	sah-**lee**-dahs
baggage check	facturar el equipaje	fahk-too-**rar** ehl ay-kee-**pah**-hay
baggage claim	reclamar el equipaje	ray-klah-**mar** ehl ay-kee-**pah**-hay
Nothing to declare.	Nada que declarar.	**nah**-dah kay day-klah-**rar**
I have only carry-on luggage.	Sólo llevo equipaje de mano.	**soh**-loh **yay**-boh ay-kee-**pah**-hay day **mah**-noh
flight number	número de vuelo	**noo**-may-roh day **bway**-loh
departure gate	puerta de salida	**pwehr**-tah day sah-**lee**-dah
duty free	libre de impuestos	**lee**-bray day eem-**pway**-stohs
luggage cart	carro de equipaje	**kah**-roh day ay-kee-**pah**-hay
jet lag	jet lag	"jet lag"

Getting to/from the Airport

Approximately how much is a taxi ride...?	¿Cuánto cuesta más o menos un taxi...?	**kwahn**-toh **kway**-stah mahs oh **may**-nohs oon **tahk**-see
...to downtown	...al centro	ahl **thayn**-troh
...to the train station	...a la estación de trenes	ah lah ay-stah-thee-**ohn** day **tray**-nays
...to the airport	...al aeropuerto	ahl ah-ay-roh-**pwehr**-toh

Does a bus (or train) run...?	*¿Va un autobús (o un tren)...?*	bah oon ow-toh-**boos** (oh oon trayn)
...from the airport to downtown	*...desde el aeropuerto al centro*	**dehs**-day ehl ah-ay-roh-**pwehr**-toh ahl **thayn**-troh
...to the airport from downtown	*...al aeropuerto desde el centro*	ahl ah-ay-roh-**pwehr**-toh **dehs**-day ehl **thayn**-troh
How much is it?	*¿Cuánto cuesta?*	**kwahn**-toh **kway**-stah
Where does it leave from...?	*¿De dónde sale...?*	day **dohn**-day **sah**-lay
...at the airport?	*...desde el aeropuerto?*	**dehs**-day ehl ah-ay-roh-**pwehr**-toh
...downtown?	*...desde el centro?*	**dehs**-day ehl **thayn**-troh
How often does it run?	*¿Con qué frecuencia sale?*	kohn kay fray-**kwayn**-thee-ah **sah**-lay

Trains

The Train Station

Where is the...?	*¿Dónde está la...?*	**dohn**-day ay-**stah** lah
...train station	*...estación de tren*	ay-stah-thee-**ohn** day trayn
Spanish Railways	*R.E.N.F.E.*	**rehn**-fay
train information	*información de trenes*	een-for-mah-thee-**ohn** day **tray**-nays
train	*tren*	trayn
high-speed trains	*Talgo, AVE*	**tahl**-goh, **ah**-vay
fast / faster	*rápido / más rápido*	**rah**-pee-doh / mahs **rah**-pee-doh
arrival	*llegada*	yay-**gah**-dah
departure	*salida*	sah-**lee**-dah
delay	*retraso*	ray-**trah**-soh
toilets	*aseos*	ah-**say**-ohs
waiting room	*sala de espera*	**sah**-lah day ay-**spay**-rah

TRAVELING

lockers	casilleros	kah-see-**yay**-rohs
baggage check room	consigna	kohn-**seen**-yah
lost and found office	oficina de objetos perdidos	oh-fee-**thee**-nah day ohb-**hay**-tohs pehr-**dee**-dohs
tourist information office	Oficina de Turismo	oh-fee-**thee**-nah day too-**rees**-moh
to the platforms	a los andenes	ah lohs **ahn**-deh-nays
platform	andén	ahn-**dayn**
track	vía	**bee**-ah
train car	vagón, coche	bah-**gohn**, **koh**-chay
dining car	coche comedor	**koh**-chay koh-may-**dor**
sleeper car	coche cama	**koh**-chay **kah**-mah
conductor	conductor	kohn-dook-**tor**

KEY PHRASES: TRAINS

train station	estación de tren	ay-stah-thee-**ohn** day trayn
train	tren	trayn
ticket	billete	bee-**yeh**-tay
transfer	transbordo	trahns-**bor**-doh
supplement	suplemento	soo-play-**mehn**-toh
arrival	llegada	yay-**gah**-dah
departure	salida	sah-**lee**-dah
platform	andén	ahn-**dayn**
track	vía	**bee**-ah
train car	vagón, coche	bah-**gohn**, **koh**-chay
A ticket to ___.	Un billete para ___.	oon bee-**yeh**-tay **pah**-rah
Two tickets to ___.	Dos billetes para ___.	dohs bee-**yeh**-tays **pah**-rah
When is the next train?	¿Cuándo es el siguiente tren?	**kwahn**-doh ays ehl see-**gehn**-tay trayn
Where does the train leave from?	¿Desde dónde sale el tren?	**dehs**-day **dohn**-day **sah**-lay ehl trayn
Which train to ___?	¿Qué tren para ___?	kay trayn **pah**-rah

The trains in Spain (which run mainly on the plain) come in several types. Along with the various local (*Cercania*) and milk-run (*Regional* and *Correo*) trains, there are:

- the slow *Rápido, Tranvía, Semi-directo,* and *Expreso* trains
- the medium-speed *Intercity* and *Electro* trains
- the fast *Talgo* trains
- several super-fast "bullet" trains (about 140 mph) that have different names depending on the route: *AVE (Alta Velocidad Española), Talgo 2000, Alaria, Ataris,* and *Euromed.*

Spanish trains require reservations for longer trips (even if you have a Eurailpass and the train is empty). When you arrive in a town, make your out-bound reservation right away. In bigger cities, the downtown RENFE (Spanish Railways) office is sometimes more efficient at making reservations than the train station.

Trains get more expensive as they pick up speed, but all are cheaper per mile than their Northern European counterparts. Franco left Spain a train system that didn't fit Europe's gauge. The high-speed *AVE* trains run on European-gauge tracks, whisking travelers between Madrid and Sevilla in less than three hours (you'll pay an extra $15 second-class supplement with a railpass). A Madrid-Barcelona link may also be built. *AVE* trains can be priced differently according to their time of departure. Peak hours (*punta*) are most expensive, followed by *llano* and *valle* (quietest and cheapest times).

Getting a Ticket

Where can I buy a ticket?	¿Dónde puedo comprar un billete?	**dohn**-day **pway**-doh kohm-**prar** oon bee-**yeh**-tay
A ticket to ___.	Un billete para ___.	oon bee-**yeh**-tay **pah**-rah
Where can we buy tickets?	¿Dónde podemos comprar billetes?	**dohn**-day poh-**day**-mohs kohm-**prar** bee-**yeh**-tays

Two tickets to ___.	Dos billetes para ___.	dohs bee-**yeh**-tays **pah**-rah
Is this the line for...?	¿Es ésta la fila para...?	ays **ay**-stah lah **fee**-lah **pah**-rah
...tickets	...billetes	bee-**yeh**-tays
...reservations	...reservas	ray-**sehr**-bahs
How much is a ticket to ___?	¿Cuánto cuesta el billete a ___?	**kwahn**-toh **kway**-stah ehl bee-**yeh**-tay ah
Is this ticket valid for ___?	¿Es este billete válido para ___?	ays **ay**-stay bee-**yeh**-tay **bah**-lee-doh **pah**-rah
How long is this ticket valid?	¿Cuándo expira este billete?	**kwahn**-doh ehk-**spee**-rah **ay**-stay bee-**yeh**-tay
When is the next train?	¿Cuándo es el siguiente tren?	**kwahn**-doh ays ehl see-**gehn**-tay trayn
Do you have a schedule for all trains departing for ___ today / tomorrow?	¿Tienen un horario de todas las salidas de los trenes para ___ hoy / mañana?	tee-**ehn**-ehn oon oh-**rah**-ree-oh day **toh**-dahs lahs sah-**lee**-dahs day lohs **tray**-nays **pah**-rah ___ oy / mahn-**yah**-nah
I / We would like to leave...	Me / Nos gustaría salir...	may / nohs goo-stah-**ree**-ah sah-**leer**
I / We would like to arrive...	Me / Nos gustaría llegar...	may / nohs goo-stah-**ree**-ah yay-**gar**
...by ___.	...a las ___.	ah lahs
...in the morning.	...por la mañana.	por lah mahn-**yah**-nah
...in the afternoon.	...por la tarde.	por lah **tar**-day
...in the evening.	...por la noche.	por lah **noh**-chay
Is there a...?	¿Hay un...?	ī oon
...earlier train	...tren más temprano	trayn mahs tehm-**prah**-noh
...later train	...tren más tarde	trayn mahs **tar**-day
...overnight train	...tren nocturno	trayn nohk-**toor**-noh
...cheaper train	...tren más barato	trayn mahs bah-**rah**-toh
...local train	...tren local	trayn loh-**kahl**
...express train	...tren expreso	trayn ehk-**spray**-soh
Is there a cheaper option?	¿Hay una opción más barata?	ī **oo**-nah ohp-thee-**ohn** mahs bah-**rah**-tah

What track does it leave from?	*¿Desde qué andén sale?*	**dehs**-day kay ahn-**dayn sah**-lay
What track?	*¿Qué vía?*	kay **bee**-ah
On time?	*¿Puntual?*	poon-too-**ahl**
Late?	*¿Tarde?*	**tar**-day

Reservations, Supplements, and Discounts

Is a reservation required?	*¿Se requiere reserva?*	say ray-kee-**eh**-ray ray-**sehr**-bah
I'd like to reserve...	*Me gustaría reservar...*	may goo-stah-**ree**-ah ray-sehr-**bar**
...a seat.	...un asiento.	oon ah-see-**ehn**-toh
...a berth (couchette).	...una litera.	**oo**-nah **lee**-tay-rah
...a first-class sleeper.	...un coche cama.	oon **koh**-chay **kah**-mah
...the entire train.	...todo el tren.	**toh**-doh ehl trayn
We'd like to reserve...	*Nos gustaría reservar...*	nohs goo-stah-**ree**-ah ray-sehr-**bar**
...two seats.	...dos asientos.	dohs ah-see-**ehn**-tohs
...two berths (couchettes).	...dos literas.	dohs **lee**-tay-rahs
...two beds in a sleeper car.	...dos camas en un coche cama.	dohs **kah**-mahs ayn oon **koh**-chay **kah**-mah
Is there a supplement?	*¿Hay un suplemento?*	ī oon soo-play-**mehn**-toh
Does my railpass cover the supplement?	*¿Mi railpass incluye el suplemento?*	mee **rayl**-pahs een-**kloo**-yay ehl soo-play-**mehn**-toh
Is there a discount for...?	*¿Tienen descuento para...?*	tee-**ehn**-ehn days-**kwehn**-toh **pah**-rah
...youths	...jóvenes	**hoh**-beh-nays
...seniors	...la tercera edad	lah tehr-**thay**-rah ay-**dahd**
...families	...familias	fah-**mee**-lee-ahs

TRAVELING

Ticket Talk

ticket window	*venta de billetes*	**bayn**-tah day bee-**yeh**-tays
reservations window	*reservas*	ray-**sehr**-bahs
national / international	*nacional / internacional*	nah-thee-oh-**nahl** / een-tehr-nah-thee-oh-**nahl**
ticket	*billete*	bee-**yeh**-tay
one way	*de ida*	day **ee**-dah
roundtrip	*de ida y vuelta*	day **ee**-dah ee **bwehl**-tah
first class	*primera clase*	pree-**may**-rah **klah**-say
second class	*segunda clase*	say-**goon**-dah **klah**-say
non-smoking	*no fumadores*	noh foo-mah-**doh**-rays
validate	*validar*	bah-lee-**dar**
schedule	*horario*	oh-**rah**-ree-oh
departure	*salida*	sah-**lee**-dah
direct	*directo*	dee-**rehk**-toh
transfer	*transbordo*	trahns-**bor**-doh
connection	*enlace*	ayn-**lah**-thay
with supplement	*con suplemento*	kohn soo-play-**mehn**-toh
reservation	*reserva*	ray-**sehr**-bah
seat by the aisle / window	*asiento de pasillo / ventana*	ah-see-**ehn**-toh day pah-**see**-yoh / vayn-**tah**-nah
berth...	*litera...*	**lee**-tay-rah
...upper	*...alta*	**ahl**-tah
...middle	*...media*	**may**-dee-ah
...lower	*...baja*	**bah**-hah
refund	*devolución*	day-voh-loo-thee-**ohn**
reduced fare	*tarifa reducida*	tah-**ree**-fah ray-doo-**thee**-dah

Changing Trains

Is it direct?	*¿Es directo?*	ays dee-**rehk**-toh
Must I transfer?	*¿Tengo que cambiar?*	**tayn**-goh kay kahm-bee-**ar**

Must we transfer?	¿Tenemos que cambiar?	tay-**nay**-mohs kay kahm-bee-**ar**
When? Where?	¿Cuándo? ¿Dónde?	**kwahn**-doh **dohn**-day
Do I / Do we change here for ___?	¿Tengo / Tenemos que cambiar aquí para ___?	**tayn**-goh / tay-**nay**-mohs kay kahm-bee-**ar** ah-**kee pah**-rah
Where do I / do we change for ___?	¿Dónde cambio / cambiamos para ___?	**dohn**-day **kahm**-bee-oh / kahm-bee-**ah**-mohs **pah**-rah
At what time...?	¿A qué hora...?	ah kay **oh**-rah
From what track does my / our connecting train leave ?	¿De qué vía sale mi / nuestro tren de conexión?	day kay **bee**-ah sah-lay mee / **nway**-stroh trayn day koh-nehk-thee-**ohn**
How many minutes in ___ to change trains?	¿Cuántos minutos en ___ para cambiar de tren?	**kwahn**-tohs mee-**noo**-tohs ehn ___ **pah**-rah kahm-bee-**ar** day trayn

On the Platform

Where is...?	¿Dónde está.....?	**dohn**-day ay-**stah**
Is this...?	¿Es éste...?	ays **ay**-stay
...the train to ___?	...el tren a ___?	ehl trayn ah
Which train to ___?	¿Qué tren para ___?	kay trayn **pah**-rah
Which train car to ___?	¿Qué vagón para ___?	kay bah-**gohn pah**-rah
Where is first class?	¿Dónde está primera clase?	**dohn**-day ay-**stah** pree-**may**-rah **klah**-say
...front / middle / back	...frente / centro / detrás	**frayn**-tay / **thayn**-troh / day-**trahs**
Where can I validate my ticket?	¿Dónde puedo validar mi billete?	**dohn**-day **pway**-doh bah-lee-**dar** mee bee-**yeh**-tay

On the Train

Is this (seat) free?	¿Está libre?	ay-**stah lee**-bray
May I / May we...?	¿Puedo / Podemos...?	**pway**-doh / poh-**day**-mohs
...sit here (I / we)	...sentarme / sentarnos aquí?	sayn-**tar**-may / sayn-**tar**-nohs ah-**kee**
...open the window	...abrir la ventana	ah-**breer** lah behn-**tah**-nah
...eat your meal	...comer su comida	koh-**mehr** soo koh-**mee**-dah
Save my place?	¿Guárdeme mi asiento?	**gwar**-day-may mee ah-see-**ehn**-toh
Save our places?	¿Guárdenos nuestros asientos?	**gwar**-day-nohs **nway**-strohs ah-see-**ehn**-tohs
That's my seat.	Ése es mi asiento.	**ay**-say ays mee ah-see-**ehn**-toh
These are our seats.	Éstes son nuestros asientos.	**ay**-stays sohn **nway**-strohs ah-see-**ehn**-tohs
Where are you going?	¿A dónde va?	ah **dohn**-day bah
I'm going to ___.	Voy a ___.	boy ah
We're going to ___.	Vamos a ___.	**bah**-mohs ah
Tell me when to get off?	¿Dígame cuándo tengo que bajarme?	**dee**-gah-may **kwahn**-doh **tayn**-goh kay bah-**har**-may
Tell us when to get off?	¿Díganos cuándo tenemos que bajarnos?	**dee**-gah-nohs **kwahn**-doh tay-**nay**-mohs kay bah-**har**-nohs
Where is a (good looking) conductor?	¿Dónde hay un conductor (guapo)?	**dohn**-day ī oon kohn-dook-**tor** (**gwah**-poh)
Does this train stop in ___?	¿Para el tren en ___?	**pah**-rah ehl trayn ayn
When will it arrive in ___?	¿Cuándo llegará a ___?	**kwahn**-doh yay-gah-**rah** ah
When will it arrive?	¿Cuándo llegará?	**kwahn**-doh yay-gah-**rah**

Reading Train and Bus Schedules

a	to
aviso	advisory (listing changes)
con retraso	late
clase	class
coche	car
de	from
destino	destination
diario	daily
días	days
días de semana	weekdays
días laborales	workdays (Monday-Saturday)
domingo	Sunday
festivos	holidays
excepto	except
fecha	date
hasta	until
hora salida	departure time
llegadas	arrivals
no	not
plaza	seat, place
sábado	Saturday
salidas	departures
salidas inmediatas	immediate departures
sólo	only
también	too
tipo de tren	type of train
todos	every
vía	track (or via)
1-5, 6, 7	Monday-Friday, Saturday, Sunday

Spanish schedules use the 24-hour clock. It's like American time until noon. After that, subtract twelve and add p.m. So 13:00 is 1 p.m., 19:00 is 7 p.m., and midnight is 24:00. If your train is scheduled to depart at 00:01, it'll leave one minute after midnight.

Major Rail Lines in Iberia

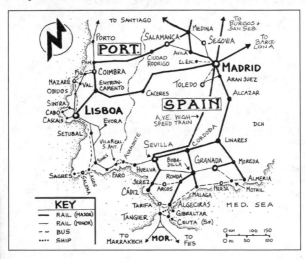

Going Places

Spain	España	ay-**spahn**-yah
Madrid	Madrid	mah-**dreed**
Seville	Sevilla	seh-**vee**-yah
Gibraltar	Gibraltar	hee-brahl-**tar**
Portugal	Portugal	por-too-**gahl**
Lisbon	Lisboa	lees-**boh**-ah
Morocco	Marruecos	mar-**way**-kohs
Austria	Austria	**ow**-stree-ah
Belgium	Bélgica	**bayl**-hee-kah
Czech Republic	República	ray-**poob**-lee-kah
	Checa	**chay**-kah
France	Francia	**frahn**-thee-ah
Germany	Alemania	ah-lay-**mah**-nee-yah
Great Britain	Gran Bretaña	grahn bray-**tahn**-yah
Greece	Grecia	**gray**-thee-ah

Ireland	*Irlanda*	eer-**lahn**-dah
Italy	*Italia*	ee-**tah**-lee-ah
Netherlands	*Holanda*	oh-**lahn**-dah
Scandinavia	*Escandinavia*	ay-skahn-dee-**nah**-bee-ah
Switzerland	*Suiza*	**swee**-thah
Turkey	*Turquía*	toor-**kee**-ah
Europe	*Europa*	ay-oo-**roh**-pah
EU (European Union)	*UE (Unión Europea)*	oo ay (oo-nee-**ohn** ay-oo-roh-**pay**-ah)
Russia	*Rusia*	**roo**-see-ah
Africa	*Africa*	**ah**-free-kah
United States	*Estados Unidos*	ay-**stah**-dohs oo-**nee**-dohs
Canada	*Canadá*	kah-nah-**dah**
Mexico	*Méjico*	**may**-hee-koh

Buses and Subways

At the Bus Station or Metro Stop

ticket	*billete*	bee-**yeh**-tay
city bus	*autobús*	ow-toh-**boos**
long-distance bus	*autocar*	ow-toh-**kar**
bus stop	*parada de autobús*	pah-**rah**-dah day ow-toh-**boos**
bus station	*estación de autobuses*	ay-stah-thee-**ohn** day ow-toh-**boo**-says
subway	*metro*	**may**-troh
subway station	*estación de metro*	ay-stah-thee-**ohn** day **may**-troh
subway map	*mapa*	**mah**-pah
subway entrance	*entrada al metro*	ayn-**trah**-dah ahl **may**-troh

subway stop	*parada*	pah-**rah**-dah
subway exit	*salida de*	sah-**lee**-dah day
	metro	**may**-troh
direct	*directo*	dee-**rehk**-toh
connection	*conexión*	koh-nehk-thee-**ohn**
pickpocket	*carterista*	kar-tay-**ree**-stah

Taking Buses and Subways

How do I get to___?	*¿Cómo llego a ___?*	**koh**-moh **yay**-goh ah
How do we get to ___?	*¿Cómo llegamos a ___?*	**koh**-moh yay-**gah**-mohs ah
How much is a ticket?	*¿Cuánto cuesta el billete?*	**kwahn**-toh **kway**-stah ehl bee-**yeh**-tay
Where can I buy a ticket?	*¿Dónde puedo comprar un billete?*	**dohn**-day **pway**-doh kohm-**prar** oon bee-**yeh**-tay
Where can we buy tickets?	*¿Dónde podemos comprar unos billetes?*	**dohn**-day poh-**day**-mohs kohm-**prar** **oo**-nohs bee-**yeh**-tays
One ticket, please.	*Un billete, por favor*	oon bee-**yeh**-tay por fah-**bor**
Two tickets.	*Dos billetes*	dohn bee-**yeh**-tays
Is this ticket valid (for___)?	*¿Es este billete válido (para ___)?*	ays **ay**-stay bee-**yeh**-tay **bah**-lee-doh (**pah**-rah___)
Is there a one-day pass?	*¿Hay un pase para todo el día?*	ī oon **pah**-say **pah**-rah **toh**-doh ehl **dee**-ah
Which bus to ___?	*¿Qué autocar para ___?*	kay ow-toh-**kar** **pah**-rah
Does it stop at ___?	*¿Tiene parada en ___?*	tee-**ehn**-ay pah-**rah**-dah ayn
Which metro stop for ___?	*¿Qué parada de metro para ___?*	kay pah-**rah**-dah day **may**-troh **pah**-rah
Which direction for___?	*¿Qué dirección para ___?*	kay dee-rehk-thee-**ohn** **pah**-rah
Must I transfer?	*¿Tengo que cambiar?*	**tayn**-goh kay kahm-bee-**ar**
Must we transfer?	*¿Tenemos que cambiar?*	tay-**nay**-mohs kay kahm-bee-**ar**

When does the... leave?	¿Cuándo sale el ...?	**kwahn**-doh **sah**-lay ehl
...first	...primero	pree-**may**-roh
...next	...siguiente	see-**gehn**-tay
...last	...último	**ool**-tee-moh
...bus / subway	...autobús / metro	ow-toh-**boos** / **may**-troh
What's the frequency per hour / day?	¿Con qué frecuencia pasa por hora / día?	kohn kay fray-**kwayn**-thee-ah **pah**-sah por **oh**-rah / **dee**-ah
Where does it leave from?	¿Desde dónde sale?	**dehs**-day **dohn**-day **sah**-lay
What time does it leave?	¿A qué hora sale?	ah kay **oh**-rah **sah**-lay
I'm going to___.	Voy a ___.	boy ah
We are going to ___.	Vamos a ___.	**bah**-mohs ah
Tell me when to get off?	¿Dígame cuándo tengo que bajarme?	**dee**-gah-may **kwahn**-doh **tayn**-goh kay bah-**har**-may
Tell us when to get off?	¿Díganos cuándo tenemos que bajarnos?	**dee**-gah-nohs **kwahn**-doh tay-**nay**-mohs kay bah-**har**-nohs

Buses (*autocars*) connect many smaller towns better and cheaper than trains. *Autopistas* are fast buses that take freeway routes. Tourist information offices have bus schedules. Subways are handy in Madrid and Barcelona.

TRAVELING

KEY PHRASES: BUSES AND SUBWAYS

bus	autobús	ow-toh-**boos**
subway	metro	**may**-troh
ticket	billete	bee-**yeh**-tay
How do I get to ___?	¿Cómo llego a ___?	**koh**-moh **yay**-goh ah
How do we get to ___?	¿Cómo llegamos a ___?	**koh**-moh yay-**gah**-mohs ah
Which stop for ___?	¿Qué parada para...?	kay pah-**rah**-dah **pah**-rah
Tell me when to get off?	¿Dígame cuándo tengo que bajarme?	**dee**-gah-may **kwahn**-doh **tayn**-goh kay bah-**har**-may

Taxis

Getting a Taxi

Taxi!	*¡Taxi!*	**tahk**-see
Can you call a taxi?	*¿Puede llamarme un taxi?*	**pway**-day yah-**mar**-may oon **tahk**-see
Where is a taxi stand?	*¿Dónde está una parada de taxi?*	**dohn**-day ay-**stah oo**-nah pah-**rah**-dah day **tahk**-see
Where can I get a taxi?	*¿Dónde puedo coger un taxi?*	**dohn**-day **pway**-doh koh-**hehr** oon **tahk**-see
Where can we get a taxi?	*¿Dónde podemos coger un taxi?*	**dohn**-day poh-**day**-mohs koh-**hehr** oon **tahk**-see
Are you free?	*¿Está libre?*	ay-**stah lee**-bray
Occupied.	*Ocupado.*	oh-koo-**pah**-doh
To ___, please.	*A ___, por favor.*	ah ___ por fah-**bor**
To this address.	*A esta dirección.*	ah **ay**-stah dee-rehk-thee-**ohn**
Take me to ___.	*Lléveme a ___.*	**yay**-bay-may ah
Take us to ___.	*Llévenos a ___.*	**yay**-bay-nohs ah
Approximately how much will it cost to go...?	*¿Más o menos cuánto me costará...?*	mahs oh **may**-nohs **kwahn**-toh may koh-stah-**rah**
...to ___	*...a ___*	ah
...the airport	*...al aeropuerto*	ahl ah-ay-roh-**pwehr**-toh
...the train station	*...a la estación de trenes*	ah lah ay-stah-thee-**ohn** day **tray**-nays
...this address	*...a esta dirección*	ah **ay**-stah dee-rehk-thee-**ohn**
Any extra supplement?	*¿Hay un suplemento extra?*	ī oon soop-lay-**mayn**-toh **ayk**-strah
Too much.	*Demasiado.*	day-mah-see-**ah**-doh
Can you take ___ people?	*¿Puede llevar a ___ personas?*	**pway**-day yay-**bar** ah ___ pehr-**soh**-nahs

Any extra fee?	¿Hay una tarifa extra?	ī **oo**-nah tah-**ree**-fah **ayk**-strah
Do you have an hourly rate?	¿Tiene una tarifa por hora?	tee-**ehn**-ay oo-nah tah-**ree**-fah por **oh**-rah
How much for a one-hour city tour?	¿Cuánto cuesta una excursión por la ciudad de una hora?	**kwahn**-toh **kway**-stah **oo**-nah ayk-skoor-see-**ohn** por lah thee-oo-**dahd** day **oo**-nah **oh**-rah

Taxis in Spain are cheap, except for going to and from airports (use airport buses for these trips). In Madrid and Barcelona, subways are cheap and efficient. Taxis usually take up to four people. If you have trouble flagging down a taxi, ask for directions to a *parada de taxi* (taxi stand). The simplest way to tell a cabbie where you want to go is by stating your destination followed by "please" (*"El Prado, por favor"*). Tipping isn't expected, but it's polite to round up. So if the fare is €19, round up to €20.

In the Taxi

The meter, please.	El taxímetro, por favor.	ehl tahk-**see**-may-troh por fah-**bor**
Where is the meter?	¿Dónde está el taxímetro?	**dohn**-day ay-**stah** ehl tahk-**see**-may-troh
I'm / We're in a hurry.	Tengo / Tenemos prisa.	**tayn**-goh / tay-**nay**-mohs **pree**-sah
Slow down.	Más despacio.	mahs day-**spah**-thee-oh
If you don't slow down, I'll throw up.	Si no va más despacio, voy a vomitar.	see noh bah mahs day-**spah**-thee-oh boy ah boh-mee-**tar**
Left / Right / Straight.	A la izquierda / A la derecha / Derecho.	ah lah eeth-kee-**ehr**-dah / ah lah day-**ray**-chah / day-**ray**-choh
I'd / We'd like to stop here briefly.	Me / Nos gustaría parar aquí brevemente.	may / nohs goo-stah-**ree**-ah pah-**rar** ah-**kee** bray-vay-**mehn**-tay

Please stop here for ___ minutes.	*Por favor pare aquí por ___ minutos.*	por fah-**bor pah**-ray ah-**kee** por ___ mee-**noo**-tohs
Can you wait?	*¿Puede esperar?*	**pway**-day ay-spay-**rar**
Crazy traffic, isn't it?	*Un tráfico de locos, ¿no?*	oon **trah**-fee-koh day **loh**-kohs noh
You drive like ...	*¡Usted conduce como...*	oo-**stehd** kohn-**doo**-thay **koh**-moh
...a madman!	*...un loco!*	oon **loh**-koh
...Michael Schumacher!	*...Michael Schumacher!*	"Michael Schumacher"
You drive very well.	*Usted conduce muy bien.*	oo-**stehd** kohn-**doo**-thay **moo**-ee bee-**yehn**
Where did you learn to drive?	*¿Dónde aprendió a conducir?*	**dohn**-day ah-prehn-dee-**oh** ah kohn-doo-**theer**
Stop here.	*Pare aquí.*	**pah**-ray ah-**kee**
Here is fine.	*Aquí está bien.*	ah-**kee** ay-**stah** bee-**yehn**
At this corner.	*En esta esquina.*	ayn **ay**-stah ay-**skee**-nah
The next corner.	*En la esquina siguiente.*	ayn lah ay-**skee**-nah see-**gehn**-tay
My change, please.	*Mi cambio, por favor.*	mee **kahm**-bee-oh por fah-**bor**
Keep the change.	*Quédese con el cambio.*	**kay**-day-say kohn ehl **kahm**-bee-oh
This ride is / was more fun than Disneyland.	*Este recorrido es / fue más divertido que Disneylandia.*	**ay**-stay ray-koh-**ree**-doh ays / fway mahs dee-vehr-**tee**-doh kay deez-nay-**lahn**-dee-ah

---

KEY PHRASES: TAXIS

Taxi!	*¡Taxi!*	**tahk**-see
Are you free?	*¿Está libre?*	ay-**stah lee**-bray
To ___ , please.	*A ___ , por favor.*	ah ___ por fah-**bor**
meter	*taxímetro*	tahk-**see**-may-troh
Stop here.	*Pare aquí.*	**pah**-ray ah-**kee**
Keep the change.	*Quédese con el cambio.*	**kay**-day-say kohn ehl **kahm**-bee-oh

Driving

Rental Wheels

car rental office	alquiler de coches	ahl-kee-**lehr** day **koh**-chays
I / We would like to rent...	Me / Nos gustaría alquilar...	may / nohs goo-stah-**ree**-ah ahl-kee-**lar**
...a car.	...un coche.	oon **koh**-chay
...a station wagon.	...un coche familiar.	oon **koh**-chay fah-mee-lee-**ar**
...a van.	...una frugoneta.	**oo**-nah froo-goh-**nay**-tah
...a motorcycle.	...una moto.	**oo**-nah **moh**-toh
...a motor scooter.	...una motocicleta.	**oo**-nah moh-toh-thee-**klay**-tah
How much per...?	¿Cuánto es por...?	**kwahn**-toh ays por
...hour	...hora	**oh**-rah
...half day	...medio día	**may**-dee-oh **dee**-ah
...day	...día	**dee**-ah
...week	...semana	say-**mah**-nah
Unlimited mileage?	¿Sin límite de kilómetros?	seen **lee**-mee-tay day kee-**loh**-may-trohs
When must I bring It back?	¿Cuándo tengo que traerlo de vuelta?	**kwahn**-doh **tayn**-goh kay trah-**ehr**-loh day **bwehl**-tah
Is there...?	¿Hay...?	ī
...a helmet	...un casco	oon **kah**-skoh
...a discount	...un descuento	oon days-**kwehn**-toh
...a deposit	...un depósito	oon day-**poh**-see-toh
...insurance	...seguro	say-**goo**-roh

At the Gas Station

gas station	gasolinera	gah-soh-lee-**nay**-rah
The nearest gas station?	¿La gasolinera más cercana?	lah gah-soh-lee-**nay**-rah mahs thehr-**kah**-nah
Self-service?	¿Auto-servicio?	ow-toh-sehr-**bee**-thee-oh

44

Fill the tank.	Llene el depósito.	**yay**-nay ehl day-**poh**-see-toh
Wash the windows.	Limpie el parabrisas.	**leem**-pee-ay ehl pah-rah-**bree**-sahs
I need...	Necesito...	nay-thay-**see**-toh
We need...	Necesitamos...	nay-thay-see-**tah**-mohs
...gas.	...gasolina.	gah-soh-**lee**-nah
...unleaded.	...sin plomo.	seen **ploh**-moh
...regular.	...normal.	nor-**mahl**
...super.	...super.	**soo**-pehr
...diesel.	...diesel, gasoleo.	**dee**-sehl, gah-**soh**-lee-oh
Check...	Cheque...	**chay**-kay
...the oil.	...el aceite.	ehl ah-**thay**-tay
...the air in the tires.	...el aire en las ruedas.	ehl ī-ray ayn lahs roo-**ay**-dahs
...the radiator.	...el radiador.	ehl rah-dee-ah-**dor**
...the battery.	...la batería.	lah bah-tay-**ree**-ah
...the sparkplugs.	...las bujías.	lahs boo-**hee**-ahs
...the headlights.	...los faros.	lohs **fah**-rohs
...the tail lights.	...las luces de atrás.	lahs **loo**-thays day ah-**trahs**
...the turn signal.	...el intermitente.	ehl een-tehr-mee-**tehn**-tay
...the brakes.	...los frenos.	lohs **fray**-nohs
...the transmission fluid.	...el líquido de transmisión.	ehl **lee**-kee-doh day trahns-mee-see-**ohn**
...the windshield wipers.	...los limpiapara-brisas.	lohs leem-pee-ah-pah-rah-**bree**-sahs
...the fuses.	...los fusibles.	lohs foo-**see**-blays
...the fan belt.	...la correa del ventilador.	lah koh-**ray**-ah dayl bayn-tee-lah-**dor**
...my pulse.	...mi pulso.	mee **pool**-soh
...my husband / wife.	...mi marido / esposa.	mee mah-**ree**-doh / ay-**spoh**-sah

Euros and liters replace dollars and gallons. If a euro is equal to a dollar and there are about four liters in a gallon, gas costing €1 a liter = $4 a gallon. In parts of Spain, diesel is called gasoleo.

Car Trouble

accident	*accidente*	ahk-thee-**dehn**-tay
breakdown	*averiado*	ah-bay-ree-**ah**-doh
dead battery	*batería*	bah-tay-**ree**-ah
	descargada	dehs-kar-**gah**-dah
funny noise	*ruido*	roo-**ee**-doh
	extraño	ayk-**strahn**-yoh
electrical problem	*problema*	proh-**blay**-mah
	eléctrico	ay-**lehk**-tree-koh
flat tire	*rueda*	roo-**ay**-dah
	pinchada	peen-**chah**-dah
shop with parts	*tienda de*	tee-**ehn**-dah day
	repuestos	ray-**pway**-stohs
My car won't start.	*Mi coche no*	mee **koh**-chay noh
	enciende.	ayn-thee-**ehn**-day
My car is broken.	*Mi coche está*	mee **koh**-chay ay-**stah**
	estropeado.	ay-stroh-pay-**ah**-doh
This doesn't work.	*Esto no*	**ay**-stoh noh
	funciona.	foonk-thee-**oh**-nah
It's overheating.	*Está caliente.*	ay-**stah** kahl-**yehn**-tay
It's a lemon	*Es un timo.*	ehs oon **tee**-moh
(swindle).		
I need...	*Necesito...*	nay-thay-**see**-toh
We need...	*Necesitamos...*	nay-thay-see-**tah**-mohs
...a tow truck.	*...una grúa.*	**oo**-nah **groo**-ah
...a mechanic.	*...un mecánico.*	oon may-**kah**-nee-koh
...a stiff drink.	*...un trago.*	oon **trah**-goh

For help with repair, look up "Repair" in the Services chapter on page 171.

Parking

parking lot	*aparcamiento*	ah-par-kah-mee-**ehn**-toh
parking garage	*parking, garage*	**par**-keeng, gah-**rah**-hay
Where can I park?	*¿Dónde puedo*	**dohn**-day **pway**-doh
	aparcar?	ah-par-**kar**

Is parking nearby?	¿Hay un parking cercano?	ī oon **par**-keeng thehr-**kah**-noh
Can I park here?	¿Puedo aparcar aquí?	**pway**-doh ah-par-**kar** ah-**kee**
Is this a safe place to park?	¿Es éste un sitio seguro para aparcar?	ays **ay**-stay oon **seet**-yoh say-**goo**-roh **pah**-rah ah-par-**kar**
How long can I park here?	¿Por cuánto tiempo puedo aparcar aquí?	por **kwahn**-toh tee-**ehm**-poh **pway**-doh ah-par-**kar** ah-**kee**
Must I pay to park here?	¿Tengo que pagar por aparcar aquí?	**tayn**-goh kay pah-**gar** por ah-par-**kar** ah-**kee**
How much per hour / day?	¿Cuánto cuesta por hora / día?	**kwahn**-toh **kway**-stah por **oh**-rah / **dee**-ah

Parking in Spain can be hazardous. Park legally. Many towns require parking permits, sold at tobacco shops. To give your car a local profile, cover the rental decal and put a local newspaper inside the back window. Leave the car empty and, some would advise, unlocked overnight. If it's a hatchback, remove the shelf behind the back seat to show thieves you have *nada* in the trunk. Get safe parking tips from your hotel.

TRAVELING

KEY PHRASES: DRIVING

car	coche	**koh**-chay
gas station	gasolinera	gah-soh-lee-**nay**-rah
parking lot	aparcamiento	ah-par-kah-mee-**ehn**-toh
accident	accidente	ahk-thee-**dehn**-tay
left / right	izquierda / derecha	eeth-kee-**ehr**-dah / day-**ray**-chah
straight ahead	derecho	day-**ray**-choh
downtown	centro ciudad	**thayn**-troh thee-oo-**dahd**
How do I get to ___?	¿Cómo llego a ___?	**koh**-moh **yay**-goh ah
Where can I park?	¿Dónde puedo aparcar?	**dohn**-day **pway**-doh ah-par-**kar**

Finding
Your Way

English	Spanish	Pronunciation
I'm going to ___.	Voy a ___.	boy ah
We're going to ___.	Vamos a ___.	**bah**-mohs ah
How do I get to ___?	¿Cómo llego a ___?	**koh**-moh **yay**-goh ah
How do we get to ___?	¿Cómo llegamos a ___?	**koh**-moh yay-**gah**-mohs ah
Do you have a...?	¿Tiene un...?	tee-**ehn**-ay oon
...city map	...mapa de la ciudad	**mah**-pah day lah thee-oo-**dahd**
...road map	...mapa de carretera	**mah**-pah day kah-ray-**tay**-rah
How many minutes / hours...?	¿Cuántos minutos / horas...?	**kwahn**-tohs mee-**noo**-tohs / **oh**-rahs
...on foot	...a pie	ah pee-**ay**
...by bicycle	...en bicicleta	ayn bee-thee-**klay**-tah
...by car	...en coche	ayn **koh**-chay
How many kilometers to ___?	¿Cuántos kilómetros a ___?	**kwahn**-tohs kee-**loh**-may-trohs ah
What's the... route to Madrid?	¿Cuál es la ruta... para Madrid?	kwahl ays lah **roo**-tah... **pah**-rah mah-**dreed**
...most scenic	...más panorámica	mahs pah-noh-**rah**-mee-kah
...fastest	...más rápida	mahs **rah**-pee-dah
...most interesting	...más interesante	mahs een-tay-ray-**sahn**-tay
Point it out?	¿Señálelo?	sayn-**yah**-lay-loh
I'm lost.	Estoy perdido[a].	ay-**stoy** pehr-**dee**-doh
Where am I?	¿Dónde estoy?	**dohn**-day ay-**stoy**
Where is...?	¿Dónde está...?	**dohn**-day ay-**stah**
The nearest...?	¿El más cercano...?	ehl mahs thehr-**kah**-noh
Where is this address?	¿Dónde se encuentra esta dirección?	**dohn**-day say ayn-**kwehn**-trah **ay**-stah dee-rehk-thee-**ohn**

TRAVELING

Route-Finding Words

city map	mapa de la ciudad	**mah**-pah day lah thee-oo-**dahd**
road map	mapa de carretera	**mah**-pah day kah-ray-**tay**-rah
downtown	centro ciudad	**thayn**-troh thee-oo-**dahd**
straight ahead	derecho	day-**ray**-choh
left	izquierda	eeth-kee-**ehr**-dah
right	derecha	day-**ray**-chah
first	primero	pree-**may**-roh
next	siguiente	see-**gehn**-tay
intersection	intersección	een-tehr-sehk-thee-**ohn**
corner	esquina	ay-**skee**-nah
block	manzana	mahn-**thah**-nah
roundabout	glorieta	gloh-ree-**eh**-tah
stoplight	semáforo	say-**mah**-foh-roh
(main) square	plaza (principal)	**plah**-thah (preen-thee-**pahl**)
street	calle	**kah**-yay
bridge	puente	**pwehn**-tay
tunnel	tunnel	**too**-nehl
highway	carretera	kah-ray-**tay**-rah
freeway	autopista	ow-toh-**pee**-stah
north	norte	**nor**-tay
south	sur	soor
east	este	**ay**-stay
west	oeste	oh-**ay**-stay

The Police

In any country, the flashing lights of a patrol car are a sure sign that someone's in trouble. If it's you, try this handy phrase: "*Lo siento, soy un turista.*" (Sorry, I'm a tourist.) Or, for the adventurous: "*Si no le gusta como conduzco, quítese de la acera.*" (If you don't like how I drive, stay off the sidewalk.)

I'm late for my tour.	*Llego tarde a mi excursión.*	**yay**-goh **tar**-day ah mee ehk-skoor-see-**ohn**
Can I buy your hat?	*¿Puedo comprar su sombrero?*	**pway**-doh kohm-**prar** soo sohm-**bray**-roh
What seems to be the problem?	*¿Cuál puede ser el problema?*	kwahl **pway**-day sehr ehl proh-**blay**-mah
Sorry, I'm a tourist.	*Lo siento, soy un turista.*	loh see-**ehn**-toh soy oon too-**ree**-stah

Reading Road Signs

ceda el paso	yield
centro de la ciudad	to the center of town
construcción	construction
cuidado	caution
despacio	slow
desvío	detour
dirección única	one-way street
entrada	entrance
estacionamiento prohibido	no parking
obras	workers ahead
próxima salida	next exit
peage	toll road
peatones	pedestrians
salida	exit
stop	stop
todas direcciones	out of town (all directions)

Other Signs You May See

abierto	open
abierto de... a...	open from... to...
agua no potable	undrinkable water
alquilo	for rent
averiado	out of service
caballeros	men
camas	vacancy

cerrado	closed
cerrado por vacaciones	closed for vacation
cerrado por obras	closed for restoration
completo	no vacancy
empujar / tirar	push / pull
entrada libre	free admission
habitaciones	vacancy
hay...	we have...
no fumar	no smoking
no tocar	do not touch
ocupado	occupied
paso prohibido	no entry
peligro	danger
perro molesto	mean dog
prohibido	forbidden
salida de emergencia	emergency exit
señoras	women
servicios	toilets
tirar / empujar	pull / push
turismo	tourist information office
vendo	for sale

Standard Road Signs

 AND LEARN THESE ROAD SIGNS

Speed Limit (km/hr)

Yield

No Passing

End of No Passing Zone

One Way

Intersection

Main Road

Freeway

Danger

No Entry

No Entry for Cars

All Vehicles Prohibited

Parking

No Parking

Customs

Peace

SLEEPING

Places to Stay

hotel	*hotel*	oh-**tehl**
small, family-run hotel	*pensión*	payn-see-**ohn**
fancy historic hotel	*parador*	pah-rah-**dor**
room in private home	*habitación*	ah-bee-tah-thee-**ohn**
youth hostel	*albergue de juventud*	ahl-**behr**-gay day hoo-behn-**tood**
vacancy sign (literally "rooms," "beds")	*habitaciones, camas*	ah-bee-tah-thee-**oh**-nays, **kah**-mahs
no vacancy	*completo*	kohm-**play**-toh

Spanish hotels come with a handy government-regulated classification system. Look for a blue and white plaque by the hotel door indicating the category:

Hotel (H) and **Hostal (Hs)**—The most comfortable and expensive (rated with stars). Don't confuse *hostales* with youth hostels.

Hotel-Residencia (HR) and **Hostal-Residencia (HsR)**—Hotels without restaurants.

Pensión (P), Casa de Huéspedes (CH), and **Fonda (F)—**
Cheaper, usually family-run places. If you're on a tight
budget, these can be a good value.

Parador—Government-run hotels, often in refurbished cas-
tles or palaces. They can be a good value, particularly for
travelers under 30 or over 60, who enjoy discounted rates
(see www.parador.es).

Reserving a Room

I like to reserve rooms a few days in advance as I travel.
But if my itinerary is set, I reserve before I leave home. To
reserve from the U.S. by e-mail or fax, use the handy form
in the Appendix (online at www.ricksteves.com/reservation).

Hello.	*Hola.*	**oh**-lah
Do you speak English?	*¿Habla usted inglés?*	**ah**-blah oo-**stehd** een-**glays**
Do you have a room...?	*¿Tiene una habitación libre...?*	tee-**ehn**-ay **oo**-nah ah-bee-tah-thee-**ohn lee**-bray
...for one person	*...para una persona*	**pah**-rah **oo**-nah pehr-**soh**-nah
...for two people	*...para dos personas*	**pah**-rah dohs pehr-**soh**-nahs
...for today / tomorrow	*...para hoy / mañana*	**pah**-rah oy / mahn-**yah**-nah
...for the day after tomorrow	*...para pasado mañana*	**pah**-rah pah-**sah**-doh mahn-**yah**-nah
...for two nights	*...para dos noches*	**pah**-rah dohs **noh**-chays
...for this Friday	*...para este viernes*	**pah**-rah **ay**-stay bee-**ehr**-nays
...for June 21	*...para el veintiuno de junio*	**pah**-rah ehl bayn-tee-**oo**-noh day **h**oon-yoh
Yes or no?	*¿Sí o no?*	see oh noh
I would like...	*Me gustaría...*	may goo-stah-**ree**-ah
...a private bathroom.	*...un baño privado.*	oon **bahn**-yoh pree-**vah**-doh

SLEEPING

...your cheapest room.	...su habitación más barata.	soo ah-bee-tah-thee-**ohn** mahs bah-**rah**-tah
..._ bed(s) for _ person(s) in _ room(s).	..._ cama(s) para _ persona(s) en _ habitación(es).	_ **kah**-mah(s) **pah**-rah _ pehr-**soh**-nah(s) ayn _ ah-bee-tah-thee-**ohn**(ays)
How much is it?	¿Cuánto cuesta?	**kwahn**-toh **kway**-stah
Anything cheaper?	¿Nada más barato?	**nah**-dah mahs bah-**rah**-toh
I'll take it.	La quiero.	lah kee-**ehr**-oh
My name is ___.	Me llamo ___.	may **yah**-moh
I'll stay / We'll stay...	Me quedaré / Nos quedaremos...	may kay-dah-**ray** / nohs kay-dah-**ray**-mohs
...for _ night(s).	...para _ noche(s).	**pah**-rah _ **noh**-chay(s)
I'll come / We'll come...	Vendré / Vendremos...	bayn-**dray** / bayn-**dray**-mohs
...in the morning.	...por la mañana.	por lah mahn-**yah**-nah
...in the afternoon.	...por la noche.	por lah **noh**-chay
...in the evening.	...por la tarde.	por lah **tar**-day
...in one hour.	...en una hora.	ayn **oo**-nah **oh**-rah
...before 4:00 in the afternoon.	...antes de las cuatro de la tarde.	**ahn**-tays day lahs **kwah**-troh day lah **tar**-day
...Friday before 6 p.m.	...el viernes antes de las seis de la tarde.	ehl bee-**ehr**-nays **ahn**-tays day lahs says day lah **tar**-day
Thank you.	Gracias.	**grah**-thee-ahs

Using a Credit Card

If you need to secure your reservation with a credit card, here's the lingo.

Is a deposit required?	¿Se requiere un depósito?	say ray-kee-**ay**-ray oon day-**poh**-see-toh
Credit card O.K.?	¿Tarjeta de crédito O.K.?	tar-**hay**-tah day **kray**-dee-toh "O.K."
credit card	tarjeta de crédito	tar-**hay**-tah day **kray**-dee-toh

debit card	*tarjeta de débito*	tar-**hay**-tah day **day**-bee-toh
The name on the card is...	*El nombre en la tarjeta es...*	ehl **nohm**-bray ayn lah tar-**hay**-tah ays
The credit card number is...	*El número de la tarjeta de crédito es...*	ehl **noo**-may-roh day lah tar-**hay**-tah day **kray**-dee-toh ays
0	*cero*	**theh**-roh
1	*uno*	**oo**-noh
2	*dos*	dohs
3	*tres*	trehs
4	*cuatro*	**kwah**-troh
5	*cinco*	**theen**-koh
6	*seis*	says
7	*siete*	see-**eh**-tay
8	*ocho*	**oh**-choh
9	*nueve*	**nway**-bay
The expiration date is...	*La fecha de expiración es...*	lah **fay**-chah day ehk-spee-rah-thee-**ohn** ays
January	*enero*	ay-**nay**-roh
February	*febrero*	fay-**bray**-roh
March	*marzo*	**mar**-thoh
April	*abril*	ah-**breel**
May	*mayo*	**mah**-yoh
June	*junio*	**hoon**-yoh
July	*julio*	**hool**-yoh
August	*agosto*	ah-**goh**-stoh
September	*scptiembre*	sehp-tee-**ehm**-bray
October	*octubre*	ohk-**too**-bray
November	*noviembre*	noh-bee-**ehm**-bray
December	*diciembre*	dee-thee-**ehm**-bray
2003	*dos mil tres*	dohs meel trehs
2004	*dos mil cuatro*	dohs meel **kwah**-troh
2005	*dos mil cinco*	dohs meel **theen**-koh
2006	*dos mil seis*	dohs meel says
2007	*dos mil siete*	dohs meel see-**eh**-tay
2008	*dos mil ocho*	dohs meel **oh**-choh

2009	*dos mil nueve*	dohs meel **nway**-bay
2010	*dos mil diez*	dohs meel dee-**ayth**
Can I reserve with a credit card and pay in cash?	*¿Puedo reservar con una tarjeta de crédito y pagar en efectivo?*	**pway**-doh ray-sehr-**bar** kohn **oo**-nah tar-**hay**-tah day **kray**-dee-toh ee pah-**gar** ayn ay-fehk-**tee**-voh
I have another card.	*Tengo otra tarjeta de crédito.*	**tayn**-goh **oh**-trah tar-**hay**-tah day **kray**-dee-toh

If your *tarjeta de crédito* is not approved, say "*Tengo otra tarjeta de crédito*" (I have another card)—if you do.

KEY PHRASES: SLEEPING

I'd like to make / confirm a reservation.	*Me gustaría hacer / confirmar una reserva.*	may goo-stah-**ree**-ah ah-**thehr** / kohn-feer-**mar** **oo**-nah ray-**sehr**-bah
I'd like a room (for two people), please.	*Me gustaría una habitación (para dos personas), per favor.*	may goo-stah-**ree**-ah **oo**-nah ah-bee-tah-thee-**ohn** (**pah**-rah dohs pehr-**soh**-nahs) por fah-**bor**
...with / without / and	*...con / sin / y*	kohn / seen / ee
...toilet	*...aseo*	ah-**say**-oh
...shower	*...ducha*	**doo**-chah
Can I see the room?	*¿Puedo ver la habitación?*	**pway**-doh behr lah ah-bee-tah-thee-**ohn**
How much is it?	*¿Cuánto cuesta?*	**kwahn**-toh **kway**-stah
Credit card O.K.?	*¿Tarjeta de crédito O.K.?*	tar-**hay**-tah day **kray**-dee-toh "O.K."

El Alfabeto

If phoning, you can use the code alphabet below to spell out your name if necessary. Unless you're giving the hotelier your name as it appears on your credit card, consider using a shorter version of your name to make things easier.

A	ah	*América*	ah-**may**-ree-kah
B	bay	*Barcelona*	bar-thay-**loh**-nah
C	thay	*Carlos*	**kar**-lohs
D	day	*Dinamarca*	dee-nah-**mar**-kah
E	ay	*España*	ay-**spahn**-yah
F	**ayf**-fay	*Francia*	**frahn**-thee-ah
G	gay	*Gerona*	hay-**roh**-nah
H	**ah**-chay	*Holanda*	oh-**lahn**-dah
I	ee	*Italia*	ee-**tah**-lee-ah
J	**hoh**-tah	*Jota*	**hoh**-tah
K	kah	*Kilo*	**kee**-loh
L	**ayl**-yay	*Lola*	**loh**-lah
M	**aym**-ay	*Madrid*	mah-**dreed**
N	**ayn**-yay	*Noruega*	nor-**way**-gah
O	oh	*Oslo*	**oh**-sloh
P	pay	*Portugal*	por-too-**gahl**
Q	koo	*Queso*	**kay**-soh
R	**ayr**-ay	*Ramón*	rah-**mohn**
S	**ays**-ay	*Sevilla*	seh-**vee**-yah
T	tay	*Toledo*	toh-**lay**-doh
U	oo	*Uruguay*	oo-roo-**gwī**
V	vay	*Valencia*	bah-**layn**-thee-ah
W	bay **doh**-blay	*Washington*	**wah**-sheeng-tohn
X	**ay**-hees	*Equix*	**ay**-keeks
Y	ee-**gryay**-gah	*Yoga*	**yoh**-gah
Z	**thay**-tah	*Zamora*	thah-**moh**-rah

SLEEPING

Just the Fax, Ma'am

If you're booking a room by fax...

I would like to send a fax.	*Me gustaría enviar un fax.*	may goo-stah-**ree**-ah ayn-bee-**ar** oon fahks
What is your fax number?	*¿Cuál es su número de fax?*	kwahl ays soo **noo**-may-roh day fahks
Your fax number is not working.	*Su número de fax no funciona.*	soo **noo**-may-roh day fahks noh foonk-thee-**oh**-nah
Please turn on your fax machine.	*Por favor, enchufe su máquina de fax.*	por fah-**bor** ayn-**choo**-fay soo **mah**-kee-nah day fahks

Getting Specific

I / We would like a room...	*Me / Nos gustaría una habitación...*	may / nohs goo-stah-**ree**-ah **oo**-nah ah-bee-tah-thee-**ohn**
...with / without / and	*...con / sin / y*	kohn / seen / ee
...toilet	*...aseo*	ah-**say**-oh
...shower	*...ducha*	**doo**-chah
...shower down the hall	*...ducha al fondo del pasillo*	**doo**-chah ahl **fohn**-doh dayl pah-**see**-yoh
...bathtub	*...bañera*	bahn-**yay**-rah
...double bed	*...cama de matrimonio*	**kah**-mah day mah-tree-**moh**-nee-oh
...twin beds	*...dos camas*	dohs **kah**-mahs
...balcony	*...balcón*	bahl-**kohn**
...view	*...vista*	**bee**-stah
...with only a sink	*...sólo con lavabo*	**soh**-loh kohn lah-**bah**-boh
...on the ground floor	*...en el piso bajo*	ayn ehl **pee**-soh **bah**-hoh
...television	*...televisión*	tay-lay-bee-see-**ohn**
...telephone	*...teléfono*	tay-**lay**-foh-noh
...air conditioning	*...aire acondicionado*	ī-ray ah-kohn-dee-thee-oh-**nah**-doh
...kitchenette	*...cocina*	koh-**thee**-nah

SLEEPING

Do you have...?	*¿Tiene...?*	tee-**ehn**-ay
...an elevator	*...un ascensor*	oon ah-thehn-**sor**
...a swimming pool	*...una piscina*	**oo**-nah pee-**thee**-nah
I arrive Monday, depart Wednesday.	*Llego el lunes, salgo el miércoles.*	**yay**-goh ehl **loo**-nays, **sahl**-goh ehl mee-**ehr**-koh-lays
We arrive Monday, depart Wednesday.	*Llegamos el lunes, salimos el miércoles.*	yay-**gah**-mohs ehl **loo**-nays, sah-**lee**-mohs ehl mee-**ehr**-koh-lays
I am desperate.	*Estoy desesperado[a].*	ay-**stoy** day-say-spay-**rah**-doh
We are desperate.	*Estamos desesperados[as].*	ay-**stah**-mohs day-say-spay-**rah**-dohs
I can / We can sleep anywhere.	*Puedo / Podemos dormir en cualquier sitio.*	**pway**-doh / poh-**day**-mohs **dor**-meer ayn kwahl-kee-**ehr** seet-yoh
I have a sleeping bag.	*Tengo un saco de dormir.*	**tayn**-goh oon **sah**-koh day dor-**meer**
We have sleeping bags.	*Tenemos unos sacos de dormir.*	tay-**nay**-mohs **oo**-nohs **sah**-kohs day dor-**meer**
Will you call another hotel for me?	*¿Llamaría a otro hotel para mi?*	yah-mah-**ree**-ah ah **oh**-troh oh-**tehl** **pah**-rah mee

Families

Do you have...?	*¿Tiene...?*	tee-**ehn**-ay
...a family room	*...una habitación familiar*	**oo**-nah ah-bee-tah-thee-**ohn** fah-mee-lee-**ar**
...family rates	*...precios familiares*	**pray**-thee-ohs fah-mee-lee-**ah**-rays
...discounts for children	*...descuentos para niños*	days-**kwehn**-tohs **pah**-rah **neen**-yohs
I have / We have...	*Tengo / Tenemos...*	**tayn**-goh / tay-**nay**-mohs
...one child,	*...un niño, de*	oon **neen**-yoh day

age ___ months / years.	edad ___ meses / años.	ay-**dahd** ___ may-says / **ahn**-yohs
...two children, ages ___ and ___ years.	...dos niños, de de edad ___ y ___ años.	dohs **neen**-yohs day ay-**dahd** ___ ee ___ **ahn**-yohs
I'd / We'd like...	Me / Nos gustaría...	may / nohs goo-stah-**ree**-ah
...a crib.	...una cuna.	**oo**-nah **koo**-nah
...a small extra bed.	...una cama plegable extra.	**oo**-nah **kah**-mah play-**gah**-blay **ayk**-strah
...bunk beds.	...una litera.	**oo**-nah lee-**tay**-rah
babysitting service	...servicio de canguro.	sehr-**bee**-thee-oh day kahn-**goo**-roh
Is a... nearby?	¿Hay cerca un...?	ī **thehr**-kah oon
...park	...parque	**par**-kay
...playground	...área para jugar	**ah**-ray-ah **pah**-rah hoo-**gar**
...swimming pool	...piscina	pee-**thee**-nah

For fun, the Spanish call kids *mono* (monkey) and *mondada* (peel).

Mobility Issues

Stairs are...	Las escaleras son...	lahs ay-skah-**lay**-rahs sohn
...impossible	...imposibles	eem-poh-**seeb**-lays
...difficult	...difíciles	dee-**fee**-thee-lays
...for me / us.	...para mí / nosotros.	**pah**-rah mee / noh-**soh**-trohs
...for my husband / my wife.	...para mi marido / mi esposa.	**pah**-rah mee mah-**ree**-doh / mee ay-**spoh**-sah
Do you have...?	¿Tiene...?	tee-**ehn**-ay
...an elevator	...un ascensor	oon ah-thehn-**sor**
...a ground floor room	...una habitación en la planta baja	**oo**-nah ah-bee-tah-thee-**ohn** ayn lah **plahn**-tah **bah**-hah
...a wheelchair-accessible room	...acceso de silla de ruedas	ahk-**say**-soh day **see**-yah day roo-**ay**-dahs

Confirming, Changing, and Canceling Reservations

You can use this template for your telephone call.

I have / We have a reservation.	Tengo / Tenemos la reserva hecha.	**tayn**-goh / tay-**nay**-mohs lah ray-**sehr**-bah **ay**-chah
My name is ___.	Me llamo ___.	may **yah**-moh
I'd like to... my reservation.	Me gustaría... mi reserva.	may goo-stah-**ree**-ah... mee ray-**sehr**-bah
...confirm	...confirmar	kohn-feer-**mar**
...reconfirm	...reconfirmar	ray-kohn-feer-**mar**
...cancel	...cancelar	kahn-thay-**lar**
...change	...cambiar	kahm-bee-**ar**
The reservation is / was for...	La reserva es / era para...	lah ray-**sehr**-bah ehs / **eh**-rah **pah**-rah
...one person	...una persona	**oo**-nah pehr-**soh**-nah
...two people	...dos personas	dohs pehr-**soh**-nahs
...today / tomorrow	...hoy / mañana	oy / mahn-**yah**-nah
...August 13	...el trece de agosto	ehl **tray**-thay day ah-**goh**-stoh
...one night / two nights	...una noche / dos noches	**oo**-nah **noh**-chay / dohs **noh**-chays
Did you find my / our reservation?	¿Encontró mi / nuestra reserva?	ayn-kohn-**troh** mee / **nway**-strah ray-**sehr**-bah
What is your cancellation policy?	¿Cuál es la norma de cancelación?	kwahl ays lah **nor**-mah day kahn-thay-lah-thee-**ohn**
Will I be billed for the first night if I can't make it?	¿Me cobrarán la primera noche si no puedo llegar?	may koh-brah-**rahn** lah pree-**mehr**-ah **noh**-chay see noh **pway**-doh yay-**gar**
I'd like to arrive instead on...	Me gustaría llegar en vez del...	may goo-stah-**ree**-ah yay-**gar** ayn bayth dehl
We'd like to arrive instead on...	Nos gustaría llegar en vez del...	nohs goo-stah-**ree**-ah yay-**gar** ayn bayth dehl
Is everything O.K.?	¿Está todo bien?	ay-**stah toh**-doh bee-**yehn**

Thank you.	Gracias.	**grah**-thee-ahs
See you then.	Hasta entonces.	**ah**-stah ayn-**tohn**-thays
I'm sorry I need	Lo siento que	loh see-**ehn**-toh kay
to cancel.	necesito	nay-thay-**see**-toh
	cancelar.	kahn-thay-**lar**

Nailing Down the Price

How much is...?	¿Cuánto cuesta...?	**kwahn**-toh **kway**-stah
...a room for ___	...una habitación	**oo**-nah ah-bee-tah-thee-**ohn**
people	para ___ personas	**pah**-rah ___ pehr-**soh**-nahs
...your cheapest	...su habitación	soo ah-bee-tah-thee-**ohn**
room	más barata	mahs bah-**rah**-tah
Is breakfast	¿El desayuno	ehl day-sah-**yoo**-noh
included?	está incluido?	ay-**stah** een-kloo-**ee**-doh
Is breakfast	¿Se requiere	say ray-kee-**ay**-ray
required?	desayuno?	day-sah-**yoo**-noh
How much	¿Cuánto cuesta	**kwahn**-toh **kway**-stah
without breakfast?	sin desayuno?	seen day-sah-**yoo**-noh
Is half-pension	¿Se requiere	say ray-kee-**ay**-ray
required?	media pensión?	**may**-dee-ah payn-see-**ohn**
Complete price?	¿El precio	ehl **pray**-thee-oh
	completo?	kohm-**play**-toh
Is it cheaper if I	¿Es más barato	ays mahs bah-**rah**-toh
stay three nights?	si me quedo	see may **kay**-doh
	tres noches?	trehs **noh**-chays
I will stay	Me quedaré	may kay-dah-**ray**
three nights.	tres noches.	trehs **noh**-chays
We will stay	Nos quedaremos	nohs kay-dah-**ray**-mohs
three nights.	tres noches.	trehs **noh**-chays
Is it cheaper if I	¿Es más barato	ays mahs bah-**rah**-toh
pay in cash?	si pago en	see **pah**-goh ayn
	efectivo?	ay-fehk-**tee**-voh
What is the cost	¿Cuál es el costo	kwahl ays ehl **koh**-stoh
per week?	por semana?	por say-**mah**-nah

SLEEPING

Choosing a Room

Can I see the room?	*¿Puedo ver la` habitación?*	**pway**-doh behr lah ah-bee-tah-thee-**ohn**
Can we see the room?	*¿Podemos ver la habitación?*	poh-**day**-mohs behr lah ah-bee-tah-thee-**ohn**
Show me another room?	*¿Enséñeme otra habitación?*	ayn-**sayn**-yay-may **oh**-trah ah-bee-tah-thee-**ohn**
Show us another room?	*¿Enséñenos otra habitación?*	ayn-**sayn**-yay-nohs **oh**-trah ah-bee-tah-thee-**ohn**
Do you have something...?	*¿Tiene algo...?*	tee-**ehn**-ay **ahl**-goh
...larger / smaller	*...más grande / más pequeño*	mahs **grahn**-day / mahs pay-**kayn**-yoh
...better / cheaper	*...mejor / más barato*	may-**hor** / mahs bah-**rah**-toh
...brighter	*...con más claridad*	kohn mahs klah-ree-**dahd**
...in the back	*...en la parte de atrás*	ayn lah **par**-tay day ah-**trahs**
...quieter	*...más tranquillo*	mahs trahn-**kee**-yoh
Sorry, it's not right for me.	*Lo siento, no es para mí.*	loh see-**ehn**-toh no ays **pah**-rah mee
Sorry, it's not right for us.	*Lo siento, no es para nosotros.*	loh see-**ehn**-toh no ays **pah**-rah noh-**soh**-trohs
I'll take it.	*La quiero.*	lah kee-**ehr**-oh
We'll take it.	*La queremos.*	lah kay-**ray**-mohs
My key, please.	*Mi llave, por favor.*	mee **yah**-bay por fah-**bor**
Sleep well.	*Que duerma bien.*	kay **dwehr**-mah bee-**yehn**
Good night.	*Buenas noches.*	**bway**-nahs **noh**-chays

In Spain, views often come with street noise (a Spanish specialty). You can ask for a room "*con vista*" or "*tranquillo.*" If sleep is a priority, go with the latter.

Breakfast

Is breakfast included?	¿El desayuno está incluido?	ehl day-sah-**yoo**-noh ay-**stah** een-kloo-**ee**-doh
How much is breakfast?	¿Cuánto cuesta` el desayuno?	**kwahn**-toh **kway**-stah ehl day-sah-**yoo**-noh
When does breakfast start?	¿Cuándo empieza el desayuno?	**kwahn**-doh ehm-pee-**ay**-thah ehl day-sah-**yoo**-noh
When does breakfast end?	¿Cuándo acaba el desayuno?	**kwahn**-doh ah-**kah**-bah ehl day-sah-**yoo**-noh
Where is breakfast served?	¿Dónde sirven el desayuno?	**dohn**-day **seer**-behn ehl day-sah-**yoo**-noh

Hotel Help

I / We would like...	Me / Nos gustaría...	may / nohs goo-stah-**ree**-ah
...a / another	...un / otro	oon / **oh**-troh
...towel.	...toalla.	toh-**ah**-yah
...clean towel(s).	...toalla(s) limpia(s).	toh-**ah**-yah(s) **leem**-pee-ah(s)
...pillow.	...almohada.	ahl-moh-**ah**-dah
...clean sheets.	...sábanas limpias.	**sah**-bah-nahs **leem**-pee-ahs
...blanket.	...manta.	**mahn**-tah
...glass.	...vaso.	**bah**-soh
...sink stopper.	...tapón.	tah-**pohn**
...soap.	...jabón.	hah-**bohn**
...toilet paper.	...papel higiénico.	pah-**pehl** ee-hee-**ay**-nee-koh
...electrical adapter.	...adaptador eléctrico.	ah-dahp-**tor** ay-**layk**-tree-koh
...brighter light bulb.	...bombilla más brillante.	bohm-**bee**-yah mahs bree-**yahn**-tay
...lamp.	...lámpara.	**lahm**-pah-rah
...chair.	...silla.	**see**-yah
...table.	...mesa.	**may**-sah

SLEEPING

English	Spanish	Pronunciation
...modem.	...modem.	**moh**-dehm
...Internet access.	...acceso a Internet.	ah-**say**-soh ah **een**-tehr-neht
...different room.	...habitación diferente.	ah-bee-tah-thee-**ohn** dee-fay-**rehn**-tay
...silence.	...silencio.	see-**lehn**-thee-oh
...to speak to the manager.	...hablar con el encargado.	ah-**blar** kohn ehl ayn-kar-**gah**-doh
I've fallen and I can't get up.	Me he caído y no puedo levantarme.	may ay kah-**ee**-doh ee noh **pway**-doh lay-vahn-**tar**-may
How can I make the room cooler / warmer?	¿Cómo puedo enfríar / calentar la habitación?	**koh**-moh **pway**-doh ayn-free-**ar** / kah-lehn-**tar** lah ah-bee-tah-thee-**ohn**
Where can I wash / hang my laundry?	¿Dónde puedo lavar / tender mi ropa?	**dohn**-day **pway**-doh lah-**bar** / tehn-**dehr** mee **roh**-pah
Is a...nearby?	¿Hay una... cerca?	ī **oo**-nah... **thehr**-kah
...full-service laundry	...lavandería	lah-vahn-deh-**ree**-ah
...self-service laundry	...lavandería de autoservicio	lah-vahn-deh-**ree**-ah day ow-toh-sehr-**bee**-thee-oh
I would like to stay another night.	Me gustaría quedarme otra noche.	may goo-stah-**ree**-ah kay-**dar**-may **oh**-trah **noh**-chay
We would like to stay another night.	Nos gustaría quedarnos otra noche.	nohs goo-stah-**ree**-ah kay-**dar**-nohs **oh**-trah **noh**-chay
Where can I park?	¿Dónde puedo aparcar?	**dohn**-day **pway**-doh ah-par-**kar**
What time do you lock up?	¿A qué hora cierran la puerta?	ah kay **oh**-rah thee-**ay**-rahn lah **pwehr**-tah
Please wake me at 7:00.	Despiérteme a las siete, por favor.	days-pee-**ehr**-tay-may ah lahs see-**eh**-tay por fah-**bor**
Where do you go for lunch / dinner / coffee?	¿A dónde se va para almorzar / cenar / café?	ah **dohn**-day say bah **pah**-rah ahl-mor-**thar** / thay-**nar** / kah-**fay**

66

Chill Out

Many hotel rooms in the Mediterranean part of Europe come with air-conditioning—often controlled with a stick (like a TV remote). Various sticks have the same basic features:

- fan icon (click to toggle through the wind power from light to gale)
- louver icon (click to choose: steady air flow or waves)
- snowflakes and sunshine icons (heat or cold, generally just one or the other is possible: cool air in summer, heat in winter)
- two clock settings (to determine how many hours the air-conditioning will stay on before turning off, or stay off before turning on).
- temperature control (20° or 21° is a comfortable temperature in Celsius—see the thermometer on page 199).

Hotel Hassles

English	Spanish	Pronunciation
Come with me.	Venga conmigo.	**vayn**-gah kohn-**mee**-goh
I have / We have	Tengo / Tenemos	**tayn**-goh / tay-**nay**-mohs
a problem in the room.	un problema con la habitación.	oon proh-**blay**-mah kohn lah ah-bee-tah-thee-**ohn**
It smells bad.	Huele mal.	**way**-lay mahl
bugs	moscas	**moh**-skahs
mice	ratones	rah-**toh**-nays
cockroaches	cucarachas	koo-kah-**rah**-chahs
prostitutes	prostitutas	proh-stee-**too**-tahs
I'm covered with bug bites.	Estoy llena de mordeduras de moscas.	ay-**stoy yay**-nah day mor-day-**doo**-rahs day **moh**-skahs
The bed is too soft / hard.	La cama es demasiada blanda / dura.	lah **kah**-mah ays day-mah-see-**ah**-dah **blahn**-dah / **doo**-rah
I can't sleep.	No puedo dormir.	noh **pway**-doh dor-**meer**
The room is too...	La habitación está demasiado...	lah ah-bee-tah-thee-**ohn** ays-**tah** day-mah-see-**ah**-doh
...hot / cold.	...caliente / fría.	kahl-**yehn**-tay / **free**-ah

SLEEPING

...noisy / dirty.	...ruidosa / sucia.	roo-ee-**doh**-sah / **soo**-thee-ah
I can't open / shut...	No puedo abrir / cerrar...	noh **pway**-doh ah-**breer** / thay-**rar**
...the door / the window.	...la puerta / la ventana.	lah **pwehr**-tah / lah bayn-**tah**-nah
Air conditioner...	Aire acondicionado...	ī-ray ah-kohn-dee-thee-oh-**nah**-doh
Lamp...	Lámpara...	**lahm**-pah-rah
Lightbulb...	Bombilla...	bohm-**bee**-yah
Electrical outlet...	Enchufe...	ayn-**choo**-fay
Key...	Llave...	**yah**-bay
Lock...	Cerradura...	thehr-rah-**doo**-rah
Window...	Ventana...	bayn-**tah**-nah
Faucet...	Grifo...	**gree**-foh
Sink...	Lavabo...	lah-**bah**-boh
Toilet...	Aseo...	ah-**say**-oh
Shower...	Ducha...	**doo**-chah
...doesn't work.	...no funciona.	noh foonk-thee-**oh**-nah
There is no hot water.	No hay agua caliente.	noh ī **ah**-gwah kahl-**yehn**-tay
When is the water hot?	¿Cuándo hay agua caliente?	**kwahn**-doh ī **ah**-gwah kahl-**yehn**-tay

If the management treats you like a *cucaracha* (cockroach), ask to see the hotel's *libro de reclamaciones* (the government-required complaint book). Your problems will generally get solved in a jiffy.

Checking Out

When is check-out time?	¿Cuándo es la hora de salida?	**kwahn**-doh ays lah **oh**-rah day sah-**lee**-dah
I'll leave...	Me iré...	may ee-**ray**
We'll leave...	Nos iremos...	nohs ee-**ray**-mohs
...today / tomorrow.	...hoy / mañana.	oy / mahn-**yah**-nah
...very early.	...muy temprano.	**moo**-ee tehm-**prah**-noh
Can I pay now?	¿Le pago ahora?	lay **pah**-goh ah-**oh**-rah
Can we pay now?	¿Le pagamos ahora?	lay pah-**gah**-mohs ah-**oh**-rah

The bill, please.	*La cuenta, por favor.*	lah **kwayn**-tah por fah-**bor**
Credit card O.K.?	*¿Tarjeta de crédito O.K.?*	tar-**hay**-tah day **kray**-dee-toh "O.K."
Everything was great.	*Todo estuvo muy bien.*	**toh**-doh ay-**stoo**-boh **moo**-ee bee-**yehn**
I slept like a log. (Sleep grabbed me.)	*Dormí de un tirón.*	dor-**mee** day oon tee-**rohn**
I slept like an angel.	*Dormí como un angelito.*	dor-**mee koh**-moh oon ahn-*hay*-**lee**-toh
Will you call my next hotel...?	*¿Podría llamar a mi próximo hotel...?*	poh-**dree**-ah yah-**mar** ah mee **prohk**-see-moh oh-**tehl**
...for tonight	*...para esta noche*	**pah**-rah **ay**-stah **noh**-chay
...to make a reservation	*...para hacer una reserva*	**pah**-rah ah-**thehr oo**-nah ray-**sehr**-bah
...to confirm a reservation	*...para confirmar una reserva*	**pah**-rah kohn-feer-**mar oo**-nah ray-**sehr**-bah
I will pay for the call.	*Pagaré por la llamada.*	pah-gah-**ray** por lah yah-**mah**-dah
Can I / Can we...?	*¿Puedo / Podemos...?*	**pway**-doh / poh-**day**-mohs
...leave baggage here until ___	*...guardar aquí las maletas hasta ___*	gwar-**dar** ah-**kee** lahs mah-**lay**-tahs **ah**-stah

Camping

camping	*camping*	**kahm**-peeng
campsite	*camping*	**kahm**-peeng
tent	*tienda*	tee-**ayn**-dah
The nearest campground?	*¿El camping más cercano?*	ehl **kahm**-peeng mahs thehr-**kah**-noh
Can I...?	*¿Puedo...?*	**pway**-doh
Can we...?	*¿Podemos...?*	poh-**day**-mohs
...camp here for one night	*...acampar aquí por una noche*	ah-kahm-**par** ah-**kee** por **oo**-nah **noh**-chay
Are showers included?	*¿Están las duchas incluídas?*	ay-**stahn** lahs **doo**-chahs een-kloo-**ee**-dahs

EATING

Restaurants

Types of Restaurants

Contrary to what many Americans assume, Spanish cuisine is nothing like Mexican cuisine. Spanish food—usually not spicy, often fried, and heavy on seafood—was influenced by 700 years of Muslim rule. The Moors, who were great horticulturists, introduced new herbs, spices, fruits, and vegetables. The Moorish legacy is well represented by Spain's national dish, *paella*, combining saffron (an Eastern flavor) with rice and various types of seafood. Spain's most significant contribution to world culinary culture is *tapas*—a wide variety of tasty appetizers that can add up to a handy meal.

There are many types of eateries to try. Below are some suggestions to help you find your way:

Restaurante—Serves traditional food, usually offers a fixed-price tourist meal (*menú de turista*), and is rated by the government (based more on the number of menu items than on quality)

Fonda, hostería, venta, or *posada*—Inns, of varying degrees of formality, serving regional Spanish food with hearty portions

Cafetería—Coffee shop with counter or table service (not the same as self-service cafeterias in America)

Merendero—Seafood stall or restaurant near the sea

Pastelería or *confitería*—Pastry shop

Taberna (tavern), *tasca* (tapas bar), or *bar*—Bars serving small snacks and drinks

Cervecería—Beer bar

Bodega—Wine bar

Finding a Restaurant

Where's a good...	¿Dónde hay un buen	**dohn**-day ī oon bwayn
restaurant nearby?	restaurante cerca...?	ray-stoh-**rahn**-tay **thehr**-kah
...cheap	...barato	bah-**rah**-toh
...local-style	...regional	ray-hee-oh-**nahl**
...untouristy	...que no sea un sitio de turistas	kay noh **say**-ah oon **seet**-yoh day too-**ree**-stahs
...vegetarian	...vegetariano	bay-hay-tah-ree-**ah**-noh
...fast food	...comida rápida	koh-**mee**-dah **rah**-pee-dah
...self-service buffet	...buffet de autoservicio	boo-**fay** day ow-toh-sehr-**bee**-thee-oh
...Chinese	...chino	**chee**-noh
beer garden	cervecería	thehr-bay-thehr-**ee**-ah
with terrace	con terraza	kohn tehr-**rah**-thah
with a salad bar	con ensaladas	kohn ayn-sah-**lah**-dahs
with candles	con velas	kohn **bay**-lahs
romantic	romántico	roh-**mahn**-tee-koh
moderate price	precio moderado	**pray**-thee-oh moh-day-**rah**-doh
a splurge	una extravagancia	**oo**-nah ehk-strah-bah **gahn**-thee-ah
Is it better than McDonald's?	¿Es mejor que McDonald?	ays may-**hor** kay meek-**doh**-nahld

The Spanish eating schedule frustrates many visitors. Many restaurants close during August. When restaurants are open, they serve meals "late." Lunch (*almuerzo*), eaten later than in the U.S. (1:00–4:00 p.m.), is the largest meal of the day. Because most Spaniards work until 7:30 p.m., a light supper (*cena*) is usually served around 9:00 or 10:00 p.m. Generally, no good restaurant serves meals at American hours. But to eat early, well, and within even the tightest budget, you can duck into a bar, where you can stab toothpicks into local munchies (see "Tapas," below).

Getting a Table

English	Spanish	Pronunciation
What time does this open / close?	¿A qué hora abren / cierran?	ah kay **oh**-rah **ah**-brehn / thee-**ay**-rahn
Are you open...?	¿Están abierto...?	ay-**stahn** ah-bee-**ehr**-toh
...today / tomorrow	...hoy / mañana	oy / mahn-**yah**-nah
...for lunch / dinner	...para almuerzo / cena	**pah**-rah ahlm-**wehr**-thoh / **thay**-nah
Are reservations recommended?	¿Se debe reservar?	say **day**-bay ray-sehr-**bar**
I / We would like...	Me / Nos gustaría...	may / nohs goo-stah-**ree**-ah
...a table for one / two.	...una mesa para uno / dos.	**oo**-nah **may**-sah **pah**-rah **oo**-noh / dohs
...to reserve a table for two people...	...reservar una mesa para dos personas...	ray-sehr-**bar oo**-nah **may**-sah **pah**-rah dohs per-**soh**-nahs
...for today / tomorrow	...para hoy / mañana	**pah**-rah oy / mahn-**yah**-nah
...at 8:00 p.m.	...a las ocho de la tarde.	ah lahs **oh**-choh day lah **tar**-day
My name is ___.	Me llamo ___.	may **yah**-moh
I have a reservation for ___ people.	Tengo una reserva para ___ personas.	**tayn**-goh **oo**-nah ray-**sehr**-bah **pah**-rah ___ per-**soh**-nahs

EATING

I would like to sit...	*Me gustaría sentarme...*	may goo-stah-**ree**-ah sehn-**tar**-may
We would like to sit...	*Nos gustaría sentarnos...*	nohs goo-stah-**ree**-ah sehn-**tar**-nohs
...inside / outside.	*...dentro / fuera.*	**dayn**-troh / **fwehr**-ah
...by the window.	*...cerca de la ventana.*	**thehr**-kah day lah behn-**tah**-nah
...with a view.	*...con vistas.*	kohn **bee**-stahs
...where it's quiet.	*...donde sea tranquilo.*	**dohn**-day **say**-ah trahn-**kee**-loh
Non-smoking (if possible).	*no fumadores (si es posible).*	noh foo-mah-**doh**-rays (see ays poh-**see**-blay)
Is this table free?	*¿Está esta mesa libre?*	ay-**stah ay**-stah **may**-sah **lee**-bray
Can I sit here?	*¿Puedo sentarme aquí?*	**pway**-doh sehn-**tar**-may ah-**kee**
Can we sit here?	*¿Podemos sentarnos aquí?*	poh-**day**-mohs sehn-**tar**-nohs ah-**kee**

Better restaurants routinely take reservations. Guidebooks include phone numbers and the process is simple. If you want to eat at a normal Spanish dinnertime (around 9:00 p.m.), it's smart to reserve a table. Many of my favorite restaurants are filled with tourists at 7:30 p.m. and feel less authentic. If you drop in (or call ahead) at 8:30 or 9:00 p.m., when the Spanish eat, the restaurants feel completely local.

The Menu

menu	*carta*	**kar**-tah
special of the day	*especial del día*	ay-spay-thee-**ahl** dayl **dee**-ah
specialty of the house	*especialidad de la casa*	ay-spay-thee-ah-lee-**dahd** day lah **kah**-sah
menu of the day	*menú del día*	may-**noo** dayl **dee**-ah
tourist menu	*menú de turista*	may-**noo** day too-**ree**-stah
combination plate	*plato combinado*	**plah**-toh kohm-bee-**nah**-doh
breakfast	*desayuno*	day-sah-**yoo**-noh

lunch	*almuerzo*	ahlm-**wehr**-thoh
dinner	*cena*	**thay**-nah
appetizers	*aperitivos*	ah-pay-ree-**tee**-bohs
sandwiches	*bocadillos*	boh-kah-**dee**-yohs
bread	*pan*	pahn
salad	*ensalada*	ayn-sah-**lah**-dah
soup	*sopa*	**soh**-pah
first course	*primer plato*	pree-**mehr plah**-toh
main course	*segundo plato*	say-**goon**-doh **plah**-toh
side dishes	*a parte*	ah **par**-tay
egg dishes	*tortillas*	tor-**tee**-yahs
meat	*carne*	**kar**-nay
poultry	*aves*	**ah**-bays
fish	*pescado*	pay-**skah**-doh
seafood	*marisco*	mah-**ree**-skoh
children's plate	*plato de niños*	**plah**-toh day **neen**-yohs
vegetables	*verduras*	behr-**doo**-rahs
cheese	*queso*	**kay**-soh
dessert	*postres*	**poh**-strays
munchies	*tapas*	**tah**-pahs
drink menu	*carta de bebidas*	**kar**-tah day bay-**bee**-dahs
beverages	*bebidas*	bay-**bee**-dahs
beer	*cerveza*	thehr-**bay**-thah
wine	*vino*	**bee**-noh
cover charge	*precio de entrada*	**pray**-thee-oh day ayn-**trah**-dah
service included	*servicio incluido*	sehr-**bee**-thee-oh een-kloo-**ee**-doh
service not included	*servicio no incluido*	sehr-**bee**-thee-oh noh een-kloo-**ee**-doh
hot / cold	*caliente / frío*	kahl-**yehn**-tay / **free**-oh
with / and / or / without	*con / y / o / sin*	kohn / ee / oh / seen

For a budget meal in a restaurant, try a *plato combinado* (a combination plate that includes portions of one or two main dishes, vegetables, and bread) or the *menú del día* (menu of the day, a substantial three- to four-course meal that usually comes with a carafe of house wine).

EATING

KEY PHRASES: RESTAURANTS

Where's a good restaurant nearby?	¿Dónde hay un buen restaurante cerca?	dohn-day ī oon bwayn ray-stoh-**rahn**-tay **thehr**-kah
I / We would like...	Me / Nos gustaría...	may / nohs goo-stah-**ree**-ah
...a table for one / two.	...una mesa para uno / dos.	**oo**-nah **may**-sah **pah**-rah **oo**-noh / dohs
Non-smoking (if possible).	no fumadores (si es posible).	noh foo-mah-**doh**-rays (see ays poh-**see**-blay)
Is this table free?	¿Está esta mesa libre?	ay-**stah ay**-stah **may**-sah **lee**-bray
The menu (in English), please.	La carta (en inglés), por favor.	lah **kar**-tah (ayn een-**glays**) por fah-**bor**
The bill, please.	La cuenta, por favor.	lah **kwayn**-tah por fah-**bor**
Credit card O.K.?	¿Tarjeta de crédito O.K.?	tar-**hay**-tah day **kray**-dee-toh "O.K."

Ordering

waiter	camarero	kah-mah-**ray**-roh
waitress	camarera	kah-mah-**ray**-rah
I'm / We're ready to order.	Me / Nos gustaría pedir.	may / nohs goo-stah-**ree**-ah pay-**deer**
I / We would like...	Me / Nos gustaría...	may / nohs goo-stah-**ree**-ah
...just a drink.	...sólo una bebida.	**soh**-loh **oo**-nah bay-**bee**-dah
...a snack.	...un pincho.	oon **peen**-choh
...just a salad.	...sólo una ensalada.	**soh**-loh **oo**-nah ayn-sah-**lah**-dah
...a half portion.	...media ración.	**may**-dee-ah rah-thee-**ohn**
...a tourist menu.	...un menú de turista.	oon meh-**noo** day too-**ree**-stah
...to see the menu.	...ver la carta.	behr lah **kar**-tah
...to order.	...pedir.	pay-**deer**

EATING

...to eat.	...comer.	koh-**mehr**
...to pay.	...pagar.	pah-**gar**
...to throw up.	...vomitar.	boh-mee-**tar**
Do you have...?	¿Tiene...?	tee-**ehn**-ay
...an English menu	...una carta en inglés	**oo**-nah **kar**-tah ayn een-**glays**
...a lunch special	...un menú especial	oon may-**noo** ay-spay-thee-**ahl**
What do you recommend?	¿Qué recomienda?	kay ray-koh-mee-**ehn**-dah
What's your favorite dish?	¿Cuál es su plato favorito?	kwahl ays soo **plah**-toh fah-boh-**ree**-toh
Is it...?	¿Es ésto...?	ays **ay**-stoh
...good	...bueno	**bway**-noh
...expensive	...caro	**kah**-roh
...light	...ligero	lee-**hay**-roh
Is it filling?	¿Esto le llena?	**ay**-stoh lay **yay**-nah
What is...?	¿Qué es...?	kay ays
...that	...esto	**ay**-stoh
...local	...típico	**tee**-pee-koh
...fresh	...fresco	**fray**-skoh
...cheap and filling	...lo que llene y sea barato	loh kay **yay**-nay ee **say**-ah bah-**rah**-toh
...fast	...lo más rápido	loh mahs **rah**-pee-doh
Can we split this and have an extra plate?	¿Podemos compartir esto y tener un plato extra?	poh-**day**-mohs kohm-par-**teer ay**-stoh ee tay-**nehr** oon **plah**-toh **ayk**-strah
I've changed my mind.	Cambié de idea.	kahm-bee-**ay** day ee-**day**-ah
Nothing with eyeballs.	Nada con ojos.	**nah**-dah kohn **oh**-hohs
Can I substitute (anything) for the ___?	¿Puedo sustituir (algo) por el ___?	**pway**-doh soo-stee-too-**eer** (**ahl**-goh) por ehl
Can I / we get it "to go"?	¿Me / Nos lo empaqueta para llevar?	may / nohs loh aym-pah-**kay**-tah **pah**-rah yay-**bar**
"To go"?	Para llevar?	**pah**-rah yay-**bar**

This is the sequence of a typical restaurant experience: To get your server's attention, simply say, *"Por favor."* The waiter will give you a menu (*carta*) and then ask if he can help you (*¿Cómo puedo servirles?* or simply *Dígame*), what you'd like to drink or eat (*¿Qué quiere beber / comer?*), and if you're finished (*¿Han acabado?*). You ask for the bill (*La cuenta, por favor*).

Tableware and Condiments

plate	*plato*	**plah**-toh
extra plate	*otro plato*	**oh**-troh **plah**-toh
napkin	*servilleta*	sehr-bee-**yay**-tah
silverware	*cubiertos*	koo-bee-**yehr**-tohs
knife	*cuchillo*	koo-**chee**-yoh
fork	*tenedor*	tay-nay-**dor**
spoon	*cuchara*	koo-**chah**-rah
cup	*taza*	**tah**-thah
glass	*vaso*	**bah**-soh
carafe	*garrafa*	gah-**rah**-fah
water	*agua*	**ah**-gwah
bread	*pan*	pahn
butter	*mantequilla*	mahn-tay-**kee**-yah
margarine	*margarina*	mar-gah-**ree**-nah
salt / pepper	*sal / pimienta*	sahl / pee-mee-**ehn**-tah
sugar	*azúcar*	ah-**thoo**-kar
artificial sweetener	*edulcorante*	ay-dool-koh-**rahn**-tay
honey	*miel*	mee-**ehl**
mustard	*mostaza*	moh-**stah**-thah
mayonnaise	*mayonesa*	mah-yoh-**nay**-sah
toothpick	*palillo*	pah-**lee**-yoh

The Food Arrives

Is this included with the meal?	*¿Está esto incluido con la comida?*	ay-**stah ay**-stoh een-kloo-**ee**-doh kohn lah koh-**mee**-dah

EATING

I did not order this.	No pedí esto.	noh pay-**dee ay**-stoh
We did not order this.	No pedimos esto.	noh pay-**dee**-mohs **ay**-stoh
Can you heat this up?	¿Me puede calentar esto?	may **pway**-day kah-lehn-**tar ay**-stoh
A little.	Un poco.	oon **poh**-koh
More. / Another.	Más. / Otro.	mahs / **oh**-troh
One more, please.	Uno más, por favor.	**oo**-noh mahs por fah-**bor**
The same.	El mismo.	ehl **mees**-moh
Enough.	Suficiente.	soo-fee-thee-**ehn**-tay
Finished.	Terminado.	tehr-mee-**nah**-doh
I'm full.	Estoy lleno[a].	ay-**stoy yay**-noh
I'm stuffed! (I put on my boots!)	¡Me he puesto las botas!	may ay **pway**-stoh lahs **boh**-tahs

After serving the meal, your server might wish you a cheery
"*¡Qué aproveche!*" (pronounced kay ah-proh-**vay**-chay).

Complaints

This is...	Esto es...	**ay**-stoh ays
...dirty.	...sucio.	**soo**-thee-oh
...greasy.	...grasiento.	grah-see-**ehn**-toh
...salty.	...salado.	sah-**lah**-doh
...undercooked.	...crudo.	**kroo**-doh
...overcooked.	...muy hecho.	**moo**-ee **ay**-choh
...inedible.	...asqueroso.	ahs-kay-**roh**-soh
...cold.	...frío.	**free**-oh
Do any of your customers return?	¿Vuelven sus clientes?	**bwehl**-bayn soos klee-**ehn**-tays
Yuck!	¡Que asco!	kay **ah**-skoh

Compliments to the Chef

Yummy!	¡Que rico!	kay **ree**-koh
Delicious!	¡Delicioso!	day-lee-thee-**oh**-soh
Very tasty!	¡Muy sabroso!	**moo**-ee sah-**broh**-soh

I love Spanish / this food.	*Me encanta la comida española / esta.*	may ayn-**kahn**-tah lah koh-**mee**-dah ay-spahn-**yoh**-lah / **ay**-stah
Better than mom's cooking.	*Es mejor que la comida de mi madre.*	ays may-**hor** kay lah koh-**mee**-dah day mee **mah**-dray
My compliments to the chef!	*Felicitacio- nes al cocinero!*	fay-lee-thee-tah-thee-**oh**-nays ahl koh-thee-**nay**-roh

Paying for Your Meal

The bill, please.	*La cuenta, por favor.*	lah **kwayn**-tah por fah-**bor**
Together.	*Junto.*	**hoon**-toh
Separate checks.	*En cheques separados.*	ayn **chay**-kays say-pah-**rah**-dohs
Credit card O.K.?	*¿Tarjeta de crédito O.K.?*	tar-**hay**-tah day **kray**-dee-toh "O.K."
This is not correct.	*Esto no es correcto.*	**ay**-stoh noh ays koh-**rehk**-toh
Can you explain this?	*¿Podría explicarme esto?*	poh-**dree**-ah ayk-splee-**kar**-may **ay**-stoh
Can you explain / itemize the bill?	*¿Podría explicarme / detallarme la cuenta?*	poh-**dree**-ah ayk-splee-**kar**-may / day-tah-**yar**-may lah **kwayn**-tah
What if I wash the dishes?	*¿Qué le parece si lavo platos?*	kay lay pah-**ray**-thay see **lah**-boh **plah**-tohs
Is tipping expected?	*¿Se espera una propina?*	say ay-**spay**-rah **oo**-nah proh-**pee**-nah
What percent?	*¿Qué tanto por ciento?*	kay **tahn**-toh por thee-**ehn**-toh
tip	*propina*	proh-**pee**-nah
Keep the change.	*Quédese con el cambio.*	**kay**-day-say kohn ehl **kahm**-bee-oh
This is for you.	*Esto es para usted.*	**ay**-stoh ays **pah**-rah oo-**stehd**
Could I have a receipt, please?	*¿Podría darme un recibo, por favor?*	poh-**dree**-ah **dar**-may oon ray-**thee**-boh por fah-**bor**

If the menu says *servicio incluido*, it means just that. It's good style to leave the coins, but you don't need to tip beyond what's been added to the bill. If the menu says *servicio no incluido*, leave about 10 percent. When you're uncertain whether to tip, ask another customer if it's expected ("*¿Se espera una propina?*").

Special Concerns

In a Hurry

I'm / We're in a hurry.	Tengo / Tenemos prisa.	**tayn**-goh / tay-**nay**-mohs **pree**-sah
I need to be served quickly.	Necesito que me sirvan en seguida.	nay-thay-**see**-toh kay may **seer**-bahn ayn say-**gee**-dah
We need to be served quickly.	Necesitamos que nos sirvan en seguida.	nay-thay-see-**tah**-mohs kay nohs **seer**-bahn ayn say-**gee**-dah
Is that possible?	¿Es posible?	ays poh-**see**-blay
I must / We must...	Tengo / Tenemos que...	**tayn**-goh / tay-**nay**-mohs kay
...leave in 30 minutes / one hour.	...salir en treinta minutos / una hora.	sah-**leer** ayn **trayn**-tah mee-**noo**-tohs / **oo**-nah **oh**-rah
When will the food be ready?	¿Cuándo estará la comida lista?	**kwahn**-doh ay-stah-**rah** lah koh-**mee**-dah **lee**-stah

Dietary Restrictions

I'm allergic to...	Soy alérgico[a] a...	soy ah-**lehr**-hee-koh ah
I cannot eat...	No puedo comer...	noh **pway**-doh koh-**mehr**
He / She cannot eat...	No puede comer...	noh **pway**-day koh-**mehr**
...dairy products.	...productos lácteos.	proh-**dook**-tohs **lahk**-tay-ohs

EATING

...wheat.	...de trigo.	day **tree**-goh
...meat / pork.	...carne / cerdo.	**kar**-nay / **thehr**-doh
...salt / sugar.	...sal / azúcar.	sahl / ah-**thoo**-kar
...shellfish.	...moluscos.	moh-**loo**-skohs
...spicy foods.	...comida picante.	koh-**mee**-dah pee-**kahn**-tay
...nuts.	...productos secos.	proh-**dook**-tohs **say**-kohs
I am diabetic.	Soy diabético[a].	soy dee-ah-**bay**-tee-koh
I'd / We'd like...	Me / Nos gustaría...	may / nohs goo-stah-**ree**-ah
...a kosher meal.	...una comida kosher.	**oo**-nah koh-**mee**-dah **koh**-shehr
...a low-fat meal.	...una comida con poca grasa.	**oo**-nah koh-**mee**-dah kohn **poh**-kah **grah**-sah
I eat only insects.	Sólo como insectos.	**soh**-loh **koh**-moh een-**sayk**-tohs
No salt.	Sin sal.	seen sahl
No sugar.	Sin azúcar.	seen ah-**thoo**-kar
No fat.	Sin grasa.	seen **grah**-sah
Minimal fat.	Poca grasa.	**poh**-kah **grah**-sah
Low cholesterol.	Bajo en colesterol.	**bah**-hoh ayn koh-lay-stay-**rohl**
No caffeine.	Sin cafeína.	seen kah-**fay**-nah
No alcohol.	Sin alcohol.	seen ahl-**kohl**
Organic.	Orgánico.	or-**gah**-nee-koh
I'm a...	Soy...	soy
...vegetarian.	...vegetariano[a].	bay-hay-tah-ree-**ah**-noh
...strict vegetarian.	...vegetariano[a] estricto[a].	bay-hay-tah-ree-**ah**-noh ay-**streek**-toh
...carnivore.	...carnívoro[a].	kar-**nee**-boh-roh
...big eater.	...glotón.	gloh-**tohn**
Is any meat or animal fat used in this?	¿Se ha usado carne o grasa animal en esto?	say ah oo-**sah**-doh **kar**-nay oh **grah**-sah ah-nee-**mahl** ayn **ay**-stoh

Many Spaniards think "vegetarian" means "no red meat" or "not much meat." If you're a strict vegetarian, you'll have to make it very clear.

Children

English	Spanish	Pronunciation
Do you have...?	¿Tiene...?	tee-**ehn**-ay
...children's portions	...raciones para niños	rah-thee-**oh**-nays **pah**-rah **neen**-yohs
...half portions	...media raciones	**may**-dee-ah rah-thee-**oh**-nays
...a high chair	...una silla alta	**oo**-nah **see**-yah **ahl**-tah
...a booster seat	...un asiento alto	oon ah-see-**ehn**-toh **ahl**-toh
plain noodles	fideos sin salsa	fee-**day**-ohs seen **sahl**-sah
plain rice	arroz sin salsa	ah-**rohth** seen **sahl**-sah
with butter	con mantequilla	kohn mahn-tay-**kee**-yah
no sauce	sin salsa	seen **sahl**-sah
sauce / dressing on the side	salsa / aliño a parte	**sahl**-sah / ah-**leen**-yoh ah **par**-tay
pizza	pizza	**peet**-sah
...cheese only	...sólo queso	**soh**-loh **kay**-soh
...pepperoni and cheese	...salchichón y queso	sahl-chee-**chohn** ee **kay**-soh
peanut butter and jelly sandwich	sandwich de mantequilla de cacahuete y mermelada	**sahnd**-weech day mahn-tay-**kee**-yah day kah-kah-**way**-tay ee mehr-may-**lah**-dah
cheese sandwich...	sandwich de queso...	**sahnd**-weech day **kay**-soh
...toasted	...tostada	toh-**stah**-dah
...grilled	...a la parrilla	ah lah pah-**ree**-yah
hot dog	perrito caliente	pehr-**ree**-toh kahl-**yehn**-tay
hamburger	hamburguesa	ahm-boor-**gay**-sah
French fries	patatas fritas	pah-**tah**-tahs **free**-tahs
ketchup	ketchup	"ketchup"
crackers	galletas	gah-**yay**-tahs
Nothing spicy.	Nada picante.	**nah**-dah pee-**kahn**-tay
Not too hot.	Que no esté muy caliente.	kay noh ay-**stay** moo-ee kahl-**yehn**-tay

Please keep the food separate on the plate.	Por favor, ponga la comida separada en el plato.	por fah-**bor pohn**-gah lah koh-**mee**-dah say-pah-**rah**-dah ayn ehl **plah**-toh
He / She will share...	Él / Ella compartirá...	ehl / **ay**-yah kohm-par-tee-**rah**
They (m / f) will share...	Ellos / Elllas compartirán...	**ay**-yohs / **ay**-yahs kohm-par-tee-**rahn**
...our meal.	...nuestra comida.	**nway**-strah koh-**mee**-dah
Please bring the food quickly.	Por favor, traiga la comida en seguida.	por fah-**bor trī**-gah lah koh-**mee**-dah ayn say-**gee**-dah
Can I / Can we have an extra...?	¿Puedo / Podemos tener extra...?	**pway**-doh / poh-**day**-mohs tay-**nehr ayk**-strah
...plate	...plato	**plah**-toh
...cup	...taza	**tah**-thah
...spoon / fork	...cuchara / tenedor	koo-**chah**-rah / tay-nay-**dor**
Can I / Can we have two extra...?	¿Puedo / Podemos tener dos extra...?	**pway**-doh / poh-**day**-mohs tay-**nehr** dohs **ayk**-strah
...plates	...platos	**plah**-tohs
...cups	...tazas	**tah**-thahs
...spoons / forks	...cucharas / tenedores	koo-**chah**-rahs / tay-nay-**doh**-rays
Small milk (in a plastic cup).	Leche chiquita (en una copa plástica).	**lay**-chay chee-**kee**-tah (ayn **oo**-nah **koh**-pah **plah**-stee-kah)
straw(s)	paja(s)	**pah**-hah(s)
More napkins, please.	Más servilletas, por favor.	mahs sehr-bee-**yay**-tahs por fah-**bor**
Sorry for the mess.	Perdone el desorden.	pehr-**doh**-nay ehl day-**sor**-dehn

What's Cooking?

Breakfast

breakfast	desayuno	day-sah-**yoo**-noh
bread	pan	pahn
roll	panecillo	pah-nay-**thee**-yoh
toast	tostada	toh-**stah**-dah
butter	mantequilla	mahn-tay-**kee**-yah
jelly	mermelada	mehr-may-**lah**-dah
milk	leche	**lay**-chay
coffee / tea	café / té	kah-**feh** / tay
Is breakfast included?	¿El desayuno está incluido?	ehl day-sah-**yoo**-noh ay-**stah** een-kloo-**ee**-doh

KEY PHRASES: WHAT'S COOKING

food	comida	koh-**mee**-dah
breakfast	desayuno	day-sah-**yoo**-noh
lunch	almuerzo	ahlm-**wehr**-thoh
dinner	cena	**thay**-nah
bread	pan	pahn
cheese	queso	**kay**-soh
soup	sopa	**soh**-pah
salad	ensalada	ayn-sah-**lah**-dah
meat	carne	**kar**-nay
fish	pescado	pay-**skah**-doh
fruit	fruta	**froo**-tah
vegetables	verduras	behr-**doo**-rahs
dessert	postres	**poh**-strays
Delicious!	¡Delicioso!	day-lee-thee-**oh**-soh

EATING

What's Probably Not for Breakfast

omelet	omelet	**ohm**-leht
eggs...	huevos...	**way**-bohs
...fried	...fritos	**free**-tohs
...scrambled	...revueltos	ray-**bwehl**-tohs
ham	jamón	hah-**mohn**
cheese	queso	**kay**-soh
yogurt	yogur	yoh-**goor**
cereal	cereales	thay-ray-**ah**-lays
pastries	pasteles	pah-**stay**-lays
fruit juice	zumo de fruta	**thoo**-moh day **froo**-tah
orange juice	zumo de naranja	**thoo**-moh day nah-**rahn**-hah
hot chocolate	chocolate caliente	choh-koh-**lah**-tay kahl-**yehn**-tay

The traditional Spanish breakfast is *churros con chocolate*—greasy fritters or doughnuts dipped in a thick, warm chocolate drink. Try these at least once. For a more solid breakfast, I prefer *tortilla española,* the hearty potato omelet most cafés serve throughout the day. Add a little bread and *café con leche,* and you've got a cheap, filling meal.

Sandwiches

Bocadillos (sandwiches) are cheap and basic. A ham sandwich is just that—ham on bread, period.

I'd like a sandwich.	Me gustaría un bocadillo.	may goo-stah-**ree**-ah oon boh-kah-**dee**-yoh
We'd like two sandwiches.	Nos gustarían dos bocadillos.	nohs goo-stah-**ree**-ahn dohs boh-kah-**dee**-yohs
white bread	pan	pahn
wheat bread	pan integral	pahn een-tay-**grahl**
baguette sandwich	flauta	**flow**-tah

toasted	tostado	toh-**stah**-doh
toasted ham	tostado de	toh-**stah**-doh day
and cheese	jamón y queso	hah-**mohn** ee **kay**-soh
cheese	queso	**kay**-soh
tuna	atún	ah-**toon**
fish	pescado	pay-**skah**-doh
chicken	pollo	**poh**-yoh
turkey	pavo	**pah**-boh
ham	jamón	hah-**mohn**
salami	salami	sah-**lah**-mee
egg salad	ensalada de	ayn-sah-**lah**-dah day
	huevo	**way**-boh
lettuce	lechuga	lay-**choo**-gah
tomatoes	tomates	toh-**mah**-tays
onions	cebollas	thay-**boh**-yahs
mustard	mostaza	moh-**stah**-thah
mayonnaise	mayonesa	mah-yoh-**nay**-sah
peanut butter	mantequilla de	mahn-tay-**kee**-yah day
	cacahuete	kah-kah-**way**-tay
jelly	mermelada	mehr-may-**lah**-dah
Does this come	¿Lo sirven frío o	loh **seer**-behn **free**-oh oh
cold or warm?	caliente?	kahl-**yehn**-tay
Heated, please.	Caliente, por favor.	kahl-**yehn**-tay por fah-**bor**

Typical Sandwiches

bocadillo	boh-kah-**dee**-yoh	meat and fried egg
de carne y	day **kar**-nay ee	on a roll
huevo frito	**way**-boh **free**-toh	
bocadillo	boh-kah-**dee**-yoh	pork sandwich
de jamón	day hah-**mohn**	
pan tomáquet	pahn toh-**mah**-kayt	country bread rubbed
		with tomato and olive oil
pulguita	pool-**gee**-tah	small closed baguette
		sandwich
sandwich de	**sahnd**-weech day	Wonder bread toasted
carne / queso	**kar**-nay / **kay**-soh	with meat / cheese

EATING

Say Cheese

cheese	*queso*	**kay**-soh
...mild	*...suave*	**swah**-bay
...sharp	*...fuerte*	**fwehr**-tay
...smoked	*...ahumado*	ah-oo-**mah**-doh
May I taste a little?	*¿Podría probarlo?*	poh-**dree**-ah proh-**bar**-loh

Spanish Cheeses

burgos	**boor**-gohs	fresh, creamy ewe's milk cheese (Castile)
cabrales	kah-**brah**-lays	tangy, blue-veined goat's cheese
manchego	mahn-**chay**-goh	hard white or yellow ewe's milk cheese (La Mancha)
palitos de queso	pah-**lee**-tohs day **kay**-soh	cheese sticks or straws
perilla, teta	pay-**ree**-yah, **tay**-tah	firm, bland cow's milk cheese
requesón	ray-kay-**sohn**	type of cottage cheese
roncal	rohn-**kahl**	smoked, strong, dry, sharp ewe's milk cheese (Navarre)
San Simón	sahn see-**mohn**	smooth, mild cheese (Galicia)
villalón	bee-yah-**lohn**	ewe's milk curdled and drained, pressed into molds, and salted

Soups

soup...	*sopa...*	**soh**-pah
...of the day	*...del día*	dayl **dee**-ah
...vegetable	*...de verduras*	day behr-**doo**-rahs
broth...	*caldo...*	**kahl**-doh
...chicken	*...de pollo*	day **poh**-yoh

EATING

...meat	...de carne	day **kar**-nay
...fish	...de pescado	day pay-**skah**-doh
...with noodles	...con tallarines	kohn tah-yah-**ree**-nays
...with rice	...con arroz	kohn ah-**rohth**

Soup Specialties

cocido	koh-**thee**-doh	meat stew with beans and veggies
gazpacho	gahth-**pah**-choh	chilled, pureed tomato vegetable soup
puré de verduras	poo-**ray** day behr-**doo**-rahs	thick vegetable soup
sopa a la gitana	**soh**-pah ah lah hee-**tah**-nah	pumpkin and chickpea soup with chopped tomatoes, green beans, and pears (Andalucía)
sopa castellana	**soh**-pah kah-stay-**ah**-nah	egg soup with garlic
sopa de almendras	**soh**-pah day ahl-**mayn**-drahs	almond soup with saffron and red pepper (Granada)
sopa de espárragos	**soh**-pah day ay-**spah**-rah-gohs	asparagus soup
sopa de mariscos	**soh**-pah day mah-**ree**-skohs	seafood soup

Salads

salad...	ensalada...	ayn-sah-**lah**-dah
...green	...verde	**behr**-day
...mixed	...mixta	**meek**-stah
chef's salad...	ensalada de la casa...	ayn-sah-**lah**-dah day lah **kah**-sah
...with ham and cheese	...con queso y jamón	kohn **kay**-soh ee hah-**mohn**
...with egg	...con huevo	kohn **way**-boh
lettuce	lechuga	lay-**choo**-gah
tomato	tomate	toh-**mah**-tay
onion	cebolla	thay-**boh**-yah

cucumber	pepino	pay-**pee**-noh
oil / vinegar	aceite / vinagre	ah-**thay**-tay / bee-**nah**-gray
dressing on the side	aliño aparte	ah-**leen**-yoh ah-**par**-tay
What is in this salad?	¿Qué tiene esta ensalada?	kay tee-**ehn**-ay **ay**-stah ayn-sah-**lah**-dah

The Spaniards started the tradition of salad before the main course long before it became an American standard. In Spanish restaurants, salad dressing is normally just the oil and vinegar at the table. The bread (*pan*) is usually white with a crisp crust. Rolls are *bollos.*

Salad Specialties

ensalada de arroz	ayn-sah-**lah**-dah day ah-**rohth**	rice mixed with shellfish and fresh herbs
ensalada de pulpo	ayn-sah-**lah**-dah day **pool**-poh	octopus salad
ensalada de pimientos verdes y sardines asadas	ayn-sah-**lah**-dah day pee-mee-**ehn**-tohs **behr**-days ee sar-**dee**-nays ah-**sah**-dahs	salad with green peppers and grilled sardines
ensalada de atún, patatas, y huevo	ayn-sah-**lah**-dah day ah-**toon** pah-**tah**-tahs ee **way**-boh	salad with tuna, egg, and potatoes
ensaladilla Rusa	ayn-sah-lah-**dee**-yah **roo**-sah	veggie salad in mayonnaise dressing
esqueixada	ays-kay-**hah**-dah	salad of salted cod, onions, and peppers (Catalonia)
xato	**h**ah-toh	lettuce with tuna and anchovies in a spicy sauce

Seafood

| seafood | marisco | mah-**ree**-skoh |
| assorted seafood | marisco variado | mah-**ree**-skoh bah-ree-**ah**-doh |

English	Spanish	Pronunciation
fish	*pescado*	pay-**skah**-doh
anchovies	*anchoas*	ahn-**choh**-ahs
barnacles	*percebes*	pehr-**thay**-bays
bream (fish)	*besugo*	bay-**soo**-goh
clams	*almejas*	ahl-**may**-*h*ahs
cod	*bacalao*	bah-kahl-**ow**
crab	*cangrejo*	kahn-**greh**-*h*oh
crayfish	*cangrejo de río*	kahn-**greh**-*h*oh day **ree**-oh
cuttlefish	*sepia*	**say**-pee-ah
Dungeness crab	*centollo*	thehn-**toh**-yoh
eel	*anguila*	ahn-**gee**-lah
herring	*arenque*	ah-**rayn**-kay
lobster	*langosta*	lahn-**goh**-stah
mussels	*mejillones*	may-*h*ee-**yoh**-nays
octopus	*pulpo*	**pool**-poh
oysters	*ostras*	**oh**-strahs
prawns	*gambas*	**gahm**-bahs
large prawns	*langostinos*	lahn-goh-**stee**-nohs
salmon	*salmón*	sahl-**mohn**
sardines	*sardinas*	sar-**dee**-nahs
scad (like mackerel)	*jurel*	*h*oo-**rayl**
scallops	*veneras*	behn-**ay**-rahs
shrimp	*gamba*	**gahm**-bah
sole	*lenguado*	layn-**gwah**-doh
squid	*calamares*	kah-lah-**mah**-rays
swordfish	*pez espada*	payth ay-**spah**-dah
trout	*trucha*	**troo**-chah
tuna	*atún*	ah-**toon**
How much for a portion?	*¿Cuánto cuesta una ración?*	**kwahn**-toh **kway**-stah **oo**-nah rah-thee-**ohn**
What's fresh today?	*¿Qué hay fresco hoy?*	kay ī **fray**-skoh oy
Do you eat this part?	*¿Se come esta parte?*	say **koh**-may **ay**-stah **par**-tay
Just the head, please.	*Sólo la cabeza, por favor.*	**soh**-loh lah kah-**bay**-thah por fah-**bor**

Seafood Specialties

bacalao a la vizcaína	bah-kahl-**ow** ah lah beeth-kah-**ee**-nah	salt cod braised with peppers, tomatoes, and onions
calamares con guisantes	kah-lah-**mah**-rays kohn gee-**sahn**-tays	squid with garlic, peas, tomatoes, and mint
fidegua	fee-**day**-gwah	paella made with noodles instead of rice
mar y montaña	mar ee mohn-**tahn**-yah	chicken or rabbit with lobster or scampi in a tomato-garlic sauce (Catalonia)
marmitako	mar-mee-**tah**-koh	Basque tuna stew
paella	pah-**ay**-ah	saffron rice, usually with seafood, sausage, and veggies
romesco	roh-**may**-skoh	stewed fish and beans with tomato, green pepper, pimento, and garlic
zarzuela de mariscos	thar-**thway**-lah day mah-**ree**-skohs	seafood stew with an almond-cayenne pepper broth (Catalonia)

Poultry

poultry	*aves*	**ah**-bays
chicken	*pollo*	**poh**-yoh
duck	*pato*	**pah**-toh
turkey	*pavo*	**pah**-boh
partridge	*perdiz*	pehr-**deeth**
How long has this been dead?	*¿Cuánto tiempo hace que lo mataron?*	**kwahn**-toh tee-**ehm**-poh **ah**-thay kay loh mah-**tah**-rohn

EATING

AVOIDING MIS-STEAKS		
alive	*vivo*	**bee**-boh
raw	*crudo*	**kroo**-doh
very rare	*muy crudo*	**moo**-ee **kroo**-doh
rare	*poco hecho*	**poh**-koh **ay**-choh
medium	*medio*	**may**-dee-oh
well-done	*muy hecho*	**moo**-ee **ay**-choh
very well-done	*bastante hecho*	bah-**stahn**-tay **ay**-choh

Meat

meat	*carne*	**kar**-nay
beef	*carne de vaca*	**kar**-nay day **bah**-kah
beef steak	*biftec*	**beef**-tayk
ribsteak	*costillas*	koh-**stee**-yahs
bunny	*conejo*	koh-**nay**-hoh
a wee goat	*cabrito*	kah-**bree**-toh
ham	*jamón*	hah-**mohn**
lamb	*carnero*	kar-**nay**-roh
pork	*cerdo*	**thehr**-doh
roast beef	*carne asada*	**kar**-nay ah-**sah**-dah
sausage	*chorizo,*	choh-**ree**-thoh,
	salchichón	sahl-chee-**chon**
smoked ham	*jamón*	hah-**mohn**
	ahumado	ah-oo-**mah**-doh
suckling pig	*cochinillo*	koh-chee-**nee**-yoh
veal	*ternera*	tehr-**nay**-rah

Meat, but...

These are the cheapest items on a menu for good reason.

brains	*sesos*	say-sohs
horse meat	*caballo*	kah-bah-yoh
kidney	*riñones*	reen-yoh-nays
liver	*hígado*	ee-gah-doh
tongue	*lengua*	lehn-gwah
tripe	*tripa*	tree-pah

EATING

Main Course Specialties

butifarra	boo-tee-**fah**-rah	pork sausage spiced with cinnamon, nutmeg, and cloves
cochinillo asado	koh-chee-**nee**-yoh ah-**sah**-doh	roasted suckling pig marinated in herbs, olive oil, and white wine (Segovia and Toledo)
cola de toro, rabo de toro	**koh**-lah day **toh**-roh, **rah**-boh day **toh**-roh	bull-tail stew
cordonices en hoja de parra	kor-doh-**nee**-thays ayn **oh**-*h*ah day **pah**-rah	sherry-braised quail wrapped in grape leaves and bacon
empanada gallega	aym-pah-**nah**-dah gah-**yay**-gah	pizza-like pie, usually with pork tenderloin, onions, and peppers
escudella i carn d'olla	ay-skoo-**day**-ah ee karn **doy**-ah	minced pork meatballs
fabada asturiana	fah-**bah**-dah ah-stoo-ree-**ah**-nah	pork, bean, and paprika stew
habas a la Catalana	**ah**-bahs ah lah kah-tah-**lah**-nah	fava bean and chorizo sausage stew with mint and paprika
pato con higos	**pah**-toh kohn **ee**-gohs	duck with figs
pollo en pepitoria	**poh**-yoh ayn pay-pee-**toh**-ree-ah	chicken fricassee with almonds and eggs
riñones al jerez	reen-**yoh**-nays ahl hay-**rayth**	kidneys in sherry sauce

How It's Prepared

assorted	*variado*	bah-ree-**ah**-doh
baked	*asado*	ah-**sah**-doh
boiled	*cocido*	koh-**thee**-doh
braised	*estofado*	ay-stoh-**fah**-doh

broiled	*a la parilla*	ah lah pah-**ree**-yah
cold	*frío*	**free**-oh
cooked	*cocinado*	koh-thee-**nah**-doh
deep fried	*rebozado*	ray-boh-**thah**-doh
fillet	*filete*	fee-**lay**-tay
fresh	*fresco*	**fray**-skoh
fried	*frito*	**free**-toh
grilled	*a la plancha*	ah lah **plahn**-chah
homemade	*casera*	kah-**sehr**-ah
hot	*caliente*	kahl-**yehn**-tay
in cream sauce	*en salsa blanca*	ayn **sahl**-sah **blahn**-kah
medium	*medio*	**may**-dee-oh
microwave	*microondas*	mee-kroh-**ohn**-dahs
mild	*templado*	tehm-**plah**-doh
mixed	*mixto*	**meek**-stoh
poached	*escalfado*	ay-skahl-**fah**-doh
rare	*poco hecho*	**poh**-koh **ay**-choh
raw	*crudo*	**kroo**-doh
roasted	*asado*	ah-**sah**-doh
sautéed	*salteado*	sahl-tay-**ah**-doh
smoked	*ahumado*	ah-oo-**mah**-doh
sour	*amargo*	ah-**mar**-goh
spicy hot	*picante*	pee-**kahn**-tay
steamed	*hervido*	ehr-**bee**-doh
stuffed	*relleno*	ray-**yay**-noh
sweet	*dulce*	**dool**-thay
well-done	*muy hecho*	**moo**-ee **ay**-choh
with rice	*con arroz*	kohn ah-**rohth**
with garlic sauce	*con alioli*	kohn ah-lee-**oh**-lee

Veggies

vegetables	*verduras*	behr-**doo**-rahs
mixed vegetables	*menestra*	may-**nay**-strah
artichoke	*alcachofa*	ahl-kah-**choh**-fah
asparagus	*espárragos*	ay-**spah**-rah-gohs
beans	*judías*	hoo-**dee**-ahs

beets	remolachas	ray-moh-**lah**-chahs
broccoli	brécol	**bray**-kohl
cabbage	col	kohl
carrots	zanahorias	thah-nah-**oh**-ree-ahs
cauliflower	coliflor	koh-lee-**flor**
corn	maíz	mah-**eeth**
cucumbers	pepinos	pay-**pee**-nohs
eggplant	berenjena	bay-rehn-**hay**-nah
French fries	patatas fritas	pah-**tah**-tahs **free**-tahs
garlic	ajo	**ah**-hoh
green beans	judías verdes	hoo-**dee**-ahs **behr**-days
lentils	lentejas	layn-**tay**-hahs
mushrooms	setas	**say**-tahs
olives	aceitunas	ah-thay-**too**-nahs
onions	cebollas	thay-**boh**-yahs
pasta	pasta	**pah**-stah
peas	guisantes	gee-**sahn**-tays
pepper...	pimiento...	pee-mee-**ehn**-toh
...green / red / hot	...verde / rojo / picante	**behr**-day / **roh**-hoh / pee-**kahn**-tay
pickle	pepinillo	pay-pee-**nee**-yoh
potatoes	patatas	pah-**tah**-tahs
rice	arroz	ah-**rohth**
spaghetti	espaguetis	ay-spah-**geh**-tees
spinach	espinacas	ay-spee-**nah**-kahs
tomatoes	tomates	toh-**mah**-tays
zucchini	calabacín	kah-lah-bah-**theen**

Veggie Specialties

acelgas con pasas y piñones	ah-**thayl**-gahs kohn **pah**-sahs ee peen-**yoh**-nays	Swiss chard sautéed with onions and pine nuts
champiñones rellenos	cham-peen-**yoh**-nays ray-**yay**-nohs	mushrooms stuffed with ham, cheese, and onions
escalivada	ay-skah-lee-**bah**-dah	roasted or grilled eggplant, peppers, and onions (literally "grilled")

pimientos	pee-mee-**yehn**-tohs	sweet peppers stuffed
a la	ah lah	with minced meat,
riojana	ree-oh-**hah**-nah	
pisto	**pee**-stoh	stewed zucchini, bell
		peppers, and tomatoes

Fruits

apple	*manzana*	mahn-**thah**-nah
apricot	*albaricoque*	ahl-bah-ree-**koh**-kay
banana	*plátano*	**plah**-tah-noh
berries	*bayas*	**bah**-yahs
cantaloupe	*melón*	may-**lohn**
cherry	*cereza*	thay-**ray**-thah
date	*dátil*	**dah**-teel
fig	*higo*	**ee**-goh
fruit	*fruta*	**froo**-tah
grapefruit	*pomelo*	poh-**may**-loh
grapes	*uvas*	**oo**-bahs
honeydew melon	*melón verde*	may-**lohn behr**-day
lemon	*limón*	lee-**mohn**
orange	*naranja*	nah-**rahn**-hah
peach	*melocotón*	may-loh-koh-**tohn**
pear	*pera*	**pay**-rah
persimmon	*caqui*	**kah**-kee
pineapple	*piña*	**peen**-yah
plum	*ciruela*	theer-**way**-lah
prune	*ciruela seca*	theer-**way**-lah **say**-kah
raspberry	*frambuesa*	frahm-**bway**-sah
strawberry	*fresa*	**fray**-sah
tangerine	*mandarina*	mahn-dah-**ree**-nah
watermelon	*sandía*	sahn-**dee**-ah

Nuts to You

almond	*almendra*	ahl-**mayn**-drah
cashews	*anacardos*	ah-nah-**kar**-dohs
chestnut	*castaña*	kah-**stahn**-yah

EATING

coconut	*coco*	**koh**-koh
hazelnut	*avellana*	ah-bay-**yah**-nah
peanut	*cacahuete*	kah-kah-**way**-tay
pistachio	*pistacho*	pee-**stah**-choh
walnut	*nuez*	noo-**ayth**

Just Desserts

dessert	*postres*	**poh**-strays
little tarts and cakes	*pastas*	**pah**-stahs
caramel custard	*flan*	flahn
cake	*bizcocho*	beeth-**koh**-choh
cream cake	*pastel de crema*	pah-**stayl** day **kray**-mah
cream custard	*natilla*	nah-**tee**-yah
ice cream	*helado*	ay-**lah**-doh
scoop of...	*cucharón de...*	koo-chah-**rohn** day
cone of...	*cucurucho de...*	koo-koo-**roo**-choh day
cup of...	*copa de...*	**koh**-pah day
vanilla	*vainilla*	bī -**nee**-yah
chocolate	*chocolate*	choh-koh-**lah**-tay
strawberry	*fresa*	**fray**-sah
lemon	*limón*	lee-**mohn**
ice cream cake	*tarta helada*	**tar**-tah ay-**lah**-dah
sherbet	*sorbete*	sor-**bay**-tay
cupcakes	*magdalenas*	mahg-dah-**lay**-nahs
fruit cup	*macedonia*	mah-theh-**doh**-nee-ah
tart	*tarta*	**tar**-tah
whipped cream	*nata montada*	**nah**-tah mohn-**tah**-dah
chocolate mousse	*mousse*	moos
pudding	*pudín*	poo-**deen**
rice pudding	*arroz con leche*	ah-**rohth** kohn **lay**-chay
sweet egg pudding	*natilla de huevo*	nah-**tee**-yah day **way**-boh
sweet egg rolls	*rollitos de huevo*	roh-**yee**-tohs day **way**-boh
pastry	*pasteles*	pah-**stay**-lays
cookies	*galletas*	gah-**yay**-tahs
candy	*caramelo*	kah-rah-**may**-loh

low calorie	bajo en calorías	**bah**-hoh ayn kah-loh-**ree**-ahs
homemade	hecho en casa	**ay**-choh ayn **kah**-sah
We'll split one.	Lo compartiremos.	loh kohm-par-tee-**ray**-mohs
Two forks / spoons, please.	Dos tenedores / cucharas, por favor.	dohs tay-nay-**doh**-rays / koo-**chah**-rahs por fah-**bor**
I shouldn't, but...	No debería, pero...	noh day-bay-**ree**-ah **pay**-roh
Super-tasty!	¡Riquísimo!	ree-**kee**-see-moh
Exquisite!	¡Exquisito!	ayks-kee-**see**-toh
It's heavenly!	¡Es delicioso!	ays day-lee-thee-**oh**-soh
Death by chocolate.	Muerto por el chocolate.	**mwehr**-toh por ehl choh-koh-**lah**-tay
Better than sex.	Mejor que el sexo.	may-**hor** kay ehl **sayk**-soh
A moment on the lips, forever on the hips.	Un momento en los labios, para el resto en las caderas.	oon moh-**mehn**-toh ayn lohs **lah**-bee-ohs **pah**-rah ehl **ray**-stoh ehn lahs cah-**day**-rahs

The Moors introduced Spain to pastries and treats such as *mazapán* (marzipan, the ultra-sweet almond paste) and candied fruit, previously unknown in Europe.

Dessert Specialties

arroz con leche	ah-**rohth** kohn **lay**-chay	rice pudding
brazo de gitano	**brah**-thoh day hee-**tah**-noh	sponge cake filled with butter cream (Andalucía)
canitas	kah-**nee**-tahs	fried cornets filled with cream or custard
crema Catalana	**kray**-mah kah-tah-**lah**-nah	crème caramel
cuajada	kwah-**hah**-dah	cream-based dessert with honey
flan de huevo	flahn day **way**-boh	crème caramel

mel i mató	mehl ee mah-**toh**	curd cheese drizzled with honey
panellets	pah-nay-**yayts**	sweet potato cookie with pine nuts and hazelnuts
postre de música	**poh**-stray day **moo**-see-kah	roasted nuts and dried fruit served with a cold glass of Moscatel (white dessert wine)
tocino de cielo (literally "bacon from heaven")	toh-**thee**-noh day thee-**ay**-loh	baked custard topped with caramelized sugar and often flavored with lemon
torrijas	toh-**ree**-hahs	sweet fritters

Tapas

Bars called *tascas* or *tabernas* offer delicious appetizers called *tapas* during the hours when Spanish restaurants are still closed. For a quick, tasty, inexpensive meal before the sun sets, I look for the noisy places with lots of locals, a blaring TV, and piles of napkins and food debris on the floor (go local and toss your trash, too).

Be assertive or you'll never be served. *Por favor* is a key phrase—it grabs a guy's attention. Just point to the food you want and say, "*un pincho*" for a bite-sized serving, "*una tapa*" for a larger serving, or "*una ración*" for a generous serving. Get a fun, inexpensive sampler plate. Ask for *una ración canapes variados* to get a plate of various little open-faced sandwiches. Or ask for a *surtido de* (assortment of) *charcutería* (various meats), *queso* (cheese), or *mixto* (meat and cheese). *Un surtido de jamon y queso* means a plate of different hams and cheeses. That, bread, and red wine on the right square—and you've got a romantic (and $10) dinner for two.

EATING

Don't limit yourself to what you see on the bar. A huge variety of more appetizing, interesting plates are being thrown together in the kitchen. Get a menu and explore. Handwritten signs that start out *"Hay,"* mean "Today we have ___ ," as in *"Hay caracoles"* ("Today we have snails").

If you order a *tortilla,* you'll get quiche. Spanish tortillas are egg dishes rather than flour or corn tortillas. For bread, ask for *pan* (white bread) or *picos* (small, free breadsticks).

Be careful. While veggies are cheap, seafood can be very expensive (up to $10). If you're buying seafood, confirm the cost by asking *"¿Cuánto cuesta?"* (How much is it?). Don't worry about paying until you're ready to leave (he's keeping track of your tab). To get the bill, ask, *"¿La cuenta?"* (or *la dolorosa*—meaning literally "the sadness," always draws a confused laugh). Bars come with a formidable language barrier. A small working vocabulary is essential for *tapas* proficiency.

Tapa Terms

pincho	**peen**-choh	bite-size portion
pinchito	peen-**chee**-toh	a taste (smaller than a *pincho*)
tapa	**tah**-pah	snack-size portion
1/2 ración (media ración)	**may**-dee-ah rah-thee-**ohn**	appetizer size, bigger than a tapa
ración	rah-thee-**ohn**	large portion
montadito, canape	mohn-tah-**dee**-toh, kah-**nah**-pay	tiny open-faced sandwich
pepito, bocadillo chiquito	pay-**pee**-toh, boh-kah-**dee**-yoh chee-**kee**-toh	small sandwich
surtido	soor-**tee**-doh	assortment
frito	**free**-toh	fried
la plancha	lah **plahn**-chah	grilled
con alioli	kohn ah-lee-**oh**-lee	with a sauce of garlic and olive oil

EATING

| ¿Quanto cuesta una tapa? | **kwahn**-toh **kway**-stah **oo**-nah **tah**-pah | How much per tapa? |

Not every tapa is available in every portion size. *Paella* (the popular saffron rice dish) for instance, can be served as a *tapa* or *ración,* but not as a *pincho* or *pinchito* (too messy).

Seafood Tapas

almejas a la marinera	ahl-**may**-*ha*s ah la mah-ree-**nay**-rah	clams in paprika sauce
atún	ah-**toon**	tuna
bacalao	bah-kahl-**ow**	cod
boquerones	boh-kehr-**oh**-nays	fresh anchovies
calamares a la Romana	kah-lah-**mah**-rays ah lah roh-**mah**-nah	rings of deep-fried squid
cazón en adabo	kah-**thon** ayn ah-**dah**-boh	marinated white fish
gambas a la plancha	**gahm**-bahs ah la **plahn**-chah	grilled prawns
gambas al ajillo	**gahm**-bahs ahl ah-**hee**-yoh	prawns cooked in garlic and olive oil
mejillones	may-*hee*-**yoh**-nays	mussels
merluza	mehr-**loo**-thah	hake (fish)
paella	pah-**ay**-yah	saffron rice dish with mix of seafood and meat
pescaditos fritos	pay-skah-**dee**-tohs **free**-tohs	assortment of little fried fish
pescado en adobo	pay-**skah**-doh ayn ah-**doh**-boh	marinated whitefish
pulpo	**pool**-poh	octopus
rabas	**rah**-bahs	squid tentacles
sardinas	sar-**dee**-nahs	sardines
tortillitas de camarones	tor-**tee**-yahs day kah-mah-**roh**-nays	shrimp fritters (Andalucía)
variado fritos	bah-ree-**ah**-doh **free**-tohs	typical Andalusian mix of various fried fish

Meaty Tapas

albóndigas	ahl-**bohn**-dee-gahs	spiced meatballs with sauce
bombas	**bohm**-bahs	fried ball of meat and potatoes
brocheta	broh-**chay**-tah	meat shishkebabs
cabrillas	kah-**bree**-yahs	snails (cheap and not as good as French escargot)
caracoles	kah-rah-**koh**-lays	tree snails
charcutería	char-koo-tay-**ree**-ah	cured meats
chorizo	choh-**ree**-thoh	spicy Spanish sausage
croquetas	kroh-**kay**-tahs	fried balls of meat or cornmeal
guiso	**gee**-soh	stew
empanadillas	aym-pah-nah-**dee**-yahs	pastries stuffed with meat or seafood
jamón ibérico	*h*ah-**mohn** ee-**behr**-ee-koh	best ham, from acorn-fed baby pigs
jamón serrano	*h*ah-**mohn** say-**rah**-noh	cured ham
morcilla	mor-**thee**-yah	blood sausage
morros	**moh**-rohs	pig snout
pinchos morunos	**peen**-chohs moh-**roo**-nohs	skewer of spicy lamb or pork
pollo alioli	**poh**-yoh ah-lee-**oh**-lee	chicken with garlic and olive oil sauce
sesos	**say**-sohs	lamb brains
tabla serrana	**tah**-blah say-**rah**-nah	hearty plate of meat and cheese

Veggie and Egg Tapas

aceitunas	ah-thay-**too**-nahs	olives
almendras	ahl-**mehn**-drahs	fried almonds
banderilla (literally, the spear used by matadors)	bahn-day-**ree**-yah	skewer of pickled olives, peppers, carrots, and onions

callos	**kah**-yohs	chickpeas with tripe and sauce
champiñones	chahm-peen-**yoh**-nays	mushrooms
ensalada Rusa	ayn-sah-**lah**-dah **roo**-sah	Russian salad of peas and carrots
espinacas (con garbanzos)	ay-spee-**nah**-kahs (kohn gar-**bahn**-thohs)	spinach (with garbanzo beans)
gazpacho	gahth-**pah**-choh	cold tomato soup
judías verdes	hoo-**dee**-ahs **behr**-days	green beans
patatas bravas	pah-**tah**-tahs **brah**-bahs	fried potatoes with creamy tomato sauce
pimiento (relleno)	pee-mee-**ehn**-toh (ray-**yay**-noh)	peppers (stuffed)
pinchos de queso	**peen**-chohs day **kay**-soh	pieces of cheese
queso manchego	**kay**-soh mahn-**chay**-goh	sheep cheese
revuelto de...	ray-**bwayl**-toh day	scrambled eggs with...
setas	**say**-tahs	wild mushrooms
tortilla	tor-**tee**-yah	omelet (usually made with potatoes)
tortilla de jamón / queso	tor-**tee**-yah day hah-**mohn** / **kay**-soh	potato omelet with ham / cheese
tortilla española	tor-**tee**-yah ay-spahn-**yoh**-lah	potato and onion omelet

Tapa Drinks

una caña	**oo**-nah **kahn**-yah	a small draft beer
un sangría	oon sahn-**gree**-ah	a refreshing mix of fruit juice and wine
un vinito tinto / blanco	oon bee-**nee**-toh **teen**-toh / **blahn**-koh	a small glass of red / white wine
un vaso de agua del grifo	oon **bah**-soh day **ah**-gwah dayl **gree**-foh	a glass of tap water (free)

Drinking

Water, Milk, and Juice

mineral water...	*agua mineral...*	**ah**-gwah mee-nay-**rahl**
...with / without gas	*...con / sin gas*	kohn / seen gahs
tap water	*agua del grifo*	**ah**-gwah dayl **gree**-foh
whole milk	*leche entera*	**lay**-chay ayn-**tay**-rah
skim milk	*leche desnatada*	**lay**-chay days-nah-**tah**-dah
fresh milk	*leche fresca*	**lay**-chay **fray**-skah
hot chocolate	*chocolate caliente*	choh-koh-**lah**-tay kahl-**yehn**-tay
fruit juice	*zumo de fruta*	**thoo**-moh day **froo**-tah
100% juice	*cien por cien zumo*	thee-**ehn** por thee-**ehn** **thoo**-moh
orange juice (pure)	*zumo (puro) de naranja*	**thoo**-moh (**poo**-roh) day nah-**rahn**-hah
apple juice	*zumo de manzana*	**thoo**-moh day mahn-**thah**-nah
lemonade	*limonada*	lee-moh-**nah**-dah
with / without...	*con / sin...*	kohn / seen
...sugar	*...azúcar*	ah-**thoo**-kar
...ice	*...hielo*	**yay**-loh
glass / cup	*vaso / taza*	**bah**-soh / **tah**-thah
small / large	*pequeña / grande*	pay-**kayn**-yah / **grahn**-day
bottle	*botella*	boh-**tay**-yah
Is the water safe to drink?	*¿Es el agua potable?*	ays ehl **ah**-gwah poh-**tah**-blay

Two fun Spanish beverages are the chilled almond-flavored drink called *horchata* (pron. or-**chah**-tah) and the refreshing drink of honey and water called *aloja* (pron. ah-**loh**-*h*ah).

KEY PHRASES: DRINKING

drink	*bebida*	bay-**bee**-dah
(mineral) water	*agua (mineral)*	**ah**-gwah (mee-nay-**rahl**)
tap water	*agua del grifo*	**ah**-gwah dayl **gree**-foh
milk	*leche*	**lay**-chay
juice	*zumo*	**thoo**-moh
coffee	*café*	kah-**feh**
tea	*té*	tay
wine	*vino*	**bee**-noh
beer	*cerveza*	thehr-**bay**-thah
Cheers!	*¡Salud!*	sah-**lood**

Coffee and Tea

coffee...	*café...*	kah-**feh**
...black	*...solo*	**soh**-loh
...with a little milk	*...cortado*	kor-**tah**-doh
...with a lot of milk	*...con leche*	kohn **lay**-chay
...with sugar	*...con azúcar*	kohn ah-**thoo**-kar
...iced	*...con hielo*	kohn **yay**-loh
...American-syle	*...americano*	ah-may-ree-**kah**-noh
espresso	*espreso*	ay-**spray**-soh
espresso with a touch of brandy	*carajillo*	kah-rah-**hee**-yoh
instant coffee	*Nescafé*	nehs-kah-**feh**
decaffeinated	*descafeinado*	day-skah-fay-**nah**-doh
sugar	*azúcar*	ah-**thoo**-kar
hot water	*agua caliente*	**ah**-gwah kahl-**yehn**-tay
tea / lemon	*té / limón*	tay / lee-**mohn**
tea bag	*infusión de té*	een-foo-see-**ohn** day tay
herbal tea	*té de hierbas*	tay day **yehr**-bahs
lemon tea	*té de limón*	tay day lee-**mohn**
orange tea	*té de naranja*	tay day nah-**rahn**-hah
fruit tea	*té de frutas*	tay day **froo**-tahs
mint tea	*té de menta*	tay day **mayn**-tah
small / large	*corto / largo*	**kor**-toh / **lar**-goh

EATING

small cup	*taza mediana*	**tah**-thah may-dee-**ah**-nah
large cup	*taza grande*	**tah**-thah **grahn**-day
Another cup.	*Otra taza.*	**oh**-trah **tah**-thah
Same price at	*¿Es el mismo*	ehs ehl **mees**-moh
the bar or	*precio en la*	**pray**-thee-oh ayn lah
the table?	*barra que en*	**bah**-rah kay ayn
	la mesa?	lah **may**-sah

In bigger cities, bars have menu boards that list three price levels: prices are cheapest at the *barra* (counter), higher at the *mesa* (table), and highest on the *terraza* (terrace).

Wine

I / We would like...	*Me / Nos*	may / nohs
	gustaría...	goo-stah-**ree**-ah
...a glass	*...un vaso*	oon **bah**-soh
...a small glass	*...un chato*	oon **chah**-toh
...a carafe	*...una jarra*	**oo**-nah **hah**-rah
...a bottle	*...una botella*	**oo**-nah boh-**tay**-yah
...a 5-liter jug	*...una jarra de*	**oo**-nah **hah**-rah day
	cinco litros	**theen**-koh **lee**-trohs
...a barrel	*...un barril*	oon **bah**-reel
...a vat	*...una cuba*	**oo**-nah **koo**-bah
...of red wine.	*...de vino tinto.*	day **bee**-noh **teen**-toh
...of white wine.	*...de vino blanco.*	day **bee**-noh **blahn**-koh
...of the region.	*...de la región.*	day lah ray-hee-**ohn**
...the wine list.	*...la carta de vinos.*	lah **kar**-tah day **bee**-nohs

Wine lovers will find delicious wines at reasonable prices. Rioja wines are excellent, especially the reds. Navarra, Aragón, and Castilla-La Mancha produce good budget reds. Whites and reds from the Penedés region near Barcelona are also a good value. Valdepeñas wines are usually cheap and forgettable.

A carafe of house wine with your meal is often inexpensive. In summer, red wine is served *fresco* (chilled); if you want it at room temperature, ask for *natural* (pron. nah-too-**rahl**).

EATING

Wine Words

wine	*vino*	**bee**-noh
house wine (cheap)	*vino de la casa*	**bee**-noh day lah **kah**-sah
table wine (cheap)	*vino de mesa*	**bee**-noh day **may**-sah
select wine (good year)	*vino selecto*	**bee**-noh say-**layk**-toh
local	*local*	loh-**kahl**
of the region	*de la región*	day lah ray-hee-**ohn**
red	*tinto*	**teen**-toh
white	*blanco*	**blahn**-koh
rosé	*rosado*	roh-**sah**-doh
sparkling	*espumoso*	ay-spoo-**moh**-soh
light	*ligero*	lee-**hay**-roh
sweet	*dulce*	**dool**-thay
medium	*medio*	**may**-dee-oh
semi-dry	*semi-seco*	say-mee-**say**-koh
dry	*seco*	**say**-koh
very dry	*muy seco*	**moo**-ee **say**-koh
full-bodied	*de cuerpo*	day **kwehr**-poh
mature	*maduro*	mah-**doo**-roh
cork	*corcho*	**kor**-choh
corkscrew	*sacacorchos*	sah-kah-**kor**-chohs
vineyard	*viña*	**been**-yah
harvest	*vendimia*	bayn-**dee**-mee-ah
What is a good year (vintage)?	*¿Cuál es un vino de buena cosecha?*	kwahl ays oon **bee**-noh day **bway**-nah koh-**say**-chah
What do you recommend?	*¿Qué recomienda?*	kay ray-koh-mee-**ehn**-dah

Wine Labels

Deciphering the information on a Spanish wine label can be confusing. Listed below are terms that can help you judge the quality of a wine. The words *Reserva* and *Gran Reserva* on the label are usually signs of a better quality, though these can be unreliable designations. Spanish winemaking can be old-fashioned and inconsistent.

Gran Reserva	aged two years in storage and three in the bottle	
Reserva	aged at least three years for reds and two years for whites	
DOC (DO+calificada)	highest-quality guarantee for winemaking (currently only Rioja has it)	
DO	high-quality standards for wine production	
DOP (DO+provisional)	next best in quality, after DO	
vino de la tierra	regional wine	
vino de mesa	table wine	
vino joven	new wine	

Beer

beer	*cerveza*	thehr-**bay**-thah
from the tap	*de barril*	day **bah**-reel
bottle	*botella*	boh-**tay**-yah
light / dark	*rubia / negra*	**roo**-bee-ah / **nay**-grah
local / imported	*local / importada*	loh-**kahl** / eem-por-**tah**-dah
small / large	*pequeña / grande*	pay-**kayn**-yah / **grahn**-day
small glass of draft beer	*caña*	**kahn**-yah
big, straight glass of draft beer	*tubo*	**too**-boh
large draft beer in a glass with a handle	*jarra de cerveza*	**hah**-rah day thehr-**bay**-thah
a fifth-sized bottle	*quinto, botellín*	**keen**-toh, boh-tay-**yeen**
a half-liter bottle	*mediana*	may-dee-**ah**-nah
low-calorie	*light*	"light"
alcohol-free	*sin-alcohol*	seen-ahl-**kohl**
cold	*fría*	**free**-ah
colder	*más fría*	mahs **free**-ah

A *clara* is beer with a touch of lemonade. In most bars in Spain, you pay when you leave instead of when you order. In college towns, you may find a *chupitería* (shot-shop), where students—most of them visiting from other countries—throw back *chupitos* (shots). Also popular among heavy–drinking students is the *litro* bar, where you can buy mixed drinks by the liter.

Bar Talk

Shall we go for a drink?	¿Vamos a tomar una copa?	**bah**-mohs ah toh-**mar** **oo**-nah **koh**-pah
I'll buy you a drink.	Te invito a una copa.	tay een-**bee**-toh ah **oo**-nah **koh**-pah
It's on me.	Pago yo.	**pah**-goh yoh
The next one's on me.	Invito a la próxima.	een-**bee**-toh ah lah **prohk**-see-mah
What would you like?	¿Qué quiere?	kay kee-**ay**-ray
I'll have...	Me apatece...	may ah-pah-**tay**-thay
I don't drink alcohol.	No bebo alcohol.	noh **bay**-boh ahl-**kohl**
alcohol-free	sin-alcohol	seen-ahl-**kohl**
What is the local specialty?	¿Cuál es la especialidad regional?	kwahl ays lah ay-spay-thee-ah-lee-**dahd** ray-hee-oh-**nahl**
What is a good drink for women / men	¿Cuál es una buena bebida para mujeres / hombres?	kwahl ays **oo**-nah **bway**-nah bay-**bee**-dah **pah**-rah moo-**hehr**-ays / **ohm**-brays
Straight.	Sólo.	**soh**-loh
With / Without...	Con / Sin...	kohn / seen
...alcohol.	...alcohol.	ahl-**kohl**
...ice.	...hielo.	**yay**-loh
One more.	Otro.	**oh**-troh
Cheers!	¡Salud!	sah-**lood**
Long live Spain!	¡Viva España!	**bee**-bah ay-**spahn**-yah
I'm feeling...	Me siento...	may see-**ehn**-toh
...tipsy.	...achispado[a].	ah-chee-**spah**-doh
...a little drunk.	...un poco borracho[a].	oon **poh**-koh boh-**rah**-choh
...blitzed.	...borracho[a].	boh-**rah**-choh
I'm hung over.	Tengo resaca.	**tayn**-goh ray-**sah**-kah

For a refreshing blend of red wine, seltzer, fruit, and fruit juice, try **sangría**. Brandy and triple sec are often the secret ingredients.

Cava is a champagne-like sparkling white wine produced in the northern region of Penedés. The best-known brands are Cordoniú and Freixenet. The Spaniards love a chance to celebrate with bubbly wine. *¡Salud!*

Drink Specialties

BEFORE A MEAL

Cuba libre	**koo**-bah **lee**-bray	rum and Coke
jerez...	heh-**reth**	sherry, a fortified wine from Jerez in Andalucía
...amontillado,	ah-mohn-tee-**yah**-doh,	rich, dry sherries (best-
fino,	**fee**-noh,	known *fino* brands are
manzanilla	mahn-thah-**nee**-yah	Tío Pepe and La Ina)
sidra	**see**-drah	fermented cider
tinto de	**teen**-toh day	wine and lemonade
Verono	vay-**roh**-noh	
vermut	vehr-**moot**	vermouth, red or white with soda

AFTER A MEAL

aguardiente	ah-gwar-dee-**yehn**-tay	clear grape-based liqueur
chinchón	cheen-**chohn**	anise-flavored liqueur
coñac	**kohn**-yahk	Spanish brandy (Centario, Magro, and Soberano are well-known brands)
jerez	heh-**reth**	sweet sherry
olovoso	oh-loh-**voh**-soh	
moscatel	moh-skah-**tehl**	sweet white dessert wine
pacharán	pah-chah-**rahn**	aniseed and plum liqueur

EATING

Picnicking

At the Market

Self-service?	¿Auto-servicio?	ow-toh-sehr-**bee**-thee-oh
Ripe for today?	¿Maduro para hoy?	mah-**doo**-roh **pah**-rah oy
Does it need to be cooked?	¿Esto necesita cocinarse?	**ay**-stoh nay-thay-**see**-tah koh-thee-**nar**-say
May I taste a little?	¿Podría probarlo?	poh-**dree**-ah proh-**bar**-loh
Fifty grams.	Cincuenta gramos.	theen-**kwehn**-tah **grah**-mohs
One hundred grams.	Cien gramos.	thee-**ehn grah**-mohs
More. / Less.	Más. / Menos.	mahs / **may**-nohs
A piece.	Un trozo.	oon **troh**-thoh
A slice.	Una rodaja.	**oo**-nah roh-**dah**-hah
Four slices.	Cuatro rodajas.	**kwah**-troh roh-**dah**-hahs
Sliced (fine).	En rodajas (muy finas).	ayn roh-**dah**-hahs (**moo**-ee **fee**-nahs)
Half.	Medio.	**may**-dee-oh
A small bag.	Una bolsita.	**oo**-nah bohl-**see**-tah
A bag, please.	Una bolsa, por favor.	**oo**-nah **bohl**-sah por fah-**bor**
Will you make me / us..?	¿Me / Nos puede hacer....?	may / nohs **pway**-day ah-**thehr**
...a sandwich	...un bocadillo	oon boh-kah-**dee**-yoh
...two sandwiches	...dos bocadillos	dohs boh-kah-**dee**-yohs
To take out.	Para llevar.	**pah**-rah yay-**bar**
Can I / Can we use the...?	¿Puedo / Podemos usar el...?	**pway**-doh / poh-**day**-mohs oo-**sar** ehl
...microwave	...microondas	mee-kroh-**ohn**-dahs
May I borrow a...?	¿Puedo tomar prestado un...?	**pway**-doh toh-**mar** pray-**stah**-doh oon
Do you have a...?	¿Tiene un...?	tee-**ehn**-ay oon
Where can I buy / find a...?	¿Dónde puedo comprar / encontrar un...?	**dohn**-day **pway**-doh kohm-**prar** / ayn-kohn-**trar** oon

...corkscrew	*...sacacorchos*	sah-kah-**kor**-chohs
...can opener	*...abrelatas*	ah-bray-**lah**-tahs
Is there a park nearby?	*¿Hay un parque cerca de aquí?*	ī oon **par**-kay **thehr**-kah day ah-**kee**
Where is a good place to picnic?	*¿Dónde hay un buen sitio para hacer un picnic?*	**dohn**-day ī oon bwayn **seet**-yoh **pah**-rah ah-**thehr** oon peek-**neek**
Is picnicking allowed here?	*¿Se puede hacer picnic aquí?*	say **pway**-day ah-**thehr** peek-**neek** ah-**kee**

Picnic Prose

open air market	*mercado municipal*	mehr-**kah**-doh moo-nee-thee-**pahl**
supermarket	*supermercado*	soo-pehr-mehr-**kah**-doh
delicatessen	*charcutería*	char-soo-teh-**ree**-ah
bakery	*panadería*	pah-nah-deh-**ree**-ah
pastry shop	*pastelería*	pah-stay-leh-**ree**-ah
sweets shop	*tienda de dulces*	tee-**ehn**-dah day **dool**-thays
picnic	*picnic*	peek-**neek**
sandwich	*bocadillo*	boh-kah-**dee**-yoh
bread	*pan*	pahn
whole-wheat bread	*pan integral, pan de trigo*	pahn een-tay-**grahl**, pahn day **tree**-goh
roll	*panecillo*	pah-nay-**thee**-yoh
ham	*jamón*	hah-**mohn**
smoked ham	*jamón serrano*	hah-**mohn** say-**rah**-noh
sausage	*salchichón*	sahl-chee-**chohn**
cheese	*queso*	**kay**-soh
mustard...	*mostaza...*	mohs-**tah**-thah
mayonnaise...	*mayonesa...*	mah-yoh-**nay**-sah
...in a tube	*...en tubo*	ayn **too**-boh
yogurt	*yogur*	yoh-**goor**
fruit	*fruta*	**froo**-tah
box of juice	*lata de zumo*	**lah**-tah day **thoo**-moh

EATING

cold drinks	*bebidas frías*	bay-**bee**-dahs **free**-ahs
spoon / fork...	*cuchara /*	koo-**chah**-rah /
	tenedor...	tay-nay-**dor**
...made of plastic	*...de plástico*	day **plah**-stee-koh
cup / plate...	*vaso / plato...*	**bah**-soh / **plah**-toh
...made of paper	*...de papel*	day pah-**pehl**

While you can opt for the one-stop *supermercado*, it's more fun to assemble your picnic and practice your Spanish visiting the small shops. A hundred grams of meat or cheese is about a quarter of a pound, enough for two sandwiches.

EATING

MENU DECODER

This handy Spanish-English menu decoder (followed by an English-Spanish decoder) won't unlock every word on the menu, but it'll get you *ostras* (oysters) instead of *orejas* (pigs' ears).

Spanish/English

a parte	side dish, on the side
aceite	oil
aceitunas	olives
acelgas	Swiss chard
agua	water
agua del grifo	tap water
aguardiente	clear, grape-based liqueur
ahumado	smoked
ajo	garlic
albaricoque	apricot
albóndigas	meatballs
alcachofa	artichoke
aliño	dressing
alioli	sauce of garlic and olive oil
almejas	clams
almejas a la marinera	clams in paprika sauce

almendra	almond
almuerzo	lunch
aloja	spiced water and honey drink
amontillado	dry and rich (sherry type)
anacardos	cashews
anchoas	anchovies
anguila	eel
aperitivos	appetizers
arenque	herring
arroz	rice
arroz con leche	rice pudding
asado	baked
atún	tuna
avellana	hazelnut
aves	poultry
azúcar	sugar
bacalao	cod
bacalao a la vizcaína	salt cod braised with vegetables
banderilla	skewer of pickled veggies
bastante hecho	very well-done (meat)
bebida	beverage
berenjena	eggplant
besugo	bream (fish)
biftec	beef steak
bizcocho	cake
blanco	white
bocadillo	sandwich
bocadillo chiquito	tiny sandwich
bomba	fried ball of meat and potatoes
boquerones	fresh anchovies
botella	bottle
brazo di gitano	sponge cake filled with cream
brécol	broccoli
brocheta	meat shish kebabs
burbujas	carbonation
burgos	creamy ewe's milk cheese
butifarra	sweetly spiced pork sausage
caballo	horse

cabrales	tangy, goat's bleu cheese
cabrillas	snails
cabrito	a wee goat
cacahuete	peanut
café	coffee
café americano	American-syle coffee
café con azúcar	coffee with sugar
café con hielo	iced coffee
café con leche	coffee with a lot of milk
café cortado	coffee with a little milk
café solo	black coffee
calabacín	zucchini
calamares	squid
calamares a la Romana	rings of deep-fried squid
calamares con guisantes	squid with garlic, peas, mint, and tomatoes
caldo	broth
caliente	hot (not cold)
callos	chickpeas with tripe and sauce
canape	tiny open-faced sandwich
cangrejo	crab
cangrejo de río	crayfish
canitas	fried cornets with cream
caña	small draft beer
caracoles	tree snails
carajillo	espresso with a touch of brandy
caramelo	candy
carne	meat
carne de vaca	beef
carnero	lamb
carta	menu
carta de bebidas	drink menu
carta de vinos	wine list
casa	house
casera	homemade
castaña	chestnut
cava	sparkling white wine
cazón en adabo	marinated white fish

cebollas	onions
cena	dinner
centollo	dungeness crab
cerdo	pork
cereales	cereal
cereza	cherry
cerveza	beer
champiñones	mushrooms
champiñones rellenos	stuffed mushrooms
chinchón	anise-flavored liqueur
chino	Chinese
chorizo	sausage
chuleta	cutlet
churros	fritters
ciruela	plum
ciruela seca	prune
clara	beer with a touch of lemonade
cochinillo	suckling pig
cocido	broiled, also a name of a stew
cocinado	cooked
coco	coconut
col	cabbage
coliflor	cauliflower
colo de toro	bull-tail stew
combinado	combination
comida	food
con	with
conejo	rabbit
cono	cone
copa	cup (ice crem)
cordonices en hoja de parra	quail in grape leaves
corto	small
crema Catalana	custard and caramelized sauce
croquetas	fried meatballs
crudo	raw
cuajada	cream with honey
cuchara	spoon, scoop
cucharón	scoop (ice cream)

cucurucho	cone (ice cream)
dátile	date
de cuerpo	full-bodied (wine)
del día	of the day
delicioso	delicious
desayuno	breakfast
dulce	sweet
duro	hard
edulcorante	artificial sweetener
empanada	meat pie
empanada gallega	pizza-like pie
empanadillas	pastries stuffed with meat or seafood
ensalada	salad
ensalada de arroz	rice and shellfish soup
ensaladilla Rusa	vegetable salad in mayonnaise
escalfado	poached
escalivada	roasted eggplant and peppers salad
escudella i carn d'olla	minced pork meatballs
espaguetis	spaghetti
espárragos	asparagus
especial	special
espinacas	spinach
espreso	espresso
espumoso	sparkling
esqueixada	salted cod, onion, and peppers salad
fabada asturiana	pork and bean stew
fideus	paella with noodles instead of rice
filete	fillet
fino	dry and rich (sherry type)
flan	caramel custard
flauta	sandwich with very thin baguette bread
frambuesa	raspberry
fresa	strawberry
fresco	fresh
frijoles	beans
frío	cold
fritos	fried

fruta	fruit
fuerte	sharp (cheese)
galletas	cookies
gambas	prawns
gambas a la plancha	grilled prawns
garrafa	carafe
gas	carbonation
gazpacho	chilled tomato soup
gelatina	jelly
grande	large
guisantes	peas
guiso	stew
habas alla Catalana	fava bean and chorizo stew
hamburguesa	hamburger
hay ___	we have ___
hecho en casa	homemade
helado	ice cream
hervido	steamed
hielo	ice
hígado	liver
higo	fig
horchata	chilled almond drink
huevos	eggs
importada	imported
incluido	included
jamón	ham
jamón ibérico	ham from acorn-fed baby pigs
jamón serrano	cured ham
jarra	carafe or wine or large draft beer glass
jerez	sherry
judías	beans
judías verdes	green beans
jurel	scad (like mackerel)
langosta	lobster
langostinos	large prawns
leche	milk
lechuga	lettuce

lengua	tongue
lenguado	sole
lentejas	lentils
ligero	light
limón	lemon
macedonia	fruit cup
maduro	mature (wine)
magdalenas	cupcakes
maíz	corn
manchego	hard, ewe's milk cheese
mandarina	tangerine
mantequilla	butter
mantequilla de cacahuete	peanut butter
manzana	apple
manzanilla	dry and rich (sherry type)
mar y montaña / mar y terra	chicken or rabbit with lobster or scampi
margarina	margarine
marisco	seafood
marmitako	Basque tuna stew
mayonesa	mayonnaise
mediana	a half-liter bottle
medio	medium
mejillones	mussels
mel i mató	curd cheese with honey
melocotón	big, mean peach
melón	cantaloupe
menestra	mixed vegetables
merienda	afternoon tea
merluza	hake (fish)
mermelada	jam
mesa	table
microondas	microwave
miel	honey
montadito	tiny open-faced sandwich
morcilla	blood sausage
morros	pig snout
moscatel	sweet dessert wine

mostaza	mustard
muy	very
muy crudo	very rare (meat)
muy hecho	well-done (meat)
muy seco	very dry (wine)
naranja	orange
natilla	cream custard
natilla de huevo	sweet egg pudding
negra	dark
no	not
no incluido	not included
nuez	walnut
o	or
olovoso	cream sherry
orejas	pigs' ears
orgánico	organic
ostras	oysters
pacharón	liqueur of anise and sloes
paella	saffron rice and seafood dish
palillo	toothpick
palitos de queso	cheese straws or sticks
pan	bread
pan tomáquet	country bread with tomatoes
panecillo	roll
para llevar	"to go"
pastas	tarts and cakes
pasteles	pastries
patatas	potatoes
patatas bravas	fried potatoes with creamy tomato sauce
patatas fritas	French fries
pato	duck
pato con higos	duck with figs
pavo	turkey
pepinillos	pickles
pepinos	cucumber
pepito	little sandwich
pequeño	small

pera	pear
percebes	barnacles
perilla	firm, bland cow's milk cheese
perrito caliente	hot dog
pescaditos fritos	assortment of little fried fish
pescado	fish
pescado en adobo	marinated whitefish
pez espada	swordfish
picante	spicy hot
picos	little breadsticks (free)
pimiento	bell pepper
pimienta	pepper (seasoning)
pinchito	tiny *pincho*
pincho	snack
pinchos morunos	skewer of spicy lamb or pork
piña	pineapple
pistacho	pistachio
pisto	stewed zucchini, tomatoes, and peppers
plancha	grilled
plátano	banana
plato	plate
plato de niños	children's plate
poco hecho	rare (meat)
pollo	chicken
pollo en pepitoria	chicken fricassee with almonds and eggs
pomelo	grapefruit
postre de música	roasted nuts and dried fruit with a glass of moscatel wine
postres	desserts
primer	first
pudín	pudding
pulguita	small closed baguette sandwich
pulpo	octopus
queso	cheese
queso ahumado	smoked cheese
queso manchego	sheep cheese

queso rallado	grated cheese
quinto	fifth-sized bottle
rabas	squid tentacles
ración	portion
rallado	grated (cheese)
rápido	fast
recebo	receipt
relleno	stuffed
remolachas	beets
requesón	type of cottage cheese
revueltos	scrambled
riñones	kidney
riñones al jerez	kidneys in a sherry sauce
rodaja	slice
rojo	red
rollitos de huevo	sweet egg rolls
romesco	spicy sauce or fish and vegetable stew
roncal	strong, sharp, dry cheese
rosado	rosé (wine)
rubia	light
sabroso	tasty
sacacorchos	corkscrew
sal	salt
salchichón	sausage
salmón	salmon
San Simón	smooth, mild cheese
sandía	watermelon
sangría	red wine, juice and brandy
sardinas	sardines
seco	dry
segundo	second
semi-seco	semi-dry (wine)
sepia	cuttlefish
servicio	service
sesos	brains
setas	wild mushrooms
sidra	hard cider

sin	without
solo	only
sopa	soup
sopa a la gitana	pumpkin, chickpea soup
sopa de almendras	almond soup with saffron
sopa de castellana	egg, garlic soup
sopa de espárragos	asparagus soup
sopa de mariscos	seafood soup
sorbete	sherbet
suave	mild (cheese)
surtido	assortment
tabla serrana	plate of mountain meat and cheese
tallarines	noodles
tapas	appetizers
tarrina	cup
tarta	tart
taza	cup
té	tea
té de frutas	fruit tea
té de hierbas	herbal tea
té de limón	lemon tea
té de menta	mint tea
té de naranja	orange tea
templado	mild
ternera	veal
teta	firm, mild cheese
tinto	red (wine)
tinto de Verono	wine and lemonade
típico	typical
tocino de cielo	baked custard with caramelized sugar
tomates	tomatoes
torrijas	sweet fritters (bread)
tortilla	omelet
tortilla de jamón / queso	potato omelet with ham / cheese
tortilla español	potato omelet
tortillas de camarones	shrimp fritters
tostadas	toast

triguero	wheat
tripa	tripe
trozo	piece
trucha	trout
tubo	draft beer
turista	tourist
uvas	grapes
vainilla	vanilla
variado	assorted
vaso	glass
vegetales	vegetables
vegetariano	vegetarian
veneras	scallops
verde	green
verdura	vegetable
villalón	ewe's curd cheese in a mold
vinagre	vinegar
vino	wine
vino de mesa	house wine
vino joven	new wine
xato	lettuce, tuna, and anchovy salad with romesco sauce
y	and
yogur	yogurt
zanahorias	carrots
zarzuela de mariscos	shellfish stew
zumo	juice

English/Spanish

almond	almendra
anchovies	anchoas
anchovies, fresh	boquerones
and	y
appetizers	tapas, aperitivos
apple	manzana
apricot	albaricoque
artichoke	alcachofa
asparagus	espárragos
assorted	variado
assortment	surtido
baked	asado
banana	plátano
barnacles	percebes
beans	frijoles, judías
beans, green	judías verdes
beef	carne de vaca
beef steak	biftec
beer	cerveza
beer with lemonade	clara
beer, large draft	jarra, tubo
beer, small draft	caña
beets	remolachas
bell pepper	pimiento
beverage	bebida
bottle	botella
brains	sesos
bread	pan
breadsticks	picos
breakfast	desayuno
broccoli	brécol
broiled	cocido
broth	caldo
butter	mantequilla
cabbage	col

cake	bizcocho
candy	caramelo
cantaloupe	melón
carafe	garrafa, jarra
carbonation	gas, burbujas
carrots	zanahorias
cashews	anacardos
cauliflower	coliflor
cereal	cereales
cheese	queso
cheese straws or sticks	palitos de queso
cheese, curd, with honey	mel i mató
cheese, mild	suave
cheese, sheep	queso manchego
cheese, smoked	queso ahumado
cherry	cereza
chestnut	castaña
chicken	pollo
children's plate	plato de niños
Chinese	chino
cider, hard	sidra
clams	almejas
coconut	coco
cod	bacalao
coffee	café
coffee with a little milk	café cortado
coffee with a lot of milk	café con leche
coffee with sugar	café con azúcar
coffee, American-syle	café americano
coffee, black	café solo
coffee, iced	café con hielo
cold	frío
combination	combinado
cone	cono, cucurucho
cooked	cocinado
cookies	galletas
corkscrew	sacacorchos
corn	maíz

crab	cangrejo
crab, Dungeness	centollo
crayfish	cangrejo de río
cucumber	pepinos
cup	taza, tarrina
cup (ice crem)	copa
cupcakes	magdalenas
custard, caramel	flan
custard, cream	natilla
cutlet	chuleta
cuttlefish	sepia
dark	negra
date	dátile
day, of the	del día
delicious	delicioso
desserts	postres
dinner	cena
draft beer, large	tubo
draft beer, small	caña
dressing	aliño
drink menu	carta de bebidas
dry	seco
duck	pato
Dungeness crab	centollo
eel	anguila
eggplant	berenjena
eggs	huevos
espresso	espreso
espresso with a touch of brandy	carajillo
fast	rápido
fig	higo
fillet	filete
first	primer
fish	pescado
food	comida
French fries	patatas fritas
fresh	fresco

fried	fritos
fritters	churros
fruit	fruta
fruit cup	macedonia
fruit tea	té de frutas
full-bodied (wine)	de cuerpo
garlic	ajo
garlic and olive oil sauce	alioli
glass	vaso
goat, baby	cabrito
grapefruit	pomelo
grapes	uvas
grated (cheese)	rallado
green	verde
green beans	judías verdes
grilled	plancha
hake (fish)	merluza
ham	jamón
ham from acorn-fed baby pigs	jamón ibérico
ham, cured	jamón serrano
hamburger	hamburguesa
hard	duro
hard cider	sidra
hazelnut	avellana
herbal tea	té de hierbas
herring	arenque
homemade	hecho en casa, casera
honey	miel
horse	caballo
hot (not cold)	caliente
hot (spicy)	picante
hot dog	perrito caliente
house	casa
house wine	vino de mesa
ice	hielo
ice cream	helado
imported	importada
included	incluido

jam	mermelada
jelly	gelatina
juice	zumo
kidney	riñones
lamb	carnero
large	grande
lemon	limón
lemon tea	té de limón
lentils	lentejas
lettuce	lechuga
light	ligero
light-colored (beer)	rubia
liver	hígado
lobster	langosta
lunch	almuerzo
margarine	margarina
mature (wine)	maduro
mayonnaise	mayonesa
meat	carne
meat, medium	medio
meat, rare	poco hecho
meat, raw	crudo
meat, very rare	muy crudo
meat, very well-done	bastante hecho
meat, well-done	muy hecho
meatballs	albóndigas
medium	medio
microwave	microondas
mild	templado, suave
milk	leche
mineral water	agua mineral
mint tea	té de menta
mushrooms	champiñones
mushrooms, wild	setas
mussels	mejillones
mustard	mostaza
noodles	tallarines
not	no

octopus	pulpo
of the day	del día
oil	aceite
olives	aceitunas
omelet	tortilla
omelet, potato	tortilla español
omelet, potato with ham / cheese	tortilla de jamón / queso
on the side	a parte
onions	cebollas
only	solo
or	o
orange	naranja
orange tea	té de naranja
organic	orgánico
oysters	ostras
pastries	pasteles
peach	melocotón
peanut	cacahuete
peanut butter	mantequilla de cacahuete
pear	pera
peas	guisantes
pepper, bell	pimiento
pepper (seasoning)	pimienta
pickles	pepinillos
piece	trozo
pig snout	morros
pigs' ears	orejas
pineapple	piña
pistachio	pistacho
plate	plato
plum	ciruela
poached	escalfado
pork	cerdo
portion	ración
potatoes	patatas
poultry	aves
prawns	gambas

prawns, grilled	gambas a la plancha
prawns, large	langostinos
prune	ciruela seca
pudding	pudín
quail in grape leaves	cordonices en hoja de parra
rabbit	conejo
rare (meat)	poco hecho
rare, very (meat)	muy crudo
raspberry	frambuesa
raw	crudo
receipt	recebo
red	rojo
red (wine)	tinto
rice	arroz
rice pudding	arroz con leche
roll	panecillo
rosé	rosado
salad	ensalada
salmon	salmón
salt	sal
sandwich	bocadillo
sardines	sardinas
sausage	chorizo, salchichón
sausage, blood	morcilla
scad (like mackerel)	jurel
scallops	vieiras
scoop	cuchara, cucharón
scrambled	revueltos
seafood	marisco
seafood soup	sopa de mariscos
second	segundo
semi-dry (wine)	semi-seco
service	servicio
sherbet	sorbete
sherry	jerez
side dish	a parte
slice	rodaja
small	pequeño, corto

smoked	ahumado
snack	pincho
snails	cabrillas
snails, tree	caracoles
sole	lenguado
soup	sopa
soup with egg, garlic	sopa de castellana
soup, almond with saffron	sopa de almendras
soup, asparagus	sopa de espárragos
soup, chilled tomato	gazpacho
soup, seafood	sopa de mariscos
spaghetti	espaguetis
sparkling	espumoso
special	especial
spicy hot	picante
spinach	espinacas
spoon	cuchara
squid	calamares
squid tentacles	rabas
squid, deep-fried	calamares a la Romana
steamed	hervido
stew	guiso
stew of zucchini, tomatoes, and peppers	pisto
stew, bull-tail	colo de toro
stew, fava bean and chorizo	habas alla Catalana
stew, pork and bean	fabada asturiana
stew, shellfish	zarzuela de mariscos
strawberry	fresa
stuffed	relleno
suckling pig	cochinillo
sugar	azúcar
sweet	dulce
sweetener, artificial	edulcorante
swordfish	pez espada
table	mesa
tangerine	mandarina
tap water	agua del grifo

tart	tarta
tasty	sabroso
tea	té
to go	para llevar
toast	tostadas
tomatoes	tomates
tongue	lengua
toothpick	palillo
tripe	tripa
trout	trucha
tuna	atún
turkey	pavo
typical	típico
vanilla	vainilla
veal	ternera
vegetables	verduras, vegetales
vegetables, mixed	menestra
vegetarian	vegetariano
very	muy
very dry (wine)	muy seco
very rare (meat)	muy crudo
very well-done (meat)	bastante hecho
vinegar	vinagre
walnut	nuez
water	agua
water, mineral	agua mineral
water, tap	agua del grifo
watermelon	sandía
well-done (meat)	muy hecho
wheat	triguero
white	blanco
wine	vino
wine list	carta de vinos
wine, dry	seco
wine, full-bodied	de cuerpo
wine, house	vino de la casa
wine, light	ligero
wine, local	local

wine, mature	maduro
wine, medium	medio
wine, new	vino joven
wine, of the region	de la región
wine, red	tinto
wine, rosé	rosado
wine, semi-dry	semi-seco
wine, sparkling	espumoso
wine, sweet	dulce
wine, table	vino de mesa
wine, very dry	muy seco
wine, white	blanco
with	con
without	sin
yogurt	yogur
zucchini	calabacín

ACTIVITIES

Sightseeing

Where?

Where is...?	¿Dónde está...?	**dohn**-day ay-**stah**
...the best view	...la mejor vista	lah may-**hor bee**-stah
...the main square	...la plaza mayor	lah **plah**-thah **may**-yor
...the old town center	...el viejo centro	ehl bee-**ay**-hoh **thayn**-troh
...the museum	...el museo	ehl moo-**say**-oh
...the castle	...el castillo	ehl kah-**stee**-yoh
...the palace	...el palacio	ehl pah-**lah**-thee-oh
...an amusement park	...un parque de atracciones	oon **par**-kay day ah-trahk-thee-**oh**-nays
...the tourist information office	...la Oficina de Turismo	lah oh-fee-**thee**-nah day too-**rees**-moh
...the entrance / exit	...la entrada / salida	lah ayn-**trah**-dah / sah-**lee**-dah
Where are...?	¿Dónde están...?	**dohn**-day ay-**stahn**
...the toilets	...los servicios	lohs sehr-**bee**-thee-ohs
...the ruins	...las ruinas	lahs **rwee**-nahs
Is there a festival nearby?	¿Hay una fiesta cerca?	ī **oo**-nah fee-**eh**-stah **thehr**-kah

135

KEY PHRASES: SIGHTSEEING

Where is...?	¿Dónde está...?	**dohn**-day ay-**stah**
How much is it?	¿Cuánto cuesta?	**kwahn**-toh **kway**-stah
At what time does this open / close?	¿A qué hora abren / cierran?	ah kay **oh**-rah **ah**-brehn / thee-**ay**-rahn
Do you have a guided tour?	¿Tiene una visita con guía?	tee-**ehn**-ay **oo**-nah bee-**see**-tah kohn **gee**-ah
When is the next tour in English?	¿Cuándo es la siguiente visita en inglés?	**kwahn**-doh ays lah see-**gehn**-tay bee-**see**-tah ayn een-**glays**

At the Sight

Do you have...?	¿Tiene...?	tee-**ehn**-ay
...information	...información	een-for-mah-thee-**ohn**
...a guidebook	...una guía	**oo**-nah **gee**-ah
...in English	...en inglés	ayn een-**glays**
Is it free?	¿Es gratis?	ays **grah**-tees
How much is it?	¿Cuánto cuesta?	**kwahn**-toh **kway**-stah
Is the ticket good all day?	¿Es la billete válido para todo el día?	ays lah bee-**yeh**-tay **bah**-lee-doh **pah**-rah **toh**-doh ehl **dee**-ah
Can I get back in?	¿Puedo volver a entrar?	**pway**-doh bohl-**behr** ah ayn-**trar**
What time does this open / close?	¿A qué hora abren / cierran?	ah kay **oh**-rah **ah**-brehn / thee-**ay**-rahn
What time is the last entry?	¿A qué hora es la última entrada?	ah kay **oh**-rah ays lah **ool**-tee-mah ayn-**trah**-dah

Please

| PLEASE let me in. | POR FAVOR, déjeme entrar. | por fah-**bor** **day**-hay-may ayn-**trar** |
| PLEASE let us in. | POR FAVOR, déjenos entrar. | por fah-**bor** **day**-hay-nohs ayn-**trar** |

I've traveled all the way from___.	He viajado desde ___.	ay bee-ah-**hah**-doh **dehs**-day
We've traveled all the way from ___.	Hemos viajado desde ___.	**ay**-mohs bee-ah-**hah**-doh **dehs**-day
I must leave tomorrow.	Tengo que irme mañana.	**tayn**-goh kay **eer**-may mahn-**yah**-nah
We must leave tomorrow.	Tenemos que irnos mañana.	tay-**nay**-mohs kay **eer**-nohs mahn-**yah**-nah
I promise I'll be fast.	Le prometo que vendré rápido.	lay proh-**may**-toh kay bayn-**dray rah**-pee-doh
We promise we'll be fast.	Le prometemos que vendremos rápido.	lay proh-may-**tay**-mohs kay bayn-**dray**-mohs **rah**-pee-doh
It was my mother's dying wish that I see this.	Fue el último deseo de mi madre que yo viera esto.	fway ehl **ool**-tee-moh day-**say**-oh day mee **mah**-dray kay yoh bee-**eh**-rah **ay**-stoh
I've / We've always wanted to see this.	Siempre he / hemos querido ver esto.	see-**ehm**-pray ay / **ay**-mohs kay-**ree**-doh behr **ay**-stoh

Tours

Do you have...?	¿Tiene...?	tee-**ehn**-ay
...an audioguide	...una audioguía	**oo**-nah ow-dee-oh-**gee**-ah
...a guided tour	...una visita con guía	**oo**-nah bee-**see**-tah kohn **gee**-ah
...a city walking tour	...una excursión a pie por la ciudad	**oo**-nah ayk-skoor-thee-**ohn** ah pee-**ay** por lah thee-oo-**dahd**
...in English	...en ingles	ayn een-**glays**
When is the next next tour in English?	¿Cuándo es la siguiente visita en inglés?	**kwahn**-doh ays lah see-**gehn**-tay bee-**see**-tah ayn een-**glays**
Is it free?	¿Es gratis?	ays grah-**tees**
How much is it?	¿Cuánto cuesta?	**kwahn**-toh **kway**-stah
How long does it last?	¿Cuánto tiempo dura?	**kwahn**-toh tee-**ehm**-poh **doo**-rah

| Can I join a tour in progress? | ¿Puedo unirme a una excursión que ya haya empezado? | **pway**-doh oo-**neer**-may ah **oo**-nah ayk-skoor-thee-**ohn** kay yah **ah**-yah aym-pay-**thah**-doh |
| Can we join a tour in progress? | Podemos unirnos a una excursión que ya haya empezado? | poh-**day**-mohs oo-**neer**-nohs ah **oo**-nah ayk-skoor-thee-**ohn** kay yah **ah**-yah aym-pay-**thah**-doh |

To help you decipher entrance signs, an *exposición* is an exhibit, a *bono* is a combo-ticket, and the words "*Está aquí*" on a map mean "You are here."

Discounts

You may be eligible for a discount at tourist sights, hotels, or on buses and trains—ask.

Are there discounts for...?	¿Tienen descuentos para...?	tee-**ehn**-ehn days-**kwehn**-tohs **pah**-rah
...youths	...jóvenes	**h**oh-bay-nays
...students	...estudiantes	ay-stoo-dee-**ahn**-tays
...families	...familias	fah-**meel**-yahs
...seniors	...jubilados	**h**oo-bee-**lah**-dohs
...groups	...grupos	**groo**-pohs
I am...	Tengo...	**tayn**-goh
He / She is...	Él / Ella tiene...	ehl / **ay**-yah tee-**ehn**-ay
...___ years old.	...___ años.	___ **ahn**-yohs
He / She is...	Él / Ella es...	ehl / **ay**-yah ehs
...extremely old.	...demasiado viejo[a].	day-mah-see-**ah**-doh bee-**ay**-hoh

At the Bullring

bullfight	corrida de toros	koh-**ree**-dah day **toh**-rohs
bullring	plaza de toros	**plah**-thah day **toh**-rohs
the bull	el toro	ehl **toh**-roh
kill	matar	mah-**tar**
sunny / shady side	sol / sombra	sohl / **sohm**-brah
bull run	encierro	ayn-thee-**ay**-roh

The bulls run through Pamplona (and some people) every July. Bullfights occur throughout April–October, usually on Sundays. In a Spanish bullfight, *el toro* (the bull) is killed by the *matador* (literally "killer") and his assistants: *picadores* (guys on horseback) and *banderilleros* (acrobatic helpers). If you're squeamish, go to Portugal, where the bull is killed *after* the fight.

In the Museum

Where is...?	¿Dónde está...?	**dohn**-day ay-**stah**
I / We would like to see...	Me / Nos gustaría ver...	may / nohs goo-stah-**ree**-ah behr
Photo / Video O.K.?	¿Foto / Vídeo O.K.?	**foh**-toh / **bee**-day-oh "O.K."
No flash / tripod.	No flash / trípode.	noh flahsh / **tree**-poh-day
I like it.	Me gusta.	may **goo**-stah
It's so...	Es tan...	ays tahn
...beautiful.	...bonito.	boh-**nee**-toh
...ugly.	...feo.	**fay**-oh
...strange.	...extraño.	ayk-**strahn**-yoh
...boring.	...aburrido.	ah-boo-**ree**-doh
...interesting.	...interesante.	een-tay-ray-**sahn**-tay
...pretentious.	...pretencioso.	pray-tayn-thee-**oh**-soh
...thought-provoking.	...que te hace pensar.	kay tay **ah**-thay payn-**sar**
...B.S.	...mierda.	mee-**ehr**-dah
I don't get it.	No lo entiendo.	noh loh ehn-tee-**ehn**-doh
Is it upside down?	¿Está bocarriba?	ay-**stah** boh-kah-**ree**-bah
Who did this?	¿Quién lo hizo?	kee-**ehn** loh **ee**-thoh
How old is this?	¿Cuánto tiempo tiene esto?	**kwahn**-toh tee-**ehm**-poh tee-**ehn**-ay **ay**-stoh
Wow!	¡Caray!	kah-**rī**
My feet hurt!	¡Me duelen los pies!	may **dway**-lehn lohs pee-**ays**
I'm exhausted!	¡Estoy muy cansado[a]!	ay-**stoy** moo-ee kahn-**sah**-doh
We're exhausted! (m / f)	¡Estamos muy cansados[as]!	ay-**stah**-mohs **moo**-ee kahn-**sah**-dohs

Art and Architecture

art	arte	**ar**-tay
artist	artista	ar-**tee**-stah
painting	cuadro	**kwah**-droh
self portrait	autorretrato	ow-toh-ray-**trah**-toh
sculptor	escultor	ay-skool-**tor**
sculpture	escultura	ay-skool-**too**-rah
architect	arquitecto	ar-kee-**tehk**-toh
architecture	arquitectura	ar-kee-tehk-**too**-rah
original	original	oh-ree-hee-**nahl**
restored	restaurado	ray-stow-**rah**-doh
B.C.	A.C.	ah thay
A.D.	D.C.	day thay
century	siglo	**see**-gloh
style	estilo	ay-**stee**-loh
copy by ___	una copia de ___	**oo**-nah **koh**-pee-ah day
after the style of ___	de estilo de ___	day ay-**stee**-loh day
from the school of ___	de la escuela de ___	day lah ay-**skway**-lah day
abstract	Abstracto	ahb-**strahk**-toh
ancient	Antiguo	ahn-**tee**-gwoh
Art Nouveau	Modernista	moh-dehr-**nee**-stah
Baroque	Barroco	bah-**roh**-koh
classical	Clásico	**klah**-see-koh
Gothic	Gótico	**goh**-tee-koh
Impressionist	Impresionista	eem-pray-see-oh-**nee**-stah
medieval	Medieval	may-dee-ay-**vahl**
Modern	Moderno	moh-**dehr**-noh
Moorish	Moros	**moh**-rohs
Renaissance	Renacimiento	ray-nah-thee-mee-**ehn**-toh
Romanesque	Románico	roh-**mah**-nee-koh
Romantic	Romántici	roh-**mahn**-tee-**koh**

SPANISH ART TERMS

Alcazaba: A Moorish castle.
Alcazar: A Moorish fortress or palace.
Azulejo: Blue tile.
Churrigueresque (*Churrigueresco*): Super-thick Spanish Baroque, named after a local artist.
Moriscos: The Islamic Arabs (Moors) who ruled much of Spain and Portugal from 711 to 1492. The Moorish culture left a deep mark on Iberia. An understanding of the Moorish occupation will help you better understand your sightseeing.
Mozarabs (*Mozárabes*): Christians in Spain under Moorish rule.
Mudéjar: The Gothic-Islamic style of the Moors in Spain after the Christian conquest.
Plateresque (*plateresco*): The frilly late-Gothic style of Spain.

Castles and Palaces

castle	castillo	kah-**stee**-yoh
palace	palacio	pah-**lah**-thee-oh
kitchen	cocina	koh-**thee**-nah
cellar	bodega	boh-**day**-gah
dungeon	calabozo	kah-lah-**boh**-thoh
moat	foso	**foh**-soh
fortified walls	paredes fortificadas	pah-**ray**-days for-tee-fee-**kah**-dahs
tower	torre	**toh**-ray
fountain	fuente	**fwehn**-tay
garden	jardín	har-**deen**
king	rey	ray
queen	reina	ray-**ee**-nah
knights	caballería	kah-bah-yay-**ree**-ah

Religious Words

cathedral	*catedral*	kah-tay-**drahl**
church	*iglesia*	ee-**glay**-see-ah
monastery	*monasterio*	moh-nah-**stay**-ree-oh
mosque	*mezquita*	mayth-**kee**-tah
synagogue	*sinagoga*	see-nah-**goh**-gah
chapel	*capilla*	kah-**pee**-yah
altar	*altar*	ahl-**tar**
bells	*campanas*	kahm-**pah**-nahs
choir	*coro*	**koh**-roh
cloister	*claustro*	**klow**-stroh (klow rhymes with cow)
cross	*cruz*	krooth
crypt	*cripta*	**kreep**-tah
dome	*cúpula*	**koo**-poo-lah
organ	*órgano*	**or**-gah-noh
pulpit	*púlpito*	**pool**-pee-toh
relic	*reliquia*	ray-**lee**-kee-ah
treasury	*tesoro*	tay-**soh**-roh
saint	*santo[a]*	**sahn**-toh
God	*Dios*	**dee**-ohs
Christian	*cristiano*	kree-stee-**ah**-noh
Protestant	*protestante*	proh-tay-**stahn**-tay
Catholic	*católico*	kah-**toh**-lee-koh
Jewish	*judío*	hoo-**dee**-oh
Muslim	*musulmán*	moo-sool-**mahn**
agnostic	*agnóstico*	ahg-**noh**-stee-koh
atheist	*ateo*	ah-**tay**-oh
When is the mass / service?	*¿A qué hora es la misa / servicio?*	ah kay **oh**-rah ays lah **mee**-sah / sehr-**bee**-thee-oh
Are there concerts in the church?	*¿Hay conciertos en la iglesia?*	ī kohn-thee-**ehr**-tohs ayn lah ee-**glay**-see-ah

Shopping

Spanish Shops

Where is a...?	¿Dónde hay una...?	**dohn**-day ī **oo**-nah
antique shop	*anticuarios*	ahn-tee-**kwah**-ree-ohs
art gallery	*galería de arte*	gah-lay-**ree**-ah day **ar**-tay
bakery	*panadería*	pah-nah-deh-**ree**-ah
barber shop	*barbería*	bar-beh-**ree**-ah
beauty salon	*peluquería*	pay-loo-keh-**ree**-ah
book shop	*librería*	lee-bray-**ree**-ah
camera shop	*tienda de fotos*	tee-**ehn**-dah day **foh**-tohs
cell phone shop	*tienda de teléfonos móviles*	tee-**ehn**-dah day tay-**lay**-foh-nohs **moh**-bee-lays
clothing boutique	*tienda de ropa*	tee-**ehn**-dah day **roh**-pah
coffee shop	*cafetería*	kah-fay-tay-**ree**-ah
department store	*grandes almacenes*	**grahn**-days ahl-mah-**thay**-nays
delicatessen	*charcutería*	char-soo-teh-**ree**-ah
flea market	*rastro*	**rahs**-troh
flower market	*floristería*	floh-ree-steh-**ree**-ah
grocery store	*supermercado*	soo-pehr-mehr-**kah**-doh
hardware store	*ferretería*	fehr-ray-teh-**ree**-ah
Internet café	*café de Internet*	kah-**feh** day **een**-tehr-neht
jewelry shop	*joyería*	hoy-eh-**ree**-ah
launderette	*lavandería*	lah-vahn-deh-**ree**-ah
newsstand	*kiosco*	kee-**oh**-skoh
office supplies	*papelería*	pah-peh-leh-**ree**-ah
open air market	*mercado municipal*	mehr-**kah**-doh moo-nee-thee-**pahl**
optician	*óptico*	**ohp**-tee-koh
pastry shop	*pastelería*	pah-stay-leh-**ree**-ah
pharmacy	*farmacia*	far-**mah**-thee-ah
photocopy shop	*fotocopias*	foh-toh-**koh**-pee-ahs

shopping mall	*centro comercial*	**thehn**-troh koh-mehr-thee-**ahl**
souvenir shop	*tienda de souvenirs*	tee-**ehn**-dah day soo-bay-**neers**
supermarket	*supermercado*	soo-pehr-mehr-**kah**-doh
sweets shop	*tienda de dulces*	tee-**ehn**-dah day **dool**-thays
toy store	*juguetería*	hoo-gay-teh-**ree**-ah
travel agency	*agencia de viajes*	ah-**hayn**-thee-ah day bee-**ah**-hays
used bookstore	*tienda de libros usados*	tee-**ehn**-dah day **lee**-brohs oo-**sah**-dohs
...with books in English	*...de libros en inglés*	day **lee**-brohs ayn een-**glays**
wine shop	*tienda de vinos*	tee-**ehn**-dah day **bee**-nohs

In Spain, shops are closed for a long lunch between 1:30 and 4:30 p.m., and all day on Sundays. Souvenirs and postcards are cheapest in the biggest department stores, such as *El Corte Inglés*. This ultimate department store, found in the bigger cities, offers everything from trinkets to haircuts to train and theater tickets. In Madrid, it's just a block uphill from *Puerta del Sol*.

Shop Till You Drop

opening hours	*horas de apertura*	**oh**-rahs day ah-pay-**too**-rah
sale	*rebajas*	ray-**bah**-hahs
Where can I buy...?	*¿Dónde puedo comprar...?*	**dohn**-day **pway**-doh kohm-**prar**
Where can we buy...?	*¿Dónde podemos comprar...?*	**dohn**-day poh-**day**-mohs kohm-**prar**
How much is it?	*¿Cuánto cuesta?*	**kwahn**-toh **kway**-stah
I'm / We're...	*Estoy / Estamos...*	ay-**stoy** / ay-**stah**-mohs
...just browsing.	*...sólo mirando.*	**soh**-loh mee-**rahn**-doh
I would like...	*Me gustaría...*	may goo-stah-**ree**-ah
Do you have...?	*¿Tiene usted...?*	tee-**ehn**-ay oo-**stehd**
...more	*...más*	mahs

...something cheaper	...algo más barato	**ahl**-goh mahs bah-**rah**-toh
Better quality, please.	Mejor calidad, por favor.	may-**hor** kah-lee-**dahd** por fah-**bor**
genuine / imitation	genuino / imitación	hay-noo-**ee**-noh / ee-mee-tah-thee-**ohn**
Can I / Can we see more?	¿Puedo / Podemos ver más?	**pway**-doh / poh-**day**-mohs behr mahs
This one.	Éste.	**ay**-stay
Can I try it on?	¿Puedo probarlo?	**pway**-doh proh-**bar**-loh
Do you have a mirror?	¿Tiene un espejo?	tee-**ehn**-ay oon ay-**spay**-hoh
Too...	Demasiado...	day-mah-see-**ah**-doh
...big.	...grande.	**grahn**-day
...small.	...pequeño.	pay-**kayn**-yoh
...expensive.	...caro.	**kah**-roh
It's too...	Es demasiado...	ays day-mah-see-**ah**-doh
...short / long.	...corto / largo.	**kor**-toh / **lar**-goh
...tight / loose.	...apretado / ligero.	ah-pray-**tah**-doh / lee-**hay**-roh
...dark / light.	...oscuro / claro.	oh-**skoo**-roh / **klah**-roh
What is this made of?	¿De qué está hecho esto?	day kay ay-**stah** **ay**-choh **ay**-stoh
Is it machine washable?	¿Se puede lavar en la lavadora?	say **pway**-day lah-**var** ayn lah lah-vah-**doh**-rah
Will it shrink?	¿Esto se encoge?	**ay**-stoh say ayn-**koh**-hay
Will it fade in the wash?	¿Desteñirá en la lavadora?	day-stehn-yee-**rah** ayn lah lah-vah-**doh**-rah
Can you ship this?	¿Puede enviar esto?	**pway**-day ayn-bee-**ar** **ay**-stoh
Tax-free?	¿Libre de impuestos?	**lee**-bray day eem-**pway**-stohs
I'll think about it.	Voy a pensármelo.	boy ah payn-**sar**-may-loh
What time do you close?	¿A qué hora cierran?	ah kay **oh**-rah thee-**ay**-rahn
What time do you open tomorrow?	¿A qué hora abren mañana?	ah kay **oh**-rah **ah**-brehn mahn-**yah**-nah

KEY PHRASES: SHOPPING

Where can I buy...?	¿Dónde puedo comprar...?	**dohn**-day **pway**-doh kohm-**prar**
Where is...?	¿Dónde hay...?	**dohn**-day ī
...a grocery store	...un supermercado	oon soo-pehr-mehr-**kah**-doh
...a department store	...los grandes almacenes	lohs **grahn**-days ahl-mah-**thay**-nays
...an Internet café	...un café de Internet	oon kah-**feh** day **een**-tehr-neht
...a launderette	...una lavandería	**oo**-nah lah-vahn-deh-**ree**-ah
...a pharmacy	...una farmacia	**oo**-nah far-**mah**-thee-ah
How much is it?	¿Cuánto cuesta?	**kwahn**-toh **kway**-stah
I'm just browsing.	Estoy sólo mirando.	ay-**stoy soh**-loh mee-**rahn**-doh

Street Markets

Did you make this?	¿Hizo usted esto?	**ee**-thoh oo-**stehd ay**-stoh
Is that your best price?	¿Es éste su mejor precio?	ays **ay**-stay soo may-h**or** **pray**-thee-oh
Cheaper?	Más barato?	mahs bah-**rah**-toh
My last offer.	Mi última oferta.	mee **ool**-tee-mah oh-**fehr**-tah
Good price.	Buen precio.	bwayn **pray**-thee-oh
I'll take it.	Lo quiero.	loh kee-**ehr**-oh
We'll take it.	Lo queremos.	loh kay-**ray**-mohs
I'm nearly broke.	Estoy sin un duro.	ay-**stoy** seen oon **doo**-roh
We're nearly broke.	Estamos sin un duro.	ay-**stah**-mohs seen oon **doo**-roh
My male friend...	Mi amigo...	mee ah-**mee**-goh
My female friend...	Mi amiga...	mee ah-**mee**-gah
My husband...	Mi marido...	mee mah-**ree**-doh
My wife...	Mi mujer...	mee moo-h**ehr**
...has the money.	...tiene el dinero.	tee-**ehn**-ay ehl dee-**nay**-roh

If you brake for garage sales, you'll pull a U-turn for Madrid's *El Rastro* flea market. Europe's biggest flea market sprawls for miles each Sunday. It's common to bargain.

Clothes

For...	Para...	
...a male / female baby.	...un bebé varón / hembra.	oon bay-**bay** bah-**rohn** / **aym**-brah
...a male / female child.	...un niño varón / hembra.	oon **neen**-yoh bah-**rohn** / **aym**-brah
...a male / female teenager.	...un adolescente varón / hembra.	oon ah-doh-lay-**sayn**-tay bah-**rohn** / **aym**-brah
...a man.	...un hombre.	oon **ohm**-bray
...a woman.	...una mujer.	**oo**-nah moo-**hehr**
bathrobe	albornoz	ahl-**bor**-nohth
bib	peto	**pay**-toh
belt	cinturón	theen-too-**rohn**
bra	sujetador	soo-hay-tah-**dor**
clothing	ropa	**roh**-pah
dress	vestido	bays-**tee**-doh
flip-flops	chanquetas	chahn-**kay**-tahs
gloves	guantes	**gwahn**-tays
hat	sombrero	sohm-**bray**-roh
jacket	chaqueta	chah-**kay**-tah
jeans	vaqueros	bah-**kay**-rohs
nightgown	camisón	kah-mee-**sohn**
nylons	medias	**may**-dee-ahs
pajamas	pijamas	pee-**hah**-mahs
pants	pantalones	pahn-tah-**loh**-nays
raincoat	gabardina	gah-bar-**dee**-nah
sandals	sandalias	sahn-**dah**-lee-ahs
scarf	bufanda	boo-**fahn**-dah
shirt...	camisa...	kah-**mee**-sah
...long-sleeved	...de manga larga	day **mahn**-gah **lar**-gah
...short-sleeved	...de manga corta	day **mahn**-gah **kor**-tah
...sleeveless	...sin mangas	seen **mahn**-gahs

shoelaces	cordones	kor-**doh**-nays
shoes	zapatos	thah-**pah**-tohs
shorts	pantalones cortos	pahn-tah-**loh**-nays **kor**-tohs
skirt	falda	**fahl**-dah
sleeper (for baby)	canguro	kahn-**goo**-roh
slip	calzoncillo	kahl-thohn-**thee**-yoh
slippers	zapatillas	thah-pah-**tee**-yahs
socks	calcetines	kahl-thay-**tee**-nays
sweater	jersey	**h**ehr-see
swimsuit	bañador	bahn-yah-**dor**
tennis shoes	zapatillas de tenis	thah-pah-**tee**-yahs day **tay**-nees
T-shirt	camiseta	kah-mee-**say**-tah
underwear	ropa interior	**roh**-pah een-tay-ree-**or**
vest	chaleco	chah-**lay**-koh

Colors

black	negro	**nay**-groh
blue	azul	ah-**thool**
brown	marrón	mah-**rohn**
gray	gris	grees
green	verde	**behr**-day
orange	naranja	nah-**rahn**-*h*ah
pink	rosa	**roh**-sah
purple	morado	moh-**rah**-doh
red	rojo	**roh**-*h*oh
white	blanco	**blahn**-koh
yellow	amarillo	ah-mah-**ree**-yoh
dark / light	oscuro / claro	oh-**skoo**-roh / **klah**-roh
A lighter...	Más claro...	mahs **klah**-roh
A brighter...	Más brillante...	mahs bree-**yahn**-tay
A darker...	Más oscuro...	mahs oh-**skoo**-roh
...shade.	...tono.	**toh**-noh

Materials

brass	*latón*	lah-**tohn**
bronze	*bronce*	**brohn**-thay
ceramic	*cerámica*	thay-**rah**-mee-kah
copper	*cobre*	**koh**-bray
cotton	*algodón*	ahl-goh-**dohn**
glass	*cristal*	kree-**stahl**
gold	*oro*	**oh**-roh
lace	*encaje*	ayn-**kah**-*h*ay
leather	*piel*	**pee**-ehl
linen	*lino*	**lee**-noh
marble	*mármol*	**mar**-mohl
metal	*metal*	may-**tahl**
nylon	*nilón*	nee-**lohn**
paper	*papel*	pah-**pehl**
pewter	*peltre*	**pehl**-tray
plastic	*plástico*	**plah**-stee-koh
polyester	*poliester*	poh-lee-**ay**-stehr
porcelain	*porcelana*	por-thay-**lah**-nah
silk	*seda*	**say**-dah
silver	*plata*	**plah**-tah
velvet	*terciopelo*	tehr-thee-oh-**pay**-loh
wood	*madera*	mah-**day**-rah
wool	*lana*	**lah**-nah

Jewelry

bracelet	*pulsera*	pool-**say**-rah
brooch	*broche*	**broh**-chay
earrings	*pendientes*	pehn-dee-**ehn**-tays
jewelry	*joyas*	*h*oy-ahs
necklace	*collar*	koh-**yar**
ring	*anillo*	ah-**nee**-yoh
Is this...?	*¿Es esto...?*	ays **ay**-stoh
...sterling silver	*...plata de ley*	**plah**-tah day lay
...real gold	*...oro puro*	**oh**-roh **poo**-roh
...stolen	*...robado*	roh-**bah**-doh

Sports

Bicycling

bicycle / bike	*bicicleta /* *bici*	bee-thee-**klay**-tah / **bee**-thee
mountain bike	*bicicleta de* *montaña*	bee-thee-**klay**-tah day mohn-**tahn**-yah
I'd like to rent a bicycle	*Me gustaría* *alquilar una* *bicicleta.*	may goo-stah-**ree**-ah ahl-kee-**lar oo**-nah bee-thee-**klay**-tah
We would like to rent a bicycle.	*Nos gustaría* *alquilar dos* *bicicleta.*	nohs goo-stah-**ree**-ah ahl-kee-**lar** dohs bee-thee-**klay**-tahs
How much per...?	*¿Cuánto es por...?*	**kwahn**-toh ays por
...hour	*...hora*	**oh**-rah
...half day	*...medio día*	**may**-dee-oh **dee**-ah
...day	*...día*	**dee**-ah
Is a deposit required?	*¿Se requiere un* *depósito?*	say ray-kee-**ay**-ray oon day-**poh**-see-toh
deposit	*depósito*	day-**poh**-see-toh
helmet	*casco*	**kahs**-koh
lock	*candado*	kahn-**dah**-doh
air / no air	*aire / sin aire*	ī -ray / seen ī -ray
tire	*rueda*	roo-**ay**-dah
pump	*bomba de aire*	**bohm**-bah day ī -ray
map	*mapa*	**mah**-pah
How many gears?	*¿Cuántas marchas?*	**kwahn**-tahs **mar**-chahs
What is a...	*¿Cuál es una*	kwahl ays **oo**-nah
route of about ___ kilometers?	*ruta... de unos* *___ kilómetros?*	**roo**-tah... day **oo**-nohs ___ kee-**loh**-may-trohs
...good	*...buena*	**bway**-nah
...scenic	*...panorámica*	pah-noh-**rah**-mee-kah
...interesting	*...interesante*	een-tay-ray-**sahn**-tay
...easy	*...fácil*	**fah**-theel

How many minutes / hours by bicycle?	Cuántos minutos / horas en bicicleta?	kwahn-tohs mee-noo-tohs / oh-rahs ayn bee-thee-klay-tah
I (don't) like hills.	(No) me gustan las cuestas.	(noh) may goo-stahn lahs kway-stahs
I brake for bakeries.	Me paro en las pastelerías.	may pah-roh ayn lahs pah-stay-leh-ree-ahs

Swimming and Boating

Where can I / can we rent a...?	¿Dónde puedo / podemos alquilar un...?	dohn-day pway-doh / poh-day-mohs ahl-kee-lar oon
...paddleboat	...barca de pedales	bar-kah day pay-dah-lays
...rowboat	...bote de remo	boh-tay day ray-moh
...boat	...bote	boh-tay
...sailboat	...barco de vela	bar-koh day bay-lah
How much per...?	¿Cuánto es por...?	kwahn-toh ays por
...hour	...hora	oh-rah
...half day	...medio día	may-dee-oh dee-ah
...day	...día	dee-ah
beach	playa	plah-yah
nude beach	playa nudista	plah-yah noo-dee-stah
Where's a good beach?	¿Dónde hay una buena playa?	dohn-day ī oo-nah bway-nah plah-yah
Is it safe for swimming?	¿Es una zona segura para bañarse?	ays oo-nah thoh-nah say-goo-rah pah-rah bahn-yar-say
flip-flops	chancletas	chahn-klay-tahs
pool	piscina	pee-thee-nah
snorkel and mask	tubo de respiración y máscara	too-boh day ray-spee-rah-thee-ohn ee mahs-kah-rah
sunglasses	gafas de sol	gah-fahs day sohl
sunscreen	crema bronceadora	kray-mah brohn-thay-ah-doh-rah

ACTIVITIES

surfboard	tabla de surf	**tah**-blah day soorf
surfer	surfista	soor-**fee**-stah
swimsuit	bañador	bahn-yah-**dor**
towel	toalla	toh-**ah**-yah
waterskiing	esquí	ay-**skee**
	acuático	ah-**kwah**-tee-koh
windsurfing	windsurfing	**weend**-soor-feeng

In Spain, nearly any beach is topless. For a nude beach, keep your eyes peeled for a *playa nudista*.

Sports Talk

sports	deportes	day-**por**-tays
game	partido	par-**tee**-doh
championship	campeonato	kahm-pay-oh-**nah**-toh
soccer	fútbol	**foot**-bohl
basketball	baloncesto	bahl-ohn-**thehs**-toh
hockey	hockey	"hockey"
American football	fútbol	**foot**-bohl
	americano	ah-meh-ree-**kah**-noh
baseball	béisbol	**bays**-bohl
tennis	tenis	**tay**-nees
golf	golf	gohlf
skiing	esquí	ay-**skee**
gymnastics	gimnasia	heem-**nah**-zee-ah
jogging	footing	**foo**-teeng
Olympics	Olimpíada	oh-leem-**pee**-ah-dah
medal...	medalla...	may-**dah**-yah
...gold / silver / bronze	...de oro / de plata / de bronce	day **oh**-roh / day **plah**-tah / day **brohn**-thay
What is your favorite sport / athlete / team?	¿Cuál es su deporte / atleta / equipo favorito?	kwahl ays soo day-**por**-tay / aht-**lay**-tah / ay-**kee**-poh fah-voh-**ree**-toh
Where can I see a game?	¿Dónde puedo mirar un partido?	**dohn**-day **pway**-doh mee-**rar** oon par-**tee**-doh
Where's a good place to jog?	¿Dónde se puede ir de footing?	**dohn**-day say **pway**-day eer day **foo**-teeng

Entertainment

What's happening tonight?	¿Qué hay esta noche?	kay ī **ay**-stah **noh**-chay
What do you recommend?	¿Qué recomienda?	kay ray-koh-mee-**ehn**-dah
Where is it?	¿Dónde está?	**dohn**-day ay-**stah**
How do I / do we get there?	¿Cómo llego / llegamos allí?	**koh**-moh **yay**-goh / yay-**gah**-mohs ah-**yee**
Is it free?	¿Es gratis?	ays **grah**-tees
Are there seats available?	¿Hay asientos disponibles?	ī ah-see-**ehn**-tohs dee-spoh-**nee**-blays
Where can I buy a ticket?	¿Dónde puedo comprar un billete?	**dohn**-day **pway**-doh kohm-**prar** oon bee-**yeh**-tay
Do you have tickets for today / tonight?	¿Tiene billetes para hoy / esta noche?	tee-**ehn**-ay bee-**yeh**-tays **pah**-rah oy / **ay**-stah **noh**-chay
When does it start?	¿Cuándo empieza esto?	**kwahn**-doh aym-pee-**ay**-thah **ay**-stoh
When does it end?	¿Cuándo acaba esto?	**kwahn**-doh ah-**kah**-bah **ay**-stoh
Where's the best place to dance nearby?	¿Dónde está el más cercano y mejor sitio para bailar?	**dohn**-day ay-**stah** ehl mahs thehr-**kah**-noh ee may-**hor** **seet**-yoh **pah**-rah bī-**lar**
Where is the best place to stroll?	¿Dónde está el mejor paseo?	**dohn**-day ay-**stah** ehl may-**hor** pah-**say**-oh

For free, enjoyable entertainment, join the locals for a *paseo*, an evening stroll through town.

Entertaining Words

movie...	película...	pay-**lee**-koo-lah
...original version	...versión original	behr-see-**ohn** oh-ree-hee-**nahl**

...in English	...en inglés	ayn een-**glays**
...with subtitles	...con subtítulos	kohn soob-**tee**-too-lohs
...dubbed	...doblada	doh-**blah**-dah
music...	música...	**moo**-see-kah
...live	...en vivo	ayn **bee**-boh
...classical	...clásica	**klah**-see-kah
...folk	...folklórica	fohk-**loh**-ree-kah
...opera	...ópera	**oh**-pay-rah
...symphony	...sinfónica	seen-**foh**-nee-kah
...choir	...coro	**koh**-roh
...traditional	...tradicional	trah-dee-thee-oh-**nahl**
rock / jazz / blues	rock / jazz / blues	rohk / "jazz" / "blues"
singer	cantante	kahn-**tahn**-tay
concert	concierto	kohn-thee-**ehr**-toh
show	espectáculo	ay-spehk-**tah**-koo-loh
(folk) dancing	baile (folklórico)	**b ī**-lay (fohk-**loh**-ree-koh)
flamenco	flamenco	flah-**mayn**-koh
cockfight	pelea de gallos	pay-**lay**-ah day **gah**-yohs
disco	disco	**dee**-skoh
bar with live music	bar con música en vivo	bar kohn **moo**-see-kah ayn **bee**-boh
nightclub	club nocturno	kloob nohk-**toor**-noh
(no) cover charge	(no) entrada	(noh) ayn-**trah**-dah
sold out	agotadas	ah-goh-**tah**-dahs

CONNECT

Phoning

English	Spanish	Pronunciation
I'd like to buy a...	Me gustaría comprar una...	may goo-stah-**ree**-ah kohm-**prar oo**-nah
...telephone card.	...tarjeta telefónica.	tar-**hay**-tah tay-lay-**foh**-nee-kah
...cheap international telephone card.	tarjeta telefónica. barata de código.	tar-**hay**-tah tay-lay-**foh**-nee-kah bah-**rah**-tah day **koh**-dee-goh
Where is the nearest phone?	¿Dónde está el teléfono más cercano?	**dohn**-day ay-**stah** ehl tay-**lay**-foh-noh mahs thehr-**kah**-noh
It doesn't work.	No funciona.	noh foonk-thee-**oh**-nah
May I use your phone?	¿Puedo usar su teléfono?	**pway**-doh oo-**sar** soo tay-**lay**-foh-noh
Can you talk for me?	¿Puede hablar usted por mí?	**pway**-day ah-**blar** oo-**stehd** por mee
It's busy.	Está ocupado.	ay-**stah** oh-koo-**pah**-doh
Will you try again?	¿Llamará otra vez?	yah-mah-**rah oh**-trah bayth
Hello. (answering the phone)	Diga.	**dee**-gah
My name is ___.	Me llamo ___.	may **yah**-moh

156

Sorry, I speak only a little Spanish.	Lo siento, hablo sólo un poco de español.	loh see-**ehn**-toh **ah**-bloh **soh**-loh oon **poh**-koh day ay-spahn-**yohl**
Speak slowly and clearly.	Hable despacio y claro.	**ah**-blay day-**spah**-thee-oh ee **klah**-roh
Wait a moment.	Un momento.	oon moh-**mehn**-toh

In this book, you'll find the phrases you need to reserve a hotel room (page 53) or a table at a restaurant (page 71). To spell your name over the phone, refer to the code alphabet on page 57.

Make your calls using a handy phone card sold at post offices, train stations, tobacco shops (*tabacos*), and machines near phone booths. There are two kinds:

1) an insertable card (*tarjeta telefónica*) that you slide into a phone in a phone booth, and...

2) a cheaper-per-minute international phone card (with a scratch-off PIN code) that you can use from any phone, usually even in your hotel room. (If your hotel phone balks, change its setting from pulse to tone.) To get one of these cards, ask for a *tarjeta telefónica barata de código.*

At phone booths, you'll encounter these words: *inserte la tarjeta* (insert the card), *marque su número* (dial your number), and *saldo* (the value left on your card). If the number you're calling is out of service, you'll hear a recording: "*Se ha equivocado de número.*" For more tips, see "Let's Talk Telephones" starting on page 272 in the Appendix.

Telephone Words

telephone	teléfono	tay-**lay**-foh-noh
telephone card	tarjeta telefónica	tar-**hay**-tah tay-lay-**foh**-nee-kah
cheap telephone card with a PIN code	tarjeta telefónica barata de código	tar-**hay**-tah tay-lay-**foh**-nee-kah bah-**rah**-tah day **koh**-dee-goh
PIN	código, número clave	**koh**-dee-goh, **noo**-may-roh **klah**-bay

CONNECT

phone booth	cabina telefónica	kah **bee**-nah tay-lay-**foh**-nee-kah
out of service	averiado	ah-bay-ree-**ah**-doh
post office	correos	koh-**ray**-ohs
phone office	telefónica	tay-lay-**foh**-nee-kah
operator	telefonista	tay-lay-foh-**nee**-stah
international assistance	asistencia internacional	ah-see-**stehn**-thee-ah een-tehr-nah-thee-oh-**nahl**
international call	llamada internacional	yah-**mah**-dah een-tehr-nah-thee-oh-**nahl**
collect call	llamada a cobro revertido	yah-**mah**-dah ah **koh**-broh ray-behr-**tee**-doh
credit card call	llamada con tarjeta de crédito	yah-**mah**-dah kohn tar-**hay**-tah day **kray**-dee-toh
toll-free call	llamada gratuita	yah-**mah**-dah grah-**twee**-tah
fax	fax	fahks
country code	prefijo del país	pray-**fee**-hoh dayl pah-**ees**
area code	prefijo	pray-**fee**-hoh
extension	extensión	ayk-stehn-see-**ohn**
telephone book	guía de teléfonos	**gee**-ah day tay-**lay**-foh-nohs
yellow pages	páginas amarillas	**pah**-hee-nahs ah-mah-**ree**-yahs

Cell Phones

Where is a cell phone shop?	¿Donde hay una tienda de teléfonos móviles?	**dohn**-day ī **oo**-nah tee-**ehn**-dah day tay-**lay**-foh-nohs **moh**-bee-lays
I'd / We'd like...	Me / Nos gustaría...	may /nohs goo-stah-**ree**-ah
...a cell phone.	...un teléfono móvil.	oon tay-**lay**-foh-noh **moh**-beel
...a chip.	...una ficha.	**oo**-nah **fee**-chah
...to buy more time.	...comprar más minutos.	kohm-**prar** mahs mee-**noo**-tohs

How do you...?	*¿Cómo... ?*	**koh**-moh
...make calls	*...se hacen*	say **ah**-thayn
	llamadas	yah-**mah**-dahs
...receive calls	*...se reciben*	say ray-**thee**-behn
	llamadas	yah-**mah**-dahs
Will this work	*¿Funcionará*	foonk-thee-oh-nah-**rah**
outside this	*fuera del país?*	**fway**-rah dayl pah-**ees**
country?		
Where can I buy	*¿Dónde puedo*	**dohn**-day **pway**-doh
a chip for this	*comprar una*	kohm-**prar oo**-nah
service / phone?	*ficha para este*	**fee**-chah **pah**-rah **ay**-stay
	servicio /	sehr-**bee**-thee-oh /
	teléfono?	tay-**lay**-foh-noh

Many travelers now buy cell phones in Europe to make local and international calls. You'll pay under $100 for a "locked" phone that works only in the country you buy it in (includes about $20 worth of calls). You can buy additional time at a newsstand or cell phone shop. An "unlocked" phone is more expensive (over $100), but it works all over Europe: when you cross a border, buy a SIM card at a cell phone shop and insert the pop-out chip, which comes with a new phone number. Pricier tri-band phones (*teléfono a tres bandas*) also work in North America.

E-Mail and the Web

E-Mail

Can I use this	*¿Puedo usar*	**pway**-doh oo-**sar**
computer	*este ordenador*	**ay**-stay or-day-nah-**dor**
to check	*para mirar*	**pah**-rah mee-**rar**
my e-mail?	*mi correo*	mee koh-**ray**-oh
	electrónico?	ay-lehk-**troh**-nee-koh

What's your e-mail address?	¿Cuál es tu dirección de correo electrónico?	kwahl ays too dee-rehk-thee-**ohn** day koh-**ray**-oh ay-lehk-**troh**-nee-koh
Where can I / can we access the Internet?	¿Dónde puedo / podemos acceder a Internet?	**dohn**-day **pway**-doh / poh-**day**-mohs ahk-thay-**dehr** ah **een**-tehr-neht
Where is an Internet cafe?	¿Dónde hay un café de Internet?	**dohn**-day ī oon kah-**feh** day **een**-tehr-neht
How much for... minutes?	¿Cuánto cuesta... minutos?	**kwahn**-toh **kway**-stah... mee-**noo**-tohs
...10	...diez	dee-**ayth**
...15	...quince	**keen**-thay
...30	...treinta	**trayn**-tah
...60	...sesenta	say-**sehn**-tah
Help me, please.	Ayúdeme, por favor.	ah-**yoo**-day-may por fah-**bor**
How do I...?	¿Cómo....?	**koh**-moh
...start this	...empiezo esto	aym-pee-**ay**-thoh **ay**-stoh
...send a file	...envio un fichero	**ayn**-bee-oh oon fee-**chay**-roh
...print out a file	...imprimo un fichero	eem-**pree**-moh oon fee-**chay**-roh
...make this symbol	...hago este símbolo	**ah**-goh **ay**-stay **seem**-boh-loh
...type @	...escribo arroba	ay-**skree**-boh ah-**roh**-bah
This isn't working.	Esto no funciona.	**ay**-stoh noh foonk-thee-**oh**-nah

Web Words

e-mail	*correo*	koh-**ray**-oh
	electrónico	ay-lehk-**troh**-nee-koh
e-mail address	*dirección de*	dee-rehk-thee-**ohn** day
	correo	koh-**ray**-oh
	electrónico	ay-lehk-**troh**-nee-koh
Web site	*página de la red*	**pah**-hee-nah day lah rayd
Internet	*Internet*	**een**-tehr-neht
surf the Web	*navegar la red*	nah-bay-**gar** la rayd
download	*bajar*	bah-**har**
@ sign	*arroba*	ah-**roh**-bah
dot	*punto*	**poon**-toh
hyphen (-)	*guión*	gee-**ohn**
underscore (_)	*subraya*	soob-**rah**-yah
modem	*modem*	**moh**-dehm

CONNECT

On Screen

abrir	open	**guardar**	save
borrar	delete	**imprimir**	print
enviar	send	**mensaje**	message
escribir	write	**responder**	reply
fichero	file		

KEY PHRASES: E-MAIL AND THE WEB

e-mail	*correo*	koh-**ray**-oh
	electrónico	ay-lehk-**troh**-nee-koh
Internet	*Internet*	**een**-tehr-neht
Where is the	*¿Dónde está*	**dohn**-day ay-**stah**
nearest	*el café de*	ehl kah-**feh** day
Internet café?	*Internet mas*	**een**-tehr-neht mahs
	cercano?	thehr-**kah**-noh
I'd like to check	*Me gustaría*	may goo-stah-**ree**-ah
my e-mail.	*mirar mi correo*	mee-**rar** mee koh-**ray**-oh
	electrónico.	ay-lehk-**troh**-nee-koh

Mailing

Where is the post office?	¿Dónde está la oficina de correos?	**dohn**-day ay-**stah** lah oh-fee-**thee**-nah day koh-**ray**-ohs
Which window for...?	¿Cuál es la ventana para...?	kwahl ays lah bayn-**tah**-nah **pah**-rah
Is this the line for...?	¿Es ésta la fila para...?	ays **ay**-stah lah **fee**-lah **pah**-rah
...stamps	...sellos	**say**-yohs
...packages	...paquetes	pah-**kay**-tays
To the United States...	Para los Estados Unidos...	**pah**-rah lohs ay-**stah**-dohs oo-**nee**-dohs
...by air mail.	...por avión.	por ah-bee-**ohn**
...by surface mail.	...vía terrestre.	**bee**-ah tay-**ray**-stray
...slow and cheap.	...lento y barato.	**layn**-toh ee bah-**rah**-toh
How much is it?	¿Cuánto cuesta?	**kwahn**-toh **kway**-stah
How much to send a letter / postcard to...?	¿Cuánto cuesta envíar una carta / postal a...?	**kwahn**-toh **kway**-stah ayn-bee-**ar** oo-nah **kar**-tah / poh-**stahl** ah
I need stamps for ___ postcards / letters to ...	Necesito sellos para ___ postales / cartas a	nay-thay-**see**-toh **say**-yohs **pah**-rah ___ poh-**stah**-lays / **kar**-tahs ah
...the United States / Canada.	...los Estados Unidos / Canadá.	lohs ay-**stah**-dohs oo-**nee**-dohs / kah-nah-**dah**
Pretty stamps, please.	Sellos bonitos, por favor.	**say**-yohs boh-**nee**-tohs por fah-**bor**
I always choose the slowest line.	Siempre elijo la fila más lenta.	see-**ehm**-pray ay-**lee**-hoh lah **fee**-lah mahs **layn**-tah
How many days will it take?	¿Cuántos días tardará?	**kwahn**-tohs **dee**-ahs tar-dah-**rah**

You can also buy postage stamps at *tabacos* shops—very handy, as long as you know in advance the amount of postage you need.

KEY PHRASES: MAILING

post office	oficina de correos	oh-fee-**thee**-nah day koh-**ray**-ohs
stamp	sello	**say**-yoh
postcard	postal	poh-**stahl**
letter	carta	**kar**-tah
air mail	por avión	por ah-bee-**ohn**
Where is the post office?	¿Dónde está la oficina de correos?	**dohn**-day ay-**stah** lah oh-fee-**thee**-nah day koh-**ray**-ohs
I need stamps for ___ postcards / letters to the United States.	Necesito sellos para ___ postales / cartas a los Estados Unidos.	nay-thay-**see**-toh **say**-yohs **pah**-rah ___ poh-**stah**-lays / **kar**-tahs ah lohs ay-**stah**-dohs oo-**nee**-dohs

Licking the Postal Code

post office	oficina de correos	oh-fee-**thee**-nah day koh-**ray**-ohs
stamp	sello	**say**-yoh
postcard	postal	poh-**stahl**
letter	carta	**kar**-tah
envelope	sobre	**soh**-bray
package	paquete	pah-**kay**-tay
box	caja	**kah**-hah
string	cuerda	**kwehr**-dah
tape	cinta adhesiva	**theen**-tah ah-day-**see**-bah
mailbox	buzón	boo-**thohn**
air mail	por avión	por ah-bee-**ohn**
express	rápido	**rah**-pee-doh
surface mail (slow and cheap)	via terrestre (lento y barato)	**bee**-ah tay-**ray**-stray (**layn**-toh ee bah-**rah**-toh)
book rate	tarifa	tah-**ree**-fah
weight limit	peso máximo	**pay**-soh **mahk**-see-moh
registered	certificada	thehr-tee-fee-**kah**-dah

insured	asegurada	ah-say-goo-**rah**-dah
fragile	frágil	**frah**-heel
contents	contenido	kohn-teh-**nee**-doh
customs	aduana	ah-**dwah**-nah
to / from	a / desde	ah / **dehs**-day
address	dirección	dee-rehk-thee-**ohn**
zip code	código postal	**koh**-dee-goh poh-**stahl**
general delivery	entrega	ayn-**tray**-gah
	general	hay-nay-**rahl**

HELP!

Help!	¡Ayuda!	ah-**yoo**-dah
Help me!	¡Ayúdenme!	ah-**yoo**-dehn-may
Call a doctor!	Llamen a un	**yah**-mehn ah oon
	médico!	**may**-dee-koh
Call...	Llame...	**yah**-may
...the police.	...a la policía.	ah lah poh-lee-**thee**-ah
...an ambulance.	...una	**oo**-nah
	ambulancia.	ahm-boo-**lahn**-thee-ah
...the fire	...a los bomberos.	ah lohs bohm-**bay**-rohs
department.		
I'm lost.	Estoy perdido[a].	ay-**stoy** pehr-**dee**-doh
We're lost. (m / f)	Estamos	ay-**stah**-mohs
	perdidos[as].	pehr-**dee**-dohs
Thank you for	Gracias por	**grah**-thee-ahs por
your help.	su ayuda.	soo ah-**yoo**-dah
You are very kind.	Usted es muy	oo-**stehd** ays **moo**-ee
	amable.	ah-**mah**-blay

Theft and Loss

Stop, thief!	¡Detengan	day-**tayn**-gahn
	al ladrón!	ahl lah-**drohn**
I / We have	Me / Nos han	may / nohs ahn
been robbed.	robado.	roh-**bah**-doh

English	Spanish	Pronunciation
A thief / Thieves took...	Un ladrón / Ladrones se llevaron...	oon lah-**drohn** / lah-**droh**-nays say yay-**bah**-rohn
I have lost my money.	He perdido mi dinero.	ay pehr-**dee**-doh mee dee-**nay**-roh
We have lost our money.	Hemos perdido nuestro dinero.	**ay**-mohs pehr-**dee**-doh **nway**-stroh dee-**nay**-roh
I've lost my...	He perdido mi...	ay pehr-**dee**-doh mee
...passport.	...pasaporte.	pah-sah-**por**-tay
...ticket.	...billete.	bee-**yeh**-tay
...baggage.	...equipaje.	ay-kee-**pah**-hay
...purse.	...bolso.	**bohl**-soh
...wallet.	...cartera.	kar-**tay**-rah
We've lost our...	Hemos perdido nuestros...	**ay**-mohs pehr-**dee**-doh **nway**-strohs
...passports.	...pasaportes.	pah-sah-**por**-tays
...tickets.	...billetes.	bee-**yeh**-tays
...baggage.	...equipaje.	ay-kee-**pah**-hay
I would like to contact my embassy.	Me gustaría contactar a mi embajada.	may goo-stah-**ree**-ah kohn-tahk-**tar** ah mee aym-bah-**hah**-dah
I need to file a police report for my insurance.	Necesito hacer una denuncia para mi seguro.	nay-thay-**see**-toh ah-**thehr** oo-nah day-**noon**-thee-ah **pah**-rah mee say-**goo**-roh

See page 274 in the Appendix for information on the U.S. Embassy in Spain.

See page 274 in the Appendix for information on the U.S. Embassy in Spain.

KEY PHRASES: HELP!

English	Spanish	Pronunciation
accident	accidente	ahk-thee-**dehn**-tay
emergency	emergencia	ay-mehr-**hayn**-thee-ah
police	policía	poh-lee-**thee**-ah
Help!	¡Ayuda!	ah-**yoo**-dah
Call a doctor / the police!	¡Llamen a un médico / la policía!	**yah**-mehn ah oon **may**-dee-koh / lah poh-lee-**thee**-ah
Stop, thief!	¡Detengan al ladrón!	day-**tayn**-gahn ahl lah-**drohn**

HELP!

Helpful Words

ambulance	*ambulancia*	ahm-boo-**lahn**-thee-ah
accident	*accidente*	ahk-thee-**dehn**-tay
injured	*herido*	ay-**ree**-doh
emergency	*emergencia*	ay-mehr-**hayn**-thee-ah
emergency room	*urgencias*	oor-**hayn**-thee-ahs
fire	*fuego*	**fway**-goh
police	*policía*	poh-lee-**thee**-ah
smoke	*humo*	**oo**-moh
thief	*ladrón*	lah-**drohn**
pickpocket	*carterista*	kar-tay-**ree**-stah

Help for Women

Leave me alone.	*Déjame sola.*	**day**-hah-may **soh**-lah
I want to be alone.	*Me gustaría estar sola.*	may goo-stah-**ree**-ah ay-**star soh**-lah
I'm not interested.	*No estoy interesada.*	noh ay-**stoy** een-tay-ray-**sah**-dah
I'm married.	*Estoy casada.*	ay-**stoy** kah-**sah**-dah
I'm a lesbian.	*Soy lesbiana.*	soy lehs-bee-**ah**-nah
I have a contagious disease.	*Tengo una enfermedad contagiosa.*	**tayn**-goh **oo**-nah ayn-fehr-may-**dahd** kohn-tah-hee-**oh**-sah
You are bothering me.	*Me está molestando.*	may ay-**stah** moh-lay-**stahn**-doh
This man is bothering me.	*Este señor me está molestando.*	**ay**-stay sayn-**yor** may ay-**stah** moh-lay-**stahn**-doh
Don't touch me.	*No me toque.*	noh may **toh**-kay
You're disgusting.	*Es asqueroso.*	ays ah-skay-**roh**-soh
Stop following me.	*No me siga.*	noh may **see**-gah
Stop it!	*¡Párelo!*	**pah**-ray-loh
Enough!	*¡Basta!*	**bah**-stah
Go away.	*Déjeme.*	**day**-heh-may
Get lost!	*¡Váyase!*	**bah**-yah-say

HELP!

Drop dead!	*¡Piérdase` de vista!*	pee-**ehr**-dah-say day **bee**-stah
I'll call the police!	*¡Voy a llamar a la policía!*	boy ah yah-**mar** ah lah poh-lee-**thee**-ah

Whenever macho males threaten to turn leering into a contact sport, local women stroll holding hands or arm-in-arm. Wearing conservative clothes and avoiding smiley eye contact also convey a "No way, José" message.

SERVICES

Laundry

Is a... nearby?	¿Hay una... cerca?	ī **oo**-nah... **thehr**-kah
...full service laundry	...lavandería	lah-vahn-deh-**ree**-ah
...self-service laundry	...lavandería de autoservicio	lah-vahn-deh-**ree**-ah day ow-toh-sehr-**bee**-thee-oh
Help me, please.	Ayúdeme, por favor.	ah-**yoo**-day-may por fah-**bor**
How does this work?	¿Cómo funciona?	**koh**-moh foonk-thee-**oh**-nah
Where is the soap?	¿Dónde está el jabón?	**dohn**-day ay-**stah** ehl hah-**bohn**
Are these yours?	¿Son estos suyos?	sohn **ay**-stohs **soo**-yohs
This stinks.	Esto apesta.	**ay**-stoh ah-**pay**-stah
Smells like...	Huele a...	**way**-lay ah
...spring time.	...primavera.	pree-mah-**bay**-rah
...a locker room.	...sitio cerrado.	**seet**-yoh thay-**rah**-doh
...cheese.	...queso.	**kay**-soh
I need change.	Necesito cambio.	nay-thay-**see**-toh **kahm**-bee-oh
Same-day service?	¿Sirven en el mismo día?	**seer**-behn ayn ehl **mees**-moh **dee**-ah

By when do I need to drop off my clothes?	¿Cuándo tengo que traer mi ropa?	**kwahn**-doh **tayn**-goh kay trah-**ehr** mee **roh**-pah
When will my clothes be ready?	¿Cuándo estará lista la ropa?	**kwahn**-doh ay-stah-**rah lee**-stah lah **roh**-pah
Dried?	¿Seca?	**say**-kah
Folded?	¿Doblada?	doh-**blah**-dah
Hey there. What's spinning?	Oiga ¿qué está centrifugando?	**oy**-gah kay ay-**stah** thayn-tree-foo-**gahn**-doh

Clean Words

full-service laundry	lavandería	lah-vahn-deh-**ree**-ah
self-service laundry	lavandería de autoservicio	lah-vahn-deh-**ree**-ah day ow-toh-sehr-**bee**-thee-oh
wash / dry	lavar / secar	lah-**var** / say-**kar**
washer / dryer	lavadora / secadora	lah-vah-**doh**-rah / say-kah-**doh**-rah
detergent	detergente	day-tehr-**hayn**-tay
token	ficha	**fee**-chah
whites	blanca	**blahn**-kah
colors	de color	day koh-**lor**
delicates	ropa delicada	**roh**-pah day-lee-**kah**-dah
handwash	lavar a mano	lah-**var** ah **mah**-noh

Haircuts

Where is a barber / a hair salon?	¿Dónde hay un barbero / una peluquería?	**dohn**-day ī oon bar-**bay**-roh / **oo**-nah pay-loo-kay-**ree**-ah
I'd like...	Me gustaría...	may goo-stah-**ree**-ah
...a haircut.	...cortarme el pelo.	kor-**tar**-may ehl **pay**-loh
...a permanent.	...hacerme una permanente.	ah-**thehr**-may **oo**-nah pehr-mah-**nehn**-tay
...just a trim.	...un recorte.	oon ray-**kor**-tay
Cut about this much off.	Corte más o menos esto.	**kor**-tay mahs oh **may**-nohs **ay**-stoh

SERVICES

Cut my bangs here.	*Corte mi flequillo aquí.*	**kor**-tay mee flay-**kee**-yoh ah-**kee**
Longer / shorter here.	*Más largo / más corto aquí.*	mahs **lar**-goh / mahs **kor**-toh ah-**kee**
I'd like my hair...	*Me gustaría mi pelo...*	may goo-stah-**ree**-ah mee **pay**-loh
...short.	*...corto.*	**kor**-toh
...colored.	*...con color.*	kohn koh-**lor**
...shampooed.	*...lavado con champú.*	lah-**vah**-doh kohn chahm-**poo**
...blow dried.	*...secado con el secador.*	say-**kah**-doh kohn ehl say-kah-**dor**
It looks good.	*Se ve muy bien.*	say bay **moo**-ee bee-**yehn**

Repair

These handy lines can apply to any repair, whether it's a ripped rucksack, bad haircut, or crabby camera.

This is broken.	*Esto está roto.*	**ay**-stoh ay-**stah roh**-toh
Can you fix it?	*¿Lo puede arreglar?*	loh **pway**-day ah-ray-**glar**
Just do the essentials.	*Haga sólo lo esencial.*	**ah**-gah **soh**-loh loh ay-sehn-thee-**ahl**
How much will it cost?	*¿Cuánto costará?*	**kwahn**-toh koh-stah-**rah**
When will it be ready?	*¿Cuándo estará listo?*	**kwahn**-doh ay-stah-**rah lee**-stoh
I need it by ___.	*Lo necesito para___.*	loh nay-thay-**see**-toh **pah**-rah
We need it by ___.	*Lo necesitamos para ___.*	loh nay-thay-see-**tah**-mohs **pah**-rah
Without it, I'm...	*Sin esto, estoy...*	seen **ay**-stoh ay-**stoy**
...helpless.	*...perdido[a].*	pehr-**dee**-doh
...toast.	*...arreglado[a].*	ah-ray-**glah**-doh
...dead in the water.	*...ahogado[a].*	ah-oh-**gah**-doh

Filling out Forms

Sr. / Sra. / Srta.	Mr. / Mrs. / Miss
nombre	first name
apellido	last name
dirección	address
domicilio	address
calle	street
ciudad	city
estado	state
país	country
nacionalidad	nationality
origen / destino	origin / destination
edad	age
fecha de nacimiento	date of birth
lugar de nacimiento	place of birth
sexo	sex
masculino	male
femenino	female
casado / casada	married man / married woman
soltero / soltera	single man / single woman
profesión	profession
adulto	adult
niño / niña	boy / girl
niños	children
familia	family
firma	signature
fecha	date

When filling out dates, do it European-style:
day/month/year.

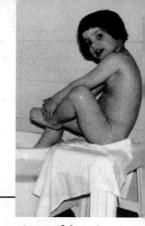

HEALTH

I am sick.	Estoy enfermo[a].	ay-**stoy** ayn-**fehr**-moh
I feel (very) sick.	Me siento (muy) enfermo[a].	may see-**ehn**-toh (**moo**-ee) ayn-**fehr**-moh
My husband / wife...	Mi marido / esposa...	mee mah-**ree**-doh / ay-**spoh**-sah
My son / daughter...	Mi hijo / hija...	mee **ee**-hoh / **ee**-hah
My male friend / female friend...	Mi amigo / amiga...	mee ah-**mee**-goh / ah-**mee**-gah
...feels (very) sick.	...está muy enfermo[a].	ay-**stah moo**-ee ayn-**fehr**-moh
It's urgent.	Es urgente.	ays oor-**hayn**-tay
I need / We need a doctor...	Necesito / Necesitamos un doctor...	nay-thay-**see**-toh / nay-thay-see-**tah**-mohs oon dohk-**tor**
...who speaks English.	...que hable inglés.	kay **ah**-blay een-**glays**
Please call a doctor.	Por favor llame al doctor.	por fah-**bor yah**-may ahl dohk-**tor**
Could a doctor come here?	¿Podría venir un doctor aquí?	poh-**dree**-ah bay-**neer** oon dohk-**tor** ah-**kee**
I am...	Soy...	soy
He / She is...	Él / Ella es...	ehl / **ay**-yah ays
...allergic to penicillin / sulfa.	...alérgico[a] a la penicilina / sulfate.	ah-**lehr**-hee-koh ah lah pay-nee-thee-**lee**-nah / sool-**fah**-tay

173

I am diabetic.	Soy diabético[a].	soy dee-ah-**bay**-tee-koh
I have cancer.	Tengo cáncer.	**tayn**-goh **kahn**-thehr
I had a heart	Tuve una ataque	**too**-bay oo-nah ah-**tah**-kay
attack __	al corazón	ahl koh-rah-**thohn**
years ago.	hace ___ años.	**ah**-thay ___ **ahn**-yohs
It hurts here.	Me duele aquí.	may **dway**-lay ah-**kee**
I feel faint.	Siento que me	see-**ehn**-toh kay may
	desmayo.	day-**smah**-yoh
It hurts to urinate.	Me hace daño	may **ah**-thay **dahn**-yoh
	al orinar.	ahl oh-ree-**nar**
I have body odor.	Huelo a sudor.	**way**-loh ah soo-**dor**
I'm going bald.	Me estoy	may ay-**stoy**
	quedando calvo.	kay-**dahn**-doh **kahl**-boh
Is it serious?	¿Es esto serio?	ays **ay**-stoh **say**-ree-oh
Is it contagious?	¿Es contagioso?	ays kohn-tah-_hee_-**oh**-soh
Aging sucks.	Hacerse viejo	ah-**thehr**-say bee-**ay**-_h_oh
	es una lata.	ays **oo**-nah **lah**-tah
Take one	Tome una	**toh**-may **oo**-nah
pill every __	pastilla cada __	pah-**stee**-yah **kah**-dah ___
hours for __	horas por __ días	**oh**-rahs por ___ **dee**-ahs
days before /	antes de / con	**ahn**-tays day / kohn
with meals.	las comidas.	lahs koh-**mee**-dahs
I need a receipt	Necesito una	nay-thay-**see**-toh **oo**-nah
for my insurance.	factura para	frahk-**too**-rah **pah**-rah
	mi seguro.	mee say-**goo**-roh

KEY PHRASES: HEALTH

doctor	doctor[a]	dohk-**tor**
hospital	hospital	oh-spee-**tahl**
pharmacy	farmacia	far-**mah**-thee-ah
medicine	medicina	may-dee-**thee**-nah
I am sick.	Estoy enfermo[a].	ay-**stoy** ayn-**fehr**-moh
I need a doctor	Necesito un	nay-thay-**see**-toh oon
(who speaks	doctor (que	dohk-**tor** (kay
English).	hable inglés).	**ah**-blay een-**glays**)
It hurts here.	Me duele aquí.	may **dway**-lay ah-**kee**

Ailments

I have...	Tengo...	**tayn**-goh
He / She has...	Él / Ella tiene...	ehl / **ay**-yah tee-**ehn**-ay
I need / We need	Necesito / Necesitamos	nay-thay-**see**-toh / nay-thay-see-**tah**-mohs
medication for...	medicina para...	may-dee-**thee**-nah **pah**-rah
...arthritis.	...artritis.	art-**ree**-tees
...asthma.	...asma.	**ahz**-mah
...athelete's foot (fungus).	...hongos en los pies.	**ohn**-gohs ayn lohs pee-**ays**
...a broken heart.	...una corazón roto.	**oo**-nah kor-ah-**thohn roh**-toh
...bad breath.	...mal aliento.	mahl ahl-**yehn**-toh
...blisters.	...rozaduras.	roh-thah-**doo**-rahs
...bug bites.	...picaduras.	pee-kah-**doo**-rahs
...a burn.	...una quemadura.	**oo**-nah kay-mah-**doo**-rah
...chest pains.	...dolor de pecho.	doh-**lor** day **pay**-choh
...chills.	...escalofríos.	ays-kah-loh-**free**-ohs
...a cold.	...un resfriado.	oon rays-free-**ah**-doh
...congestion.	...congestión.	kohn-hays-tee-**ohn**
...constipation.	...estreñimiento.	ay-strayn-yee-mee-**ehn**-toh
...a cough.	...tos.	tohs
...cramps.	...calambres.	kah-**lahm**-brays
...diabetes.	...diabetes.	dee-ah-**bay**-tays
...diarrhea.	...diarrea.	dee-ah-**ray**-ah
...dizziness.	...vértigo.	**behr**-tee-goh
...earache.	...dolor de oído.	doh-**lor** day oh-**ee**-doh
...epilepsy.	...epilepsia.	ay-pee-**lehp**-see-ah
...a fever.	...fiebre.	fee-**ay**-bray
...the flu.	...gripe.	**gree**-pay
...food poisoning.	...envenenamiento de comida.	ayn-behn-ehn-ah-mee-**ehn**-toh day koh-**mee**-dah
...hay fever.	...fiebre del heno.	fee-**ay**-bray dayl **ay**-noh
...a headache.	...dolor de cabeza.	doh-**lor** day kah-**bay**-thah

HEALTH

...a heart condition.	...problemas de corazón.	proh-**blay**-mahs day kor-ah-**thohn**
...hemorrhoids.	...hemorroides.	ay-moh-**roy**-days
...high blood pressure.	...tensión alta.	tayn-thee-**ohn ahl**-tah
...indigestion.	...indigestión.	een-dee-hay-stee-**ohn**
...an infection.	...una infección.	**oo**-nah een-fehk-thee-**ohn**
...inflammation.	...inflamación.	een-flah-mah-thee-**ohn**
...a migraine.	...una jaqueca.	**oo**-nah hah-**kay**-kah
...nausea.	...náuseas.	**now**-see-ahs
...pneumonia.	...pulmonía.	pool-moh-**nee**-ah
...a rash.	...erupción.	ay-roop-thee-**ohn**
...sinus problems.	...sinusitis.	see-noo-**see**-tees
...a sore throat.	...dolor de garganta.	doh-**lor** day gar-**gahn**-tah
...a stomach ache.	...dolor de estómago.	doh-**lor** day ay-**stoh**-mah-goh
...a swelling.	...un hinchazón.	oon een-chah-**thohn**
...a toothache.	...dolor de muelas.	doh-**lor** day moo-**ay**-lahs
...sunburn.	...quemaduras de sol.	kay-mah-**doo**-rahs day sohl
...a urinary infection.	...una infección urinaria.	**oo**-nah een-fehk-thee-**ohn** oo-ree-**nah**-ree-ah
...a venereal disease.	...una enfermedad venérea.	**oo**-nah ayn-fehr-may-**dahd** bay-**nay**-ray-ah
...vicious sunburn.	...quemaduras de sol peligrosas.	kay-mah-**doo**-rahs day sohl pay-lee-**groh**-sahs
...vomiting (projectile).	...vomitar (proyectil).	boh-mee-**tar** (proh-**yehk**-teel)
...worms.	...lombrices.	lohm-**bree**-thays

Women's Health

menstruation	menstruación	mayn-stroo-ah-thee-**ohn**
menstrual cramps	dolor de la menstruación	doh-**lor** day lay mayn-stroo-ah-thee-**ohn**
period	periodo	pay-ree-**oh**-doh

pregnancy (test)	(prueba de) embarazo	(proo-**ay**-bah day) aym-bah-**rah**-thoh
miscarriage	aborto espontáneo	ah-**bor**-toh ay-spohn-**tah**-nay-oh
abortion	aborto	ah-**bor**-toh
birth control pills	píldora anti-conceptiva	**peel**-doh-rah ahn-tee-kohn-thayp-**tee**-bah
diaphragm	diafragma	dee-ah-**frahg**-mah
I'd like to see a female...	Me gustaría ver a una...	may goo-stah-**ree**-ah behr ah **oo**-nah
...doctor.	...doctora.	dohk-**toh**-rah
...gynecologist.	...ginecóloga.	hee-nay-**koh**-loh-gah
I've missed a period.	No me vino el periodo.	noh may **bee**-noh ehl pay-ree-**oh**-doh
My last period started on ___.	Mi último periodo empezó en ___.	mee **ool**-tee-moh pay-ree-**oh**-doh aym-pay-**thoh** ayn
I am / She is...	Estoy / Está...	ay-**stoy** / ay-**stah**
pregnant.	embarazada.	aym-bah-rah-**thah**-dah
...___ months	...___ meses.	___ **may**-says

Parts of the Body

ankle	tobillo	toh-**bee**-yoh
arm	brazo	**brah**-thoh
back	espalda	ay-**spahl**-dah
bladder	vegija	bay-**hee**-yah
breast	pecho	**pay**-choh
buttocks	nalgas	**nahl**-gahs
chest	pecho	**pay**-choh
ear	oído	oh-**ee**-doh
elbow	codo	**koh**-doh
eye	ojo	**oh**-hoh
face	cara	**kah**-rah
finger	dedo	**day**-doh
foot	pie	pee-**ay**
hair	pelo	**pay**-loh

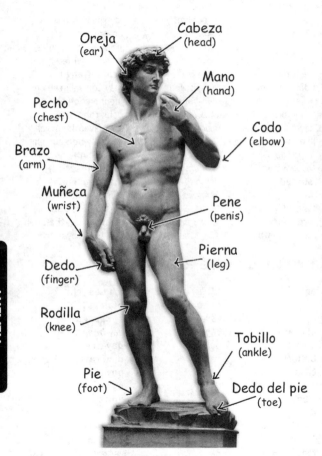

Oreja
(ear)

Cabeza
(head)

Mano
(hand)

Pecho
(chest)

Codo
(elbow)

Brazo
(arm)

Muñeca
(wrist)

Pene
(penis)

Dedo
(finger)

Pierna
(leg)

Rodilla
(knee)

Tobillo
(ankle)

Pie
(foot)

Dedo del pie
(toe)

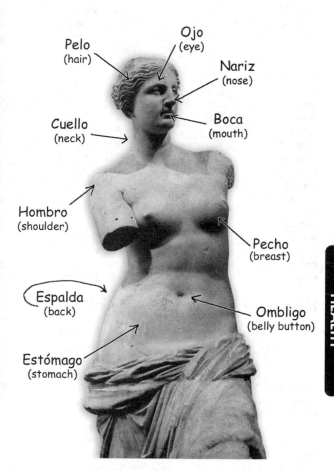

hand	mano	**mah**-noh
head	cabeza	kah-**bay**-thah
heart	corazón	kor-ah-**thohn**
intestines	intestinos	een-tay-**stee**-nohs
knee	rodilla	roh-**dee**-yah
leg	pierna	pee-**ehr**-nah
lung	pulmón	pool-**mohn**
mouth	boca	**boh**-kah
neck	cuello	**kway**-yoh
nose	nariz	nah-**reeth**
penis	pene	**pay**-nay
rectum	recto	**rayk**-toh
shoulder	hombros	**ohm**-brohs
stomach	estómago	ay-**stoh**-mah-goh
teeth	dientes	dee-**ehn**-tays
testicles	testículos	tays-**tee**-koo-lohs
throat	garganta	gar-**gahn**-tah
toe	dedo del pie	**day**-doh dayl pee-**ay**
urethra	uretra	oo-**rayt**-rah
uterus	útero	**oo**-tay-roh
vagina	vagina	bah-**hee**-nah
waist	cintura	theen-**too**-rah
wrist	muñeca	moon-**yay**-kah

Healthy Words

24-hour pharmacy	farmacia abierta las veinticuatro horas	far-**mah**-thee-ah ah-bee-**ehr**-tah lahs bayn-tee-**kwah**-troh **oh**-rahs
bleeding	sangrar	sahn-**grar**
blood	sangre	**sahn**-gray
contraceptives	anticoncep- tivos	ahn-tee-kohn-thayp- **tee**-bohs
dentist	dentista	dayn-**tee**-stah
doctor	doctor[a]	dohk-**tor**
health insurance	seguro médico	say-**goo**-roh **may**-dee-koh

hospital	hospital	oh-spee-**tahl**
medical clinic	clínica	**klee**-nee-kah
medicine	medicina	may-dee-**thee**-nah
nurse	enfermera	ayn-fehr-**may**-rah
pain	dolor	doh-**lor**
pharmacy	farmacia	far-**mah**-thee-ah
pill	pastilla	pah-**stee**-yah
prescription	receta	ray-**thay**-tah
refill	recambio	ray-**kahm**-bee-oh
unconscious	inconsciente	een-kohn-thee-**ayn**-tay
x-ray	rayos x	**rah**-yohs **ay**-kees

First-Aid Kit

antacid	antiácido	ahn-tee-**ah**-thee-doh
antibiotic	antibiótico	ahn-tee-bee-**oh**-tee-koh
aspirin	aspirina	ah-spee-**ree**-nah
non-aspirin substitute	Nolotil	**noh**-loh-teel
bandage	venda	**bayn**-dah
band-aids	tiritas	tee-**ree**-tahs
cold medicine	medicina para el resfriado	may-dee-**thee**-nah **pah**-rah ehl rays-free-**ah**-doh
cough drops	pastillas de tós	pah-**stee**-yahs day tohs
decongestant	descongestinante	day-kohn-hays-tee-**nahn**-tay
disinfectant	desinfectante	day-seen-fehk-**tahn**-tay
first-aid cream	crema de primera ayuda	**kray**-mah day pree-**may**-rah ah-**yoo**-dah
gauze / tape	gasa / esparadrapo	**gah**-sah / ays-pah-rah-**drah**-poh
laxative	laxativo	lahk-sah-**tee**-boh
medicine for diarrhea	medicina para la diarrea	may-dee-**thee**-nah **pah**-rah lah dee-ah-**ray**-ah
moleskin	lunar	loo-**nar**

HEALTH

pain killer	*analgésico*	ah-nahl-**hay**-see-koh
Preparation H	*Hemoal*	**ay**-moh-al
support bandage	*vendaje de apoyo*	bayn-**dah**-hay day ah-**poh**-yoh
thermometer	*termómetro*	tehr-**moh**-may-troh
Vaseline	*vaselina*	bah-say-**lee**-nah
vitamins	*vitaminas*	bee-tah-**mee**-nahs

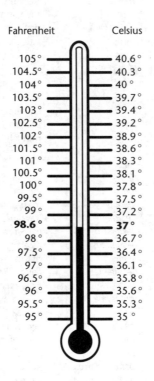

Fahrenheit	Celsius
105°	40.6°
104.5°	40.3°
104°	40°
103.5°	39.7°
103°	39.4°
102.5°	39.2°
102°	38.9°
101.5°	38.6°
101°	38.3°
100.5°	38.1°
100°	37.8°
99.5°	37.5°
99°	37.2°
98.6°	**37°**
98°	36.7°
97.5°	36.4°
97°	36.1°
96.5°	35.8°
96°	35.6°
95.5°	35.3°
95°	35°

HEALTH

Contacts and Glasses

glasses	*gafas*	**gah**-fahs
sunglasses	*gafas de sol*	**gah**-fahs day sohl
prescription	*prescripción*	pray-skreep-thee-**ohn**
contact lenses...	*lentillas...*	layn-**tee**-yahs
...soft	*...blandas*	**blahn**-dahs
...hard	*...de cristal*	day kree-**stahl**
solution...	*solución...*	soh-loo-thee-**ohn**
...cleaning	*...limpiadora*	leemp-yah-**doh**-rah
...soaking	*...de jabón*	day hah-**bohn**
20/20 vision	*vista perfecta*	**bee**-stah pehr-**fayk**-tah
all-purpose solution	*solución para*	soh-loo-thee-**ohn** pah-rah
(for cleaning	*limpiar y guardar*	leem-pee-**ar** ee gwar-**dar**
and soaking)	*las lentillas*	lahs layn-**tee**-yahs
I've lost /	*He perdido /*	ay pehr-**dee**-doh /
swallowed	*tragado una*	trah-**gah**-doh **oo**-nah
a contact lens.	*lentilla.*	layn-**tee**-yah

Toiletries

comb	*peine*	**pay**-nay
conditioner	*acondicio-nador*	ah-kohn-dee-thee-oh-nah-**dor**
condoms	*preservativos*	pray-sehr-bah-**tee**-bohs
dental floss	*seda dental*	**say**-dah dayn-**tahl**
deodorant	*desodorante*	day-soh-doh-**rahn**-tay
facial tissue	*toallitas para la cara*	toh-ah-**yee**-tahs **pah**-rah lah **kah**-rah
hairbrush	*cepillo del pelo*	thay-**pee**-yoh dayl **pay**-loh
hand lotion	*crema de manos*	**kray**-mah day **mah**-nohs
lip salve	*cacao de labios*	kah-**kah**-oh day **lah**-bee-ohs
mirror	*espejo*	ay-**spay**-hoh
nail clipper	*cortaúñas*	kor-tah-**oon**-yahs

HEALTH

razor	maquinilla de afeitar	mah-kee-**nee**-yah day ah-fay-**tar**
sanitary napkins	compresas	kohm-**pray**-sahs
scissors	tijeras	tee-*hehr*-ahs
shampoo	champú	chahm-**poo**
shaving cream	espuma de afeitar	**ay**-spoo-mah day ah-fay-**tar**
soap	jabón	hah-**bohn**
sunscreen	protección de sol	proh-tehk-thee-**ohn** day sohl
tanning lotion	crema bronceadora	**kray**-mah brohn-thay-ah-**doh**-rah
tampons	tampones	tahm-**poh**-nays
tissues	pañuelos de papel	pahn-yoo-**ay**-lohs day pah-**pehl**
toilet paper	papel higiénico	pah-**pehl** ee-*hee*-**ay**-nee-koh
toothbrush	cepillo de dientes	thay-**pee**-yoh day dee-**ehn**-tays
toothpaste	pasta de dientes	**pah**-stah day dee-**ehn**-tays
tweezers	pinzas	**peen**-thahs

Makeup

blush	brocha	**broh**-chah
eye shadow	sombra de ojos	**sohm**-brah day **oh**-*h*ohs
eyeliner	lápiz de ojos	**lah**-peeth day **oh**-*h*ohs
face cleanser	limpiadora de cara	leem-pee-ah-**doh**-rah day **kah**-rah
face powder	polvos para la cara	**pohl**-bohs **pah**-rah lah **kah**-rah
foundation	base para la cara	**bah**-say **pah**-rah lah **kah**-rah
lipstick	barra de labios	**bah**-rah day **lah**-bee-ohs
makeup	maquillaje	mah-kee-**yah**-*h*ay
mascara	máscara	**mah**-skah-rah

moisturizer...	*hidratante...*	ee-drah-**tahn**-tay
...with sun block	*...con protección solar*	kohn proh-tehk-thee-**ohn** soh-**lar**
nail polish	*esmalte de uñas*	ay-**smahl**-tay day **oon**-yahs
nail polish remover	*quitaesmaltes*	kee-tah-ay-**smahl**-tays
perfume	*perfume*	pehr-**foo**-may

For Babies

baby	*bebé*	bay-**bay**
baby food	*comida para bebé*	koh-**mee**-dah **pah**-rah bay-**bay**
bib	*babero*	bah-**bay**-roh
bottle	*biberón*	bee-bay-**rohn**
diaper	*pañal*	pahn-**yahl**
...wipes	*...paño para limpiar*	**pahn**-yoh **pah**-rah leem-pee-**ar**
...ointment	*...pomada*	poh-**mah**-dah
diapers	*pañales*	pahn-**yah**-lays
formula...	*leche...*	**lay**-chay
...powdered	*...en polvo*	ayn **pohl**-boh
...liquid	*...líquida*	**lee**-kee-dah
...soy	*...de soja*	day **soh**-yah
medication for...	*medicación para...*	may-dee-kah-thee-**ohn** **pah**-rah
...diaper rash	*...el escozor del pañal*	ehl ays-koh-**thor** dayl pahn-**yahl**
...teething	*...dentición*	dayn-tee-thee-**ohn**
nipple	*pezón*	pay-**thohn**
pacifier	*chupete*	choo-**pay**-tay
Will you refrigerate this?	*¿Podría refrigerarme esto?*	poh-**dree**-ah ray-free-*hehr*-**ar**-may **ay**-stoh
Will you warm... for a baby?	*¿Podría calentar... para un bebé?*	poh-**dree**-ah kah-lehn-**tar**... **pah**-rah oon bay-**bay**
...this	*...esto*	**ay**-stoh

...some water	...un poco de agua	oon **poh**-koh day **ah**-gwah
...some milk	...un poco de leche	oon **poh**-koh day **lay**-chay
Not too hot, please.	No demasiado caliente, por favor.	noh day-mah-see-**ah**-doh kahl-**yehn**-tay por fah-**bor**

More Baby Things

backpack to carry baby	mochila para llevar al bebé	moh-**chee**-lah **pah**-rah yay-**bar** ahl bay-**bay**
booster seat	asiento alto	ah-see-**ehn**-toh **ahl**-toh
car seat	asiento para el coche	ah-see-**ehn**-toh **pah**-rah ehl **koh**-chay
high chair	silla alta	**see**-yah **ahl**-tah
playpen	parque para niños	**par**-kay **pah**-rah **neen**-yohs
stroller	carrecoche	kah-ray-**koh**-chay

CHATTING

My name is ___.	*Me llamo ___.*	may **yah**-moh
What's your name?	*¿Cómo se llama?*	**koh**-moh say **yah**-mah
Pleased to meet you.	*Mucho gusto.*	**moo**-choh **goo**-stoh
This is ___.	*Le presenta ___.*	lay pray-**sehn**-tah
How are you?	*¿Cómo está?*	**koh**-moh ay-**stah**
Very well, thanks.	*Muy bien, gracias.*	**moo**-ee bee-**yehn** **grah**-thee-ahs
Where are you from?	*¿De dónde es?*	day **dohn**-day ays
What city?	*¿Qué ciudad?*	kay thee-oo-**dahd**
What country?	*¿Qué país?*	kay pah-**ees**
What planet?	*¿Qué planeta?*	kay plah-**nay**-tah
I am...	*Soy...*	soy
...American.	*...americano[a].*	ah-may-ree-**kah**-noh
...Canadian.	*...canadiense.*	kah-nah-dee-**ehn**-say
...a pest.	*...un pesado[a].*	oon pay-**sah**-doh
Where are you going?	*¿A dónde vas?*	ah **dohn**-day bahs
I'm / We're going to ___.	*Voy / Vamos a ___.*	boy / **bah**-mohs ah
Will you take my / our photo?	*¿Me / Nos hace una foto?*	may / nohs **ah**-thay **oo**-nah **foh**-toh
Can I take a photo of you?	*¿Puedo hacerle una foto?*	**pway**-doh ah-**thehr**-lay **oo**-nah **foh**-toh
Smile!	*¡Sonría!*	sohn-**ree**-ah

187

KEY PHRASES: CHATTING

My name is ___.	Me llamo ___.	may **yah**-moh
What's your name?	¿Cómo se llama?	**koh**-moh say **yah**-mah
Pleased to meet you.	Mucho gusto.	**moo**-choh **goo**-stoh
Where are you from?	¿De dónde es?	day **dohn**-day ays
I'm from ___.	Soy de ___.	soy day
Where are you going?	¿A dónde vas?	ah **dohn**-day bahs
I'm going to ___.	Voy a ___.	boy ah
I like...	Me gusta...	may **goo**-stah
Do you like...?	¿Le gusta...?	lay **goo**-stah
Thank you very much.	Muchas gracias.	**moo**-chahs **grah**-thee-ahs
Have a good trip!	¡Buen viaje!	bwayn bee-**ah**-hay

Nothing More Than Feelings

I am / You are...	Estoy / Está...	ay-**stoy** / ay-**stah**
He is / She is...	Él / Ella está....	ehl / **ay**-yah ay-**stah**
...happy.	...feliz.	fay-**leeth**
...sad.	...triste.	**tree**-stay
...tired.	...cansado[a].	kahn-**sah**-doh
...thirsty.	...sediento[a].	say-dee-**ehn**-toh
I am / You are...	Tengo / Tiene...	**tayn**-goh / tee-**ehn**-ay
He is / She is...	Él / Ella tiene...	ehl / **ay**-yah tee-**ehn**-ay
...hungry.	...hambre.	**ahm**-bray
...lucky.	...suerte.	**swehr**-tay
...homesick.	...morriña.	moh-**reen**-yah
...cold.	...frío.	**free**-oh
...hot.	...calor.	kah-**lor**

If you're *cansado,* you're tired. If you're *casado,* you're married. If you're both, you probably have *hijos* (children).

CHATING

Who's Who

My...	Mi...	mee
...male friend / female friend.	...amigo / amiga.	ah-**mee**-goh / ah-**mee**-gah
...boyfriend / girlfriend.	...novio / novia.	**noh**-bee-oh / **noh**-bee-ah
...husband / wife.	...marido / esposa.	mah-**ree**-doh / ay-**spoh**-sah
...son / daughter.	...hijo / hija.	**ee**-hoh / **ee**-hah
...brother / sister.	...hermano / hermana.	ehr-**mah**-noh / ehr-**mah**-nah
...father / mother.	...padre / madre.	**pah**-dray / **mah**-dray
...uncle / aunt.	...tío / tía.	**tee**-oh / **tee**-ah
...nephew / niece.	...sobrino / sobrina.	soh-**bree**-noh / soh-**bree**-nah
...male cousin / female cousin.	...primo / prima.	**pree**-moh / **pree**-mah
...grandpa / grandma.	...abuelo / abuela.	ah-**bway**-loh / ah-**bway**-lah
...grandson / granddaughter.	...nieto / nieta.	nee-**ay**-toh / nee-**ay**-tah

Family

Are you married? (asked of a man)	¿Está casado?	ay-**stah** kah-**sah**-doh
Are you married? (asked of a woman)	¿Está casada?	ay-**stah** kah-**sah**-dah
Do you have children?	¿Tiene hijos?	tee-**ehn**-ay **ee**-hohs
How many boys / girls?	¿Cuántos niños / niñas?	**kwahn**-tohs **neen**-yohs / **neen**-yahs
Do you have photos?	¿Tiene fotos?	tee-**ehn**-ay **foh**-tohs
How old is your child?	¿Cuántos años tiene su hijo[a]?	**kwahn**-tohs **ahn**-yohs tee-**ehn**-ay soo **ee**-hoh

Beautiful child!	*¡Qué niño[a] más guapo[a]!*	kay **neen**-yoh mahs **gwah**-poh
Beautiful children! (m /f)	*¡Qué niños[as] más guapos[as]!*	kay **neen**-yohs mahs **gwah**-pohs

Work

What is your occupation?	*¿En qué trabaja?*	ayn kay trah-**bah**-hah
Do you like your work?	*¿Le gusta su trabajo?*	lay **goo**-stah soo trah-**bah**-hoh
I work...	*Trabajo...*	trah-**bah**-hoh
I'm studying to work...	*Estudio para trabajar...*	ay-**stoo**-dee-oh **pah**-rah trah-bah-**har**
I used to work...	*Solía trabajar...*	soh-**lee**-ah trah-bah-**har**
I want a job...	*Busco trabajo...*	**boos**-koh trah-**bah**-hoh
...in accounting.	*...de contable.*	day kohn-**tah**-blay
...in the medical field.	*...en la medicina.*	ayn lah may-dee-**thee**-nah
...in social services.	*...en servicios sociales.*	ayn sehr-**bee**-thee-ohs soh-thee-**ah**-lays
...in the legal profession.	*...en el mundo del derecho.*	ayn ehl **moon**-doh dayl day-**ray**-choh
...in banking.	*...en la banca.*	ayn lah **bahn**-kah
...in business.	*...en los negocios.*	ayn lohs nay-**goh**-thee-ohs
...in government.	*...en el gobierno.*	ayn ehl goh-bee-**ehr**-noh
...in engineering.	*...de ingeniero.*	day een-hay-nee-**ay**-roh
...in public relations.	*...de relaciones públicas.*	day ray-lah-thee-**oh**-nays **poob**-lee-kahs
...in science.	*...en las ciencias.*	ayn lahs thee-**ehn**-thee-ahs
...in teaching.	*...en la educación.*	ayn lah ay-doo-kah-thee-**ohn**
...in the computer field.	*...en la informática.*	ayn lah een-for-**mah**-tee-kah
...in the travel industry.	*...en una agencia de viajes.*	ayn **oo**-nah ah-**hayn**-thee-ah day bee-**ah**-hays
...in the arts.	*...en el arte.*	ayn ehl **ar**-tay

...in journalism.	...de periodista.	day pay-ree-oh-**dee**-stah
...in a restaurant.	...en un restaurante.	ayn oon rehs-tow-**rahn**-tay
...in a store.	...en una tienda.	ayn **oo**-nah tee-**ehn**-dah
...in a factory.	...en una fábrica.	ayn **oo**-nah **fah**-bree-kah
I'm a professional traveler.	Soy viajante de profesión.	soy bee-ah-**hahn**-tay day proh-fay-see-**ohn**
I am / We are...	Estoy / Estamos...	ay-**stoy** / ay-**stah**-mohs
...unemployed.	...desemple-ado[a/os/as].	day-saym-play-**ah**-doh
...retired.	...jubilado[a/os/as].	hoo-bee-**lah**-doh
Do you have a...?	¿Tiene una...?	tee-**ehn**-ay oo-nah
Here is my / our...	Aquí tiene mi / nuestra...	ah-**kee** tee-**ehn**-ay mee / **nway**-strah
...business card	...tarjeta	tar-**hay**-tah
...e-mail address	...dirección de correo electrónico	dee-rehk-thee-**ohn** day koh-**ray**-oh ay-lehk-**troh**-nee-koh

Chatting with Children

What's your name?	¿Cómo te llamas?	**koh**-moh tay **yah**-mahs
My name is ___.	Me llamo ___.	may **yah**-moh
How old are you?	¿Cuántos años tienes?	**kwahn**-tohs **ahn**-yohs tee-**ehn**-ays
Do you have brothers and sisters?	¿Tienes hermanos y hermanas?	tee-**ehn**-ays ehr-**mah**-nohs ee ehr-**mah**-nahs
Do you like school?	¿Te gusta la escuela?	tay **goo**-stah lah ays-**kway**-lah
What are you studying?	¿Qué estás estudiando?	kay ay-**stahs** ay-stoo-dee-**ahn**-doh
I'm studying...	Estoy estudiando...	ay-**stoy** ay-stoo-dee-**ahn**-doh
What's your favorite subject?	¿Cúal es tu asignatura favorita?	kwahl ehs too ah-seeg-nah-**too**-rah fah-boh-**ree**-tah
Do you have pets?	¿Tienes mascotas?	tee-**ehn**-ays mah-**skoh**-tahs

CHATTING

I have / We have...	Tengo / Tenemos...	**tayn**-goh / tay-**nay**-mohs
...a cat / a dog / a fish / a bird	...un gato / un perro / un pez / un pájaro	oon **gah**-toh / oon **pehr**-roh / oon payth / oon **pah**-hah-roh
What is this / that?	¿Qué es esto / eso?	kay ays **ay**-stoh /**ay**-soh
Will you teach me / us...?	¿Me / Nos enseñas...?	may / nohs ayn-**sayn**-yahs
...some Spanish words	...algunas palabras en español	ahl-**goo**-nahs pah-**lah**-brahs ayn ay-spahn-**yohl**
...a simple Spanish song	...una canción simple en español	**oo**-nah kahn-thee-**ohn seem**-play ayn ay-spahn-**yohl**
Guess which country I live in / we live in.	Adivina en que país vivo / vivimos.	ah-dee-**bee**-nah ayn kay pah-**ees bee**-boh / bee-**bee**-mohs
How old am I?	¿Cuántos años tengo?	**kwahn**-tohs **ahn**-yohs **tayn**-goh
I'm ___ years old.	Tengo ___ años.	**tayn**-goh ___ **ahn**-yohs
Want to hear me burp?	¿Quieres oírme eructar?	kee-**ehr**-ehs oh-**eer**-may ay-rook-**tar**
Teach me a fun game.	Enséñame un juego divertido.	ayn-**sayn**-yah-may oon *h*way-goh dee-vehr-**tee**-doh
Got any candy?	¿Tienes caramelos?	tee-**ehn**-ays kah-rah-**may**-lohs
Want to thumb-wrestle?	¿Quieres hacer un pulso gitano?	kee-**ehr**-ehs ah-**thehr** oon **pool**-soh hee-**tah**-noh
Gimme five.	Choca los cinco.	**choh**-kah lohs **theen**-koh

If you do break into song, you'll find the words for *Happy Birthday* on page 24 and another song on page 270.

Travel Talk

I am / Are you...?	¿Estoy / ¿Está...?	ay-**stoy** / ay-**stah**
...on vacation	...de vacaciones	day bah-kah-thee-**oh**-nays
...on business	...de negocios	day nay-**goh**-thee-ohs
How long have you been traveling?	¿Cuánto tiempo hace que están viajando?	**kwahn**-toh tee-**ehm**-poh **ah**-thay kay ay-**stahn** bee-ah-*hahn*-doh

CHATING

English	Spanish	Pronunciation
day / week	día / semana	**dee**-ah / say-**mah**-nah
month / year	mes / año	mays / **ahn**-yoh
When are you going home?	¿Cuándo regresa a casa?	**kwahn**-doh ray-**gray**-sah ah **kah**-sah
This is my / out	Ésta es mi / nuestra	**ay**-stah ays mee / **nway**-strah
first time in ___.	primera vez en ___.	pree-**may**-rah bayth ayn
It's (not) a tourist trap.	(No) es un timo turístico.	(noh) ays oon **tee**-moh too-**ree**-stee-koh
This is paradise.	Es un paraíso.	ays oon pah-rah-**ee**-soh
Spain is wonderful.	España es preciosa.	ay-**spahn**-yah ays pray-thee-**oh**-sah
The Spanish are friendly / boring / rude.	Los españoles son amables / aburridos / maleducados.	lohs ay-spahn-**yoh**-lays sohn ah-**mah**-blays / ah-boo-**ree**-dohs / mah-lay-doo-**kah**-dohs
So far...	De momento...	day moh-**mehn**-toh
Today...	Hoy...	oy
...I / we have seen ___ and ___.	...he / hemos visto ___ y ___.	ay / **ay**-mohs **bee**-stoh ___ ee ___.
Next...	Después...	days-**pways**
Tomorrow...	Mañana...	mahn-**yah**-nah
...I / we will see ___.	...veré / veremos ___.	bay-**ray** / bay-**ray**-mohs
Yesterday...	Ayer...	ah-**yehr**
...I / we saw ___.	...vi / vimos ___.	bee / **bee**-mohs
My / Our vacation is ___ days long, starting in ___ and ending in ___.	Mis / Nuestras vacaciones son ___ días, empezando en ___ y acabando en ___.	mees / **nway**-strahs bah-kah-thee-**oh**-nays sohn ___ **dee**-ahs aym-pay-**thahn**-doh ayn ___ ee ah-kah-**bahn**-doh ayn
To travel is to live.	Viajar es vivir.	bee-ah-**har** ays bee-**beer**
Travel is enlightening.	Viajar es instructivo.	bee-ah-**har** ays een-strook-**tee**-boh
I wish all (American) politicians traveled.	Ojalá que todos los políticos (americanos) viajaran.	oh-hah-**lah** kay **toh**-dohs lohs poh-**lee**-tee-kohs (ah-may-ree-**kah**-nohs) bee-ah-**hah**-rahn
Have a good trip!	¡Buen viaje!	bwayn bee-**ah**-hay

CHATTING

Map Musings

Use the following maps to delve into family history and explore travel dreams.

I live here.	*Vivo aquí.*	**bee**-boh ah-**kee**
We live here.	*Vivimos aquí.*	bee-**bee**-mohs ah-**kee**
I was born here.	*Nací aquí.*	nah-**thee** ah-**kee**
My ancestors came from___.	*Mis familiares son de ___.*	mees fah-mee-lee-**ah**-rays sohn day
I've traveled to___.	*He viajado a ___.*	ay bee-ah-**hah**-doh ah
We've traveled to___.	*Hemos viajado a ___.*	**ay**-mohs bee-ah-**hah**-doh ah
Next I'll go to__.	*Después iré a ___.*	days-**pways** ee-**ray** ah
Next we'll go to__.	*Después iremos a ___.*	days-**pways** ee-**ray**-mohs ah
I'd / We'd like to go to ___.	*Me / Nos gustaría ir a ___.*	may / nohs goo-stah-**ree**-ah eer ah
Where do you live?	*¿Dónde vive?*	**dohn**-day **bee**-bay
Where were you born?	*¿Dónde ha nacido?*	**dohn**-day ah nah-**thee**-doh
Where did your ancestors come from?	*¿De dónde son sus familiares?*	day **dohn**-day sohn soos fah-mee-lee-**ah**-rays
Where have you traveled?	*¿Adónde ha viajado?*	ah-**dohn**-day ah bee-ah-**hah**-doh
Where are you going?	*¿Adónde va?*	ah-**dohn**-day bah
Where would you like to go?	*¿Adónde le gustaría ir?*	ah-**dohn**-day lay goo-stah-**ree**-ah eer

SPAIN

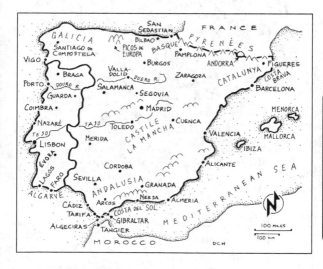

EUROPE

THE UNITED STATES

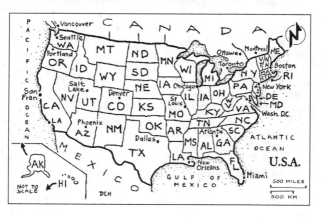

THE WORLD

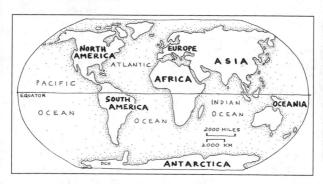

Favorite Things

What kind of...	¿Cuál tipo de...	kwahl **tee**-poh day...
do you like?	le gusta?	lay **goo**-stah
...art	...arte	**ar**-tay
...book	...libro	**lee**-broh
...hobby	...pasatiempo	pah-sah-tee-**ehm**-poh
...ice cream	...helado	ay-**lah**-doh
...food	...comida	koh-**mee**-dah
...movie	...película	pay-**lee**-koo-lah
...music	...música	**moo**-see-kah
...sport	...deporte	day-**por**-tay
...vice	...vicio	**bee**-thee-oh
Who is your...?	¿Cuál es su...?	kwahl ays soo...
...favorite male artist	...artista favorito	ar-**tee**-stah fah-boh-**ree**-toh
...favorite female artist	...artista favorita	ar-**tee**-stah fah-boh-**ree**-tah
...favorite male author	...autor favorito	ow-**tor** fah-boh-**ree**-toh
...favorite female author	...autora favorita	ow-**toh**-rah fah-boh-**ree**-tah
...favorite male singer	...cantante favorito	kahn-**tahn**-tay fah-boh-**ree**-toh
...favorite female singer	...cantante favorita	kahn-**tahn**-tay fah-boh-**ree**-tah
...favorite male movie star	...actor favorito	ahk-**tor** fah-voh-**ree**-toh
...favorite female movie star	...actriz favorita	ahk-**treeth** fah-boh-**ree**-tah
Can you recommend a good...?	¿Puede recomendarme un buen...?	**pway**-day ray-koh-mayn-**dar**-may oon bwayn
...Spanish CD	...disco compacto en español	**dees**-koh kohm-**pahk**-toh ayn ay-spahn-**yohl**
...Spanish book translated in English	...libro español traducido al inglés	**lee**-broh ay-spahn-**yohl** trah-doo-**thee**-doh ahl een-**glays**

Weather

What will the weather be like tomorrow?	*¿Qué tiempo va a hacer mañana?*	kay tee-**ehm**-poh bah ah ah-**thehr** mahn-**yah**-nah
sunny / cloudy	*soleado / nublado*	soh-lay-**ah**-doh / noo-**blah**-doh
hot / cold	*caluroso / frío*	kah-loo-**roh**-soh / **free**-oh
muggy / windy	*húmedo / ventoso*	**oo**-may-doh / vehn-**toh**-soh
rain / snow	*lluvia / nieve*	**yoov**-yah / nee-**ay**-bay
Should I bring a jacket?	*¿Debería llevar una chaqueta?*	day-bay-**ree**-ah yay-**bar oo**-nah chah-**kay**-tah

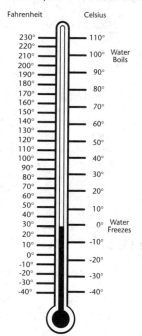

Fahrenheit

Celsius

230°	110°
220°	
210°	100° Water Boils
200°	
190°	90°
180°	80°
170°	
160°	70°
150°	
140°	60°
130°	
120°	50°
110°	
100°	40°
90°	
80°	30°
70°	20°
60°	
50°	10°
40°	
30°	0° Water Freezes
20°	
10°	-10°
0°	
-10°	-20°
-20°	-30°
-30°	
-40°	-40°

CHATING

Thanks a Million

Thank you very much.	*Muchas gracias.*	**moo**-chahs **grah**-thee-ahs
You are...	*Usted es...*	oo-**stehd** ays
...helpful, kind.	*...amable.*	ah-**mah**-blay
...wonderful.	*...maravilloso[a].*	mah-rah-bee-**yoh**-soh
...generous.	*...generoso[a].*	*h*ay-nay-**roh**-soh
You spoil me / us.	*Me / Nos mima.*	may / nohs **mee**-mah
You've been a great help.	*Me ha ayudado mucho.*	may ah ah-yoo-**dah**-doh **moo**-choh
I will / We will remember you...	*Le recordaré / Le recordaremos...*	lay ray-kor-dah-**ray** / lay ray-kor-dah-**ray**-mohs
...always.	*...siempre.*	see-**ehm**-pray
...till Tuesday.	*...hasta el martes.*	**ah**-stah ehl **mar**-tays

Smoking

Do you smoke?	*¿Fuma?*	**foo**-mah
Do you smoke pot?	*¿Fuma hierba?*	**foo**-mah **yehr**-bah
I (don't) smoke.	*(No) fumo.*	(noh) **foo**-moh
We (don't) smoke.	*(No) fumamos.*	(noh) foo-**mah**-mohs
lighter	*suaves*	**swah**-bays
cigarettes	*cigarillos*	thee-gah-**ree**-yohs
marijuana	*marihuana*	mah-ree-*h*wah-nah
hash	*hachís*	ah-**chees**
joint	*porro*	**poh**-roh
stoned	*colocado*	koh-loh-**kah**-doh
Wow!	*¡Caray!*	kah-**rī**

Responses for All Occasions

I like that.	*Eso me gusta.*	**ay**-soh may **goo**-stah
We like that.	*Eso nos gusta.*	**ay**-soh nohs **goo**-stah
I like you.	*Me cae bien.*	may **kah**-ay bee-**yehn**
We like you.	*Nos cae bien.*	nohs **kah**-ay bee-**yehn**

That's great!	¡Qué bien!	kay bee-**yehn**
What a nice place.	Que sitio más bonito.	kay **seet**-yoh mahs boh-**nee**-toh
Perfect.	Perfecto.	pehr-**fehk**-toh
Funny.	Divertido.	dee-behr-**tee**-doh
Interesting.	Interesante.	een-tay-ray-**sahn**-tay
Really?	¿De verdad?	day behr-**dahd**
Wow!	¡Caray!	kah-**rī**
Congratulations!	¡Felicidades!	fay-lee-thee-**dah**-days
Well done!	¡Bien hecho!	bee-**yehn ay**-choh
You're welcome.	De nada.	day **nah**-dah
Bless you! (after sneeze)	¡Salud!	sah-**lood**
What a pity!	¡Qué lastima!	kay **lah**-stee-mah
That's life.	Así es la vida.	ah-**see** ays lah **bee**-dah
No problem.	No hay problema.	noh ī proh-**blay**-mah
O.K.	De acuerdo / Vale.	day ah-**kwehr**-doh / **bah**-lay
This is the good life!	¡Esto sí que es vida!	**ay**-stoh see kay ays **bee**-dah
Good luck!	¡Buena suerte!	**bway**-nah **swehr**-tay
Let's go!	¡Vamos!	**bah**-mohs

The Spanish say, "*La vida es corta. No corras.*" (Life is short. Don't run.)

Conversing with Animals

rooster / cock-a-doodle-doo	gallo / cacarea	**gah**-yoh / kah-kah-**ray**-ah
bird / tweet tweet	pájaro / pío pío	**pah**-hah-roh / **pee**-oh **pee**-oh
cat / meow	gato / miau	**gah**-toh / **mee**-ow
dog / woof woof	perro / guao guao	**pehr**-roh / gwow gwow
duck / quack quack	pato / cua cua	**pah**-toh / kwah kwah
cow / moo	vaca / muh	**bah**-kah / moo
pig / oink oink	cerdo / gro gro	**thehr**-doh / (just snort)

Profanity

People make animal noises, too. These words will help you understand what the more colorful locals are saying.

bastard	*bastardo*	bah-**star**-doh
bitch	*perra*	**pay**-rah
child of a whore	*hijo[a] de puta*	ee-*hoh* day **poo**-tah
breasts (colloq.)	*tetas*	**tay**-tahs
woman's private parts (our C-word)	*coño*	**kohn**-yoh
penis (colloq.)	*polla, minga*	**poh**-yah, **meen**-gah
our F-word	*joder*	hoh-**dehr**
shit	*mierda*	mee-**ehr**-dah
drunk	*borracho[a]*	boh-**rah**-choh
idiot	*idiota*	ee-dee-**oh**-tah
imbecile	*imbécil*	eem-**bay**-theel
jerk (horned sheep)	*cabrón[a]*	kah-**brohn**
stupid	*estúpido[a]*	ay-**stoo**-pee-doh
Did someone fart?	*¿Se ha tirado alguien un pedo?*	say ah tee-**rah**-doh **ahl**-gee-ehn oon **pay**-doh
I burped.	*Eructé.*	ay-rook-**tay**
This is a piece of shit.	*Esto es una mierda.*	**ay**-stoh ays **oo**-nah mee-**ehr**-dah
Shove it up your ass.	*Métdelo en el culo.*	may-**tay**-loh ayn ehl **koo**-loh
Kiss my ass.	*Bésame el culo.*	**bay**-sah-may ehl **koo**-loh
Bullshit.	*Mierda.*	mee-**ehr**-dah
You are...	*Eres...*	**ay**-rays
Don't be...	*No seas...*	noh **say**-ahs
...a son of a bitch.	*...un hijo de puta.*	oon **ee**-*hoh* day **poo**-tah
...an asshole.	*...un gilipollas.*	oon hee-lee-**poh**-yahs
...an idiot.	*...un idiota.*	oon ee-dee-**oh**-tah
...a creep.	*...un pelota.*	oon pay-**loh**-tah
...a cretin.	*...un cretino.*	oon kray-**tee**-noh
...a pig.	*...un cerdo.*	oon **thehr**-doh

Sweet Curses

My goodness.	*Dios mío.*	**dee**-ohs **mee**-oh
Goodness gracious.	*Dios mío de*	**dee**-ohs **mee**-oh day
	mi corazón.	mee kor-ah-**thohn**
Oh, my gosh.	*¡Oh, Dios mío!*	oh **dee**-ohs **mee**-oh
Shoot.	*¡Vaya!*	**bah**-yah
Darn it!	*¡Caray!*	kah-**rī**

Spaniards are not as shy about using profanity as Americans.
Even their most extreme curses (*joder, coño*) are used far
more freely—and sound far less severe—than their American
counterparts, often even turning up around the dinner table
in mixed company.

Create Your Own Conversation

You can mix and match these words into a conversation.
Make it as deep or silly as you want.

Who

I / you	*yo / usted*	yoh / oo-**stehd**
he / she	*él / ella*	ehl / **ay**-yah
we / they	*nosotros / ellos*	noh-**soh**-trohs / **ay**-yohs
my / your...	*mi / su...*	mee / soo
...parents / children	*...padres / niños*	**pah**-drays / **neen**-yohs
men / women	*hombres /*	**ohm**-brays /
	mujeres	moo-**hehr**-ays
rich / poor	*ricos / pobres*	**ree**-kohs / **poh**-brays
young /	*joven /*	**hoh**-bayn /
middle-aged / old	*maduro[a] / viejo[a]*	mah-**doo**-roh / bee-**ay**-hoh

Spanish	españoles	ay-spahn-**yoh**-lays
Portuguese	portugueses	por-too-**gay**-says
Austrians	austriacos	ow-stree-**ah**-kohs
Belgians	belgas	**bayl**-gahs
British	británicos	bree-**tah**-nee-kohs
Czech	checos	**chay**-kohs
French	franceses	frahn-**thay**-says
Germans	alemanes	ah-lay-**mah**-nays
Irish	irlandeses	eer-lahn-**day**-says
Italians	italianos	ee-tah-lee-**ah**-nohs
Moroccans	marroquís	mah-roh-**kees**
Swiss	suizos	**swee**-thos
Europeans	europeos	ay-oo-roh-**pay**-ohs
EU (European Union)	UE (Unión Europea)	oo ay (oo-nee-**ohn** ay-oo-roh-**pay**-ah)
Americans	americanos	ah-may-ree-**kah**-nohs
liberals	liberales	lee-bay-**rah**-lays
conservatives	conservadores	kohn-sehr-bah-**doh**-rays
radicals	radicales	rah-dee-**kah**-lays
terrorists	terroristas	tay-roh-**ree**-stahs
politicians	políticos	poh-**lee**-tee-kohs
big business	gran negocio	grahn nay-**goh**-thee-oh
multinational corporations	corporaciones multinacionales	kor-poh-rah-thee-**oh**-nays mool-tee-nah-thee-oh-**nah**-lays
military	ejército	ay-**hehr**-thee-toh
mafia	mafia	**mah**-fee-ah
refugees	refugiados	ray-foo-hee-**ah**-dohs
travelers	viajantes	bee-ah-**hahn**-tays
God	Dios	**dee**-ohs
Christian	cristiano	kree-stee-**ah**-noh
Catholic	católico	kah-**toh**-lee-koh
Protestant	protestante	proh-tay-**stahn**-tay
Jew	judío	**h**oo-**dee**-oh
Muslim	musulmán	moo-sool-**mahn**
everyone	toda la gente	**toh**-dah lah **h**ehn-tay

What

buy / sell	*comprar / vender*	kohm-**prar** / bayn-**dehr**
have / lack	*tener /*	tay-**nehr** /
	carecer de	kah-ray-**thehr** day
help / abuse	*ayudar /*	ah-yoo-**dar** /
	abusar de	ah-boo-**sar** day
learn / fear	*aprender /*	ah-prehn-**dehr** /
	temer	tay-**mehr**
love / hate	*amar / odiar*	ah-**mar** / oh-dee-**ar**
prosper / suffer	*prosperar / sufrir*	proh-spay-**rar** / soof-**reer**
take / give	*coger / dar*	koh-**hehr** / dar
want / need	*querer /*	kay-**rehr** /
	necesitar	nay-thay-see-**tar**
work / play	*trabajar / jugar*	trah-bah-**har** / hoo-**gar**

The verb *coger* (to take) works fine in Spain, but it's a vulgar curse word (comparable to our F-word) in Mexico and Latin America. Try *tomar* instead.

Why

(anti-)	*(anti-)*	(**ahn**-tee)
globalization	*globalización*	gloh-bah-lee-thah-thee-**ohn**
class warfare	*guerra de clases*	**gehr**-rah day **klah**-says
corruption	*corrupción*	koh-roop-thee-**ohn**
democracy	*democracia*	day-moh-krah-**thee**-ah
education	*educación*	ay-doo-kah-thee-**ohn**
family	*familia*	fah-**meel**-yah
food	*comida*	koh-**mee**-dah
global perspective	*perspectiva*	pehr-spehk-**tee**-vah
	global	gloh-**bahl**
guns	*pistolas*	pee-**stoh**-lahs
happiness	*alegría*	ah-lay-**gree**-ah
health	*salud*	sah-**lood**
hope	*esperanza*	ay-spay-**rahn**-thah

imperialism	*imperialismo*	eem-pehr-ee-ah-**lees**-moh
lies	*mentiras*	mayn-**tee**-rahs
love / sex	*amor / sexo*	ah-**mor** / **sehk**-soh
marijuana	*marihuana*	mah-ree-*h*wah-nah
money / power	*dinero / poder*	dee-**nay**-roh / poh-**dehr**
pollution	*polución*	poh-loo-thee-**ohn**
racism	*racismo*	rah-**thees**-moh
regime change	*cambio de régimen*	**kahm**-bee-oh day **ray**-*h*ee-mayn
relaxation	*relajación*	ray-lah-*h*ah-thee-**ohn**
religion	*religion*	ray-lee-hee-**ohn**
respect	*respeto*	ray-**spay**-toh
taxes	*impuestos*	eem-**pway**-stohs
television	*televisión*	tay-lay-bee-see-**ohn**
violence	*violencia*	bee-oh-**layn**-thee-ah
war / peace	*guerra / paz*	**gehr**-rah / pahth
work	*trabajo*	trah-**bah**-*h*oh

You Be the Judge

(no) problem	*(no hay) problema*	(noh ī) proh-**blay**-mah
(not) good	*(no es) bueno*	(noh ays) **bway**-noh
(not) dangerous	*(no es) peligroso*	(noh ays) pay-lee-**groh**-soh
(not) fair	*(no es) justo*	(noh ays) *h*oo-stoh
(not) guilty	*(no es) culpable*	(noh ays) kool-**pah**-blay
(not) powerful	*(no es) poderoso*	(noh ays) poh-day-**roh**-soh
(not) stupid	*(no es) estúpido*	(noh ays) ay-**stoo**-pee-doh
(not) happy	*(no es) feliz*	(noh ays) fay-**leeth**
because / for	*porque / para*	**por**-kay / **pah**-rah
and / or / from	*y / o / de*	ee / oh / day
too much	*demasiado*	day-mah-see-**ah**-doh
(never) enough	*(nunca) suficiente*	(**noon**-kah) soo-fee-thee-**ehn**-tay
same	*igual*	ee-**gwahl**
better / worse	*mejor / peor*	may-*h*or / pay-**or**
here / everywhere	*aquí / en todas partes*	ah-**kee** / ayn **toh**-dahs **par**-tays

Beginnings and Endings

I like...	Me gusta...	may **goo**-stah
We like...	Nos gusta...	nohs **goo**-stah
I don't like...	No me gusta...	noh may **goo**-stah
We don't like...	No nos gusta...	noh nohs **goo**-stah
Do you like...?	¿Le gusta...?	lay **goo**-stah
In the past...	En el pasado...	ayn ehl pah-**sah**-doh
When I was younger,	Cuando era más joven,	**kwahn**-doh **ay**-rah mahs **hoh**-bayn
I thought...	creía...	kray-**ee**-ah
Now, I think...	Ahora, creo...	ah-**oh**-rah **kray**-oh
I am / Are you...?	Soy / ¿Eres...?	soy / **ay**-rays
...optimistic / pessimistic	...optimista / pesimista	ohp-tee-**mee**-stah / pay-see-**mee**-stah
I (don't) believe in...	Yo (no) creo en...	yoh (noh) **kray**-oh ayn
Do you believe in...?	¿Cree usted en...?	**kray**-yay oo-**stehd** ayn
...God	...Dios	**dee**-ohs
...life after death	...la vida después de la muerte	lah **bee**-dah days-**pways** day lah **mwehr**-tay
...extra-terrestrial life	...la vida extraterreste	lah **bee**-dah ayk-strah-tay-**rehs**-tay
...Santa Claus	...Papá Noel	pah-**pah** noh-**ehl**
Yes. / No.	Sí. / No.	see / noh
Maybe. / I don't know.	Tal vez. / No sé.	tahl bayth / noh say
What is most important in life?	¿Qué es lo más importante en la vida?	kay ays loh mahs eem-por-**tahn**-tay ayn lah **bee**-dah
The problem is...	El problema es...	ehl proh-**blay**-mah ays
The answer is...	La respuesta es...	lah rehs-**pway**-stah ays
We have solved the world's problems.	Hemos resuelto los problemas del mundo.	**ay**-mohs ray-**swayl**-toh lohs proh-**blay**-mahs dayl **moon**-doh

Spanish Political Terms

Basque ETA: Separatist Basque terrorist group.

Guerra Civil: The 1936-1939 Civil War, which ended with Franco's Nationalists (fascists aided by Hitler) overthrowing the Spanish Republican government (aided by the USSR and Hemingway).

Falange: Franco's fascist party.

Franco: Spain's fascist dictator from 1939 to 1975.

Guernica: Basque town destroyed by Franco during the Civil War, immortalized by a Picasso painting (now in Madrid).

Juan Carlos: Democratic Bourbon king who succeeded the dictator Franco in 1975.

OTAN: NATO

Republicanos: Supporters of Spain's democratically elected government during the Civil War, overthrown by Franco's fascists.

Nacionalistas: Supporters of Franco during the Civil War.

A Spanish Romance

Words of Love

I / me / you / we	yo / mi / tú / nosotros	yoh / mee / too / noh-**soh**-trohs
flirt	coquetear	koh-kay-tay-**ar**
kiss	beso	**bay**-soh
hug	abrazo	ah-**brah**-thoh
love	amor	ah-**mor**
make love	hacer el amor	ah-**thehr** ehl ah-**mor**
condom	preservativo	pray-sehr-bah-**tee**-boh
contraceptive	anticonceptivo	ahn-tee-kohn-thayp-**tee**-boh
safe sex	sexo sin peligro	**sehk**-soh seen pay-**lee**-groh
sexy	sexy	"sexy"
romantic	romántico	roh-**mahn**-tee-koh
honey	cariño[a]	kah-**reen**-yoh
my angel	mi ángel	mee **ahn**-hayl
my love	mi amor	mee ah-**mor**
my heaven	mi cielo	mee thee-**ay**-loh

Ah, Amor

What's the matter?	¿Qué le pasa?	kay lay **pah**-sah
Nothing.	Nada.	**nah**-dah
I am / Are you...?	Soy / ¿Eres...?	soy / **ay**-rays
...straight	...heterosexual	ay-tay-roh-sehk-soo-**ahl**
...gay	...homosexual	oh-moh-sehk-soo-**ahl**
...bisexual	...bisexual	bee-sehk-soo-**ahl**
...undecided	...indeciso[a]	een-day-**thee**-soh
...prudish	...prudente	proo-**dehn**-tay

CHATTING

I am / Are you...?	Estoy / ¿Estás...?	ay-**stoy** / ay-**stahs**
...horny	...caliente	kahl-**yehn**-tay
We are on our honeymoon.	Estamos de luna de miel.	ay-**stah**-mohs day **loo**-nah day mee-**ehl**
I have...	Tengo...	**tayn**-goh
...a boyfriend.	...un novio.	oon **noh**-bee-oh
...a girlfriend.	...una novia.	**oo**-nah **noh**-bee-ah
I'm married.	Estoy casado[a].	ay-**stoy** kah-**sah**-doh
I'm married (but...)	Estoy casado[a] (pero...)	ay-**stoy** kah-**sah**-doh (**pay**-roh)
I'm not married.	No estoy casado[a].	noh ay-**stoy** kah-**sah**-doh
Do you have a boyfriend / girlfriend?	¿Tienes novio / novia?	tee-**ehn**-ays **noh**-bee-oh / **noh**-bee-ah
I'm adventurous.	Soy aventurero.	soy ah-behn-too-**ray**-roh
I'm lonely (tonight).	Me siento solo[a] (esta noche).	may see-**ehn**-toh **soh**-loh (**ay**-stah **noh**-chay)
I'm rich and single.	Soy rico[a] y soltero[a].	soy **ree**-koh ee sohl-**tay**-roh
Do you mind if I sit here?	¿Te importa si me siento aquí?	tay eem-**por**-tah see may see-**ehn**-toh ah-**kee**
Would you like a drink?	¿Te gustaría tomar algo?	tay goo-stah-**ree**-ah toh-**mar ahl**-goh
Will you go out with me?	¿Quieres salir conmigo?	kee-**ehr**-ehs sah-**leer** kohn-**mee**-goh
Would you like to go out tonight for...?	¿Te gustaría salir esta noche para...?	tay goo-stah-**ree**-ah sah-**leer ay**-stah **noh**-chay **pah**-rah
...a walk	...dar un paseo	dar oon pah-**say**-oh
...dinner	...cenar	thay-**nar**
...a drink	...tomar algo	toh-**mar ahl**-goh
Where's the best place to dance nearby?	¿Dónde hay un lugar para bailar cerca?	**dohn**-day ī oon loo-**gar pah**-rah bī-**lar thehr**-kah
Do you want to dance?	¿Quieres bailar?	kee-**ehr**-ehs bī-**lar**
Again?	¿Otra vez?	**oh**-trah bayth

English	Spanish	Pronunciation
Let's celebrate!	¡Vamos a celebrarlo!	**bah**-mohs ah thay-lay-**brar**-loh
Let's have a wild and crazy night!	¡Tengamos una noche loca y divertida!	tayn-**gah**-mohs **oo**-nah **noh**-chay **loh**-kah ee dee-behr-**tee**-dah
I have no diseases.	No tengo enfermedades.	noh **tayn**-goh ayn-fehr-may-**dah**-days
I have many diseases.	Tengo muchas enfermedades.	**tayn**-goh **moo**-chahs ayn-fehr-may-**dah**-days
I have only safe sex.	Sólo practico sexo sin peligro.	**soh**-loh **prahk**-tee-koh **sehk**-soh seen pay-**lee**-groh
Can I take you home?	¿Puedo acompañarte a casa?	**pway**-doh ah-kohm-pahn-**yar**-tay ah **kah**-sah
Why not?	¿Por qué no?	por kay noh
How can I change your mind?	¿Cómo puedo convencerte?	**koh**-moh **pway**-doh kohn-behn-**thehr**-tay
Kiss me.	Bésame.	**bay**-sah-may
May I kiss you?	¿Puedo besarte?	**pway**-doh bay-**sar**-tay
Kiss me more.	Bésame más.	**bay**-sah-may mahs
Can I see you again?	¿Te puedo volver a ver?	tay **pway**-doh bohl-**behr** ah behr
Your place or mine?	¿Tu casa o la mía?	too **kah**-sah oh lah **mee**-ah
How does this feel?	¿Qué sientes?	kay see-**ehn**-tays
Is this an aphrodisiac?	¿Es esto un afrodisíaco?	ays **ay**-stoh oon ah-froh-dee-**see**-ah-koh
This is (not) my first time.	Ésta (no) es mi primera vez.	**ay**-stah (noh) ays mee pree-**may**-rah bayth
You are my most beautiful souvenir.	Tú eres mi mejor recuerdo.	too **ay**-rays mee may-**hor** ray-**kwehr**-doh
Do you do this often?	¿Haces esto muy a menudo?	**ah**-thays **ay**-stoh **moo**-ee ah may-**noo**-doh
How's my breath?	¿Me huele el aliento?	may **way**-lay ehl ah-**yehn**-toh
Let's just be friends.	Vamos a dejarlo como amigos.	**bah**-mohs ah day-**har**-loh **koh**-moh ah-**mee**-gohs

CHATING

I'll pay for my share.	Pagaré mi parte.	pah-gah-**ray** mee **par**-tay
Would you like	¿Te gustaría	tay goo-stah-**ree**-ah
a massage...?	un masaje...?	oon mah-**sah**-hay
...for your back	...para tu	**pah**-rah too
	espalda	ay-**spahl**-dah
...for your feet	...por tus pies	por toos pee-**ays**
Why not?	¿Por qué no?	por kay noh
Try it.	Pruébalo.	proo-**ay**-bah-loh
It tickles.	Esto me hace	**ay**-stoh may **ah**-thay
	cosquillas.	koh-**skee**-yahs
Oh my God!	¡Dios mío!	**dee**-ohs **mee**-oh
I love you.	Te quiero.	tay kee-**ehr**-oh
Darling, will you	¿Querida, te	kay-**ree**-dah tay
marry me?	casarás	kah-sah-**rahs**
	conmigo?	kohn-**mee**-goh

DICTIONARY

Spanish/English

You'll see some of the words in the dictionary listed like this: *agresivo[a]*. Use the *a* ending (pronounced "ah") if you're talking about a female.

A

a	to, at	acceso a Internet	Internet access
a través	through		
abajo	down; below	acceso de silla de ruedas	wheelchair-accessible
abierto	open (adj)		
abogado[a]	lawyer	accidente	accident
aborto	abortion	aceite	oil (n)
aborto espontáneo	miscarriage	acondicionador	conditioner (hair)
abridor de latas	can opener	acuerdo, de	agree
abril	April	adaptador eléctrico	electrical adapter
abrir	open (v)		
Abstracto	abstract	adiós	goodbye
abuela	grandmother	aduana	customs
abuelo	grandfather	adulto	adult
abusar	abuse (v)	aeropuerto	airport
acantilado	cliff	afeitar	shave (v)

213

afeitar, maquinilla de	razor	almohada	pillow
agencia de viajes	travel agency	alquilar	rent (v)
agnóstico[a]	agnostic	altar	altar
agosto	August	alto[a]	tall; high
agotado[a]	exhausted	amable	kind; nice; helpful
agresivo[a]	aggressive	amanecer	sunrise
agrio	sour	amante	lover
agua	water	amar	love (v)
agua del grifo	tap water	amarillo	yellow
agua mineral	mineral water	ambulancia	ambulance
agua potable	drinkable water	amigo[a]	friend
aguja	needle	amistad	friendship
agujero	hole	amor	love (n)
ahora	now	analgésico	pain killer
aire	air	andar	walk (v)
aire acondicionado	air-conditioned	andén	platform (train)
al natural	plain	animal de casa	pet (n)
ala	wing	año	year
albergue de juventud	youth hostel	antepasado[a]	ancestor
		antes	before
albornoz	bathrobe	antiácido	antacid
alcazaba	Moorish castle	antibiótico	antibiotic
alcazar	Moorish fortress / palace	anticonceptivos	contraceptives
		anticuarios	antiques shop
aldea	village	antigüedades	antiques
alegría	happiness	antiguo	ancient
Alemania	Germany	aparcamiento	parking lot
alergias	allergies	aparcar	park (v)
alérgico[a]	allergic	apartamento	apartment
alfiler	pin	aperitivos	appetizers
alfombra	carpet; rug	apodo	nickname
algo	some	aprender	learn
algodón	cotton	apresurarse	hurry (v)
alguna cosa	something	apretado	tight
alicates	pliers	aproximadamente	approximately
aliento	breath	apuntar	point (v)

aquí	here	ayudar	help (v)
araña	spider	azul	blue
árbol	tree	azulejo	Moorish blue tile
arco iris	rainbow		
área para jugar	playground	**B**	
arreglar	repair	babero	bib
arriba	up	bailar	dance (v)
arriba, de	upstairs	bajar	download
arroba	at sign (@)	bajo	low
arroyo	stream (n)	balcón	balcony
arte	art	baloncesto	basketball
artesanía	crafts	balsa	raft
artista	artist	bañador	swim trunks
artritis	arthritis	banco	bank
ascensor	elevator	bandera	flag
asegurado[a]	insured	bañera	bathtub
asiento	seat	baño	bathroom; bath
asiento alto	booster seat	barato	cheap
asiento para	car seat (baby)	barba	beard
el coche		barbería	barber shop
asma	asthma	barbero	barber
aspirina	aspirin	barca de pedales	paddleboat
atascado	stuck	barco	boat
ateo[a]	atheist	barco de vela	sailboat
atleta	athlete	barra de labios	lipstick
atractivo[a]	attractive	base para la cara	foundation
atravesar	go through		(makeup)
audioguía	audioguide	batería	battery
auténtico	genuine	bebé	baby
autobús	bus, city	bebé, comida para	baby food
autocar	bus, long-distance	beber	drink (v)
autopista	highway	bebida	drink (n)
auto-servicio	self-service	béisbol	baseball
auto-stop, hacer	hitchhike	Bélgica	Belgium
avión	plane	beso	kiss (n)
ayer	yesterday	biblioteca	library
ayuda	help (n)	bicicleta	bicycle

bienvenido	welcome
bigote	moustache
billete	ticket
blanco	white
boca	mouth
bocadillo	sandwich
boda	wedding
bodega	cellar
bolígrafo	pen
bolsa	bag; purse
bolsa de cremallera	zip-lock bag
bolsa de plástica	plastic bag
bolsillo	pocket
bomba	bomb
bomba de aire	pump (n)
bombilla	light bulb
bonito[a]	pretty, beautiful
borracho[a]	drunk
borrador	eraser
borrar	delete
botas	boots
bote	can (n); rowboat
botella	bottle
botón	button
bragas	panties
brazalete	bracelet
brazo	arm
brocha	blush (makeup)
broche	brooch
bronce	bronze
bronceado	suntan (n)
bronceador	tanning lotion
bueno	good
buenos días	good day (hello)
bufanda	scarf
bujías	sparkplugs
burro	donkey

C

caballería	knights
caballero	gentleman
caballo	horse
caballo, montar a	horse riding
cabeza	head
cabeza, dolor de	headache
cabina telefónica	phone booth
cacao de labios	lip salve
cada	each
caer	fall (v)
café	coffee
café de Internet	Internet café
cafetería	coffee shop
caja	box
cajera	cashier
cajero automático	cash machine
calabozo	dungeon
calambres	cramps
calcetines	socks
calendario	calendar
calidad	quality
caliente	warm (adj)
calle	street
calor	heat (n)
caloría	calorie
calzoncillo	slip
calzoncillos	underpants
cama	bed
cámara	camera
cámara de vídeo	video camera
camarera	waitress

camarero	waiter	carterista	pickpocket
cambiar	change (v);	casa	house
	transfer (v)	casa, animal de	pet (n)
cambio	change (n);	casado[a]	married
	exchange (n)	cascada	waterfall
camisa	shirt; blouse	casete	tape (cassette)
camiseta	T-shirt	casilleros	lockers
camisón	nightgown	castillo	castle
campanas	bells	catedral	cathedral
campeonato	championship	católico[a]	Catholic
camping	camping; campsite	catre	cot
campo	countryside; field	cena	dinner
Canadá	Canada	cenicero	ashtray
canal	channel; canal	centro	center; downtown
canasta	basket	centro	shopping mall
cancelar	cancel	comercial	
canción	song	cepillo de dientes	toothbrush
candela	candle	cepillo del pelo	hairbrush
canguro,	babysitting service	cerámica	ceramic
servicio de		cerca	near
canoa	canoe	cerdo	pig; pork
cansado[a]	tired	cerillas	matches
cantante	singer	cero	zero
cantar	sing	cerrado	closed
capilla	chapel	cerradura	lock (n)
capitán	captain	cerrar	lock (v)
cara	face	cerveza	beer
caramelo	candy	chaleco	vest
caravana	camper (R.V.)	champú	shampoo
carne	meat	chanquetas	flip-flops
carne de vaca	beef	chaqueta	jacket
caro	expensive	charcutería	delicatessen
carrecoche	stroller	cheque	check
carta	letter	cheque	traveler's check
carta postal	postcard	de viajero	
cartel	poster	chica	girl
cartera	wallet	chicle	gum

chico	boy	codo	elbow
chino	Chinese (adj)	coger	take; catch (v)
chiste	joke (n)	colegio	school
chupete	pacifier	colina	hill
Churrigueresco	Spanish Baroque	collar	necklace
		colocado[a]	stoned
cielo	sky; heaven	colores	colors
ciencia	science	comenzar	begin
científico[a]	scientist	comer	eat
cigarrillo	cigarette	comezón	itch (n)
cine	cinema	comida	food
cinta	tape (cassette)	comida para bebé	baby food
cinta adhesiva	tape (adhesive)	cómo	how
cintura	waist	cómodo	cozy; comfortable
cinturón	belt	completo	no vacancy
cita	appointment	complicado	complicated
ciudad	city	compras	shopping
claro	clear	compresas	sanitary napkins
clase	class	computadora	computer
clase, primera	first class	con	with
clase, segunda	second class	concha	shell
Clásico	classical	concierto	concert
claustro	cloister	conducir	drive (v)
clave, número	PIN code	conductor	driver; conductor
clínica	medical clinic	conejo	rabbit
clip	paper clip	confirmar	confirm
cobre	copper	congestión	congestion (sinus)
coche	car; train car	construcción	construction
coche cama	sleeper (train)	contador	accountant
coche comedor	dining car (train)	contagioso	contagious
		contento[a]	happy
cocido	boiled	copia	copy
cocina	kitchen	corazón	heart
cocinar	cook (v)	corcho	cork
código	PIN code	cordero	lamb
		cordón	string
código postal	zip code	cordón para ropa	clothesline

cordones	shoelaces
coro	choir
correa del ventilador	fan belt
correcto[a]	right (correct)
correo	mail (n)
correo aéreo	air mail
correo electrónico	e-mail
correr	run (v)
corrida de toros	bullfight
corrupción	corruption
corta uñas	nail clipper
corte de pelo	haircut
corto[a]	short
cosa	thing
cosa, alguna	something
costa	coast
crema de manos	hand lotion
crema de primera ayuda	first-aid cream
cremallera	zipper
cripta	crypt
cristiano[a]	Christian
crudo	raw
cruz	cross
cuaderno	notebook
cuándo	when
cuánto	how many
cuánto cuesta	how much ($)
cuarta parte	quarter (1/4)
cubo	bucket
cucaracha	cockroach
cuchara	spoon
cuchillo	knife
cuello	neck
cuenta	bill (payment)
cuerda	rope
cuero	leather

cuerpo	body
cueva	cave
cuidadoso	careful
culpable	guilty
cumpleaños	birthday
cúpula	dome

D

dar	give
de	of; from
de acuerdo	agree
de arriba	upstairs
de ida	one way (ticket)
de repente	suddenly
debajo	under
declarar	declare (customs)
dedo	finger
dedo del pie	toe
delgado[a]	skinny
demasiado	too (much)
democracia	democracy
dentición	teething (baby)
dentista	dentist
deporte	sport
depósito	deposit
derecha	right (direction)
derecho	straight
desafortunado	unfortunate
desayuno	breakfast
descongestinante	decongestant
descuento	discount
desear	wish (v)
desinfectante	disinfectant
desnudo[a]	naked
desodarante	deodorant

despacio[a]	slow
despertador	alarm clock
despertarse	wake up
después	after; afterwards
destornillador	screwdriver
desvío	detour
detergente	laundry detergent
detrás	behind
día	day
diabético[a]	diabetic
diafragma	diaphragm (birth control)
diamante	diamond
diapositiva	slide (photo)
diarrea	diarrhea
días, buenos	good day (hello)
diccionario	dictionary
diciembre	December
diente	tooth
difícil	difficult
dificultad	trouble
dinero	money
Dios	God
dirección	address; direction
dirección de correo electrónico	e-mail address
dirección única	one way (street)
directo	direct
director	manager
disculpa	apology
discutir	fight (v)
disfrutar	enjoy
diversión	fun
divertido[a]	funny
divorciado[a]	divorced
doble	double
docena	dozen

doctor[a]	doctor
dolor	pain
dolor de cabeza	headache
dolor de estómago	stomachache
dolor de garganta	sore throat
dolor de la menstruación	menstrual cramps
dolor de muelas	toothache
dolor de oído	earache
dolor de pecho	chest pains
domingo	Sunday
dónde	where
dormir	sleep (v)
dormitorio	dormitory
ducha	shower
dueño[a]	owner
dulce	sweet

E

edad	age
edad, la tercera	seniors
edificio	building
educación	education
efectivo	cash
ejemplo	example
ejército	military
él	he
ella	she
ellos	they
embajada	embassy
embarazada	pregnant
embarazo	pregnancy
embarazoso	embarrassing
emergencia	emergency
empleo, sin	unemployed
empujar	push

en	in; by (via)
en vez de	instead
encaje	lace
encendedor	lighter (n)
encierro	bull run
encima	above
enero	January
enfadado[a]	angry
enfermedad	disease
enfermedad venérea	venereal disease
enfermero[a]	nurse
enfermo[a]	sick
enlace	connection (train)
enseñar	show (v)
entender	understand
entrada	entrance
entrada	entrance (road)
entrada al metro	subway entrance
envenenamiento de comida	food poisoning
enviar	send
envolver	wrap (v)
epilepsia	epilepsy
equipaje	baggage
equipaje de mano	carry-on luggage
equipo	team
error	mistake
erupción	rash
es	is
escalera de mano	ladder
escaleras	stairs
escalofríos	chills
escandaloso	scandalous
Escandinavia	Scandinavia

escozor del pañal	diaper rash
escribir	write
escuchar	listen
escultor[a]	sculptor
escultura	sculpture
esmalte de uñas	nail polish
espalda	back
España	Spain
especialidad	specialty
espectáculo	show (n)
espejo	mirror
esperanza	hope
esperar	wait (v)
esposa	wife
espuma de afeitar	shaving cream
esquí	skiing
esquí acuático	waterskiing
esquiar	ski (v)
esquina	corner
esta noche	tonight
estacas de tienda	tent pegs
estación	station
estación de autobuses	bus station
estación de metro	subway station
estado	state
Estados Unidos	United States
este	east
estilo	style
estomago	stomach
estómago, dolor de	stomachache
estornudo	sneeze (n)
estrecho	narrow
estrella	star (in sky)

estreñimiento	constipation
estudiante	student
estúpido[a]	stupid
Europa	Europe
exactamente	exactly
excelente	excellent
excepto	except
explicar	explain
extranjero[a]	foreign
extraño[a]	strange

F

fábrica	factory
fácil	easy
facturar el equipaje	baggage check
falda	skirt
falso	false
familia	family
famoso[a]	famous
fantástico[a]	fantastic
farmacia	pharmacy
faros	headlights
favor, por	please
febrero	February
felicidades	congratulations
feliz	happy
femenino	female
feo[a]	ugly
ferretería	hardware store
ferrocarril	railway
festival	festival
festivo	holiday
ficha	token
fiebre	fever
fiebre del heno	hay fever

fiesta	party
firma	signature
flash	flash (camera)
flor	flower
floristería	flower market
fondo	bottom
footing	jogging
foso	moat
foto	photo
fotocopia	photocopy
fotocopias	photocopy shop
frágil	fragile
Francia	France
frenos	brakes
fresco	fresh; cool
frío	cold (adj)
frontera	border
fruta	fruit
fuego	fire
fuegos artificiales	fireworks
fuente	fountain
fuerte	strong
fumador	smoker
fumadores	smoking
fusibles	fuses
fútbol	soccer
fútbol americano	American football
futuro	future

G

gafas	glasses (eye)
gafas de sol	sunglasses
galería	gallery
galería de arte	art gallery
garaje	garage
garantía	guarantee

garganta	throat
garganta, dolor de	sore throat
garrafa	carafe
gasa	gauze
gaseoso	fizzy
gasolinera	gas station
gastar	spend
gato	cat
gemelos	twins
generoso[a]	generous
gente	people
Gilete	razor
gimnasia	gymnastics
ginecólogo[a]	gynecologist
glorieta	roundabout
gordo[a]	fat (adj)
gorro	cap
gotas	cough drops
para la tos	
Gótico	Gothic
gracias	thanks
gramática	grammar
Gran Bretaña	Great Britain
grande	big
grandes	department store
almacenes	
granja	farm
granjero[a]	farmer
grapadora	stapler
grasa	fat (n)
grasiento	greasy
gratis	free (no cost)
Grecia	Greece
grifo	faucet
gripe	flu
gris	gray
grúa	tow truck

grueso	thick
guantes	gloves
guapo[a]	handsome
guardar	keep (v);
	save (computer)
guerra	war
guía	guide; guidebook
guía, visita con	guided tour
guión	hyphen (-)
guitarra	guitar
gustar	like (v)

H

habitación	room
habitaciónes	vacancy sign
hablar	talk; speak
hacer	make (v)
hacer auto-stop	hitchhike
hachís	hash (drug)
hambriento[a]	hungry
hecho en casa	homemade
helado	ice cream
hemorroides	hemorrhoids
herido[a]	injured
hermana	sister
hermano	brother
hidratante	moisturizer
hidroplano	hydrofoil
hielo	ice
hija	daughter
hijo	son
hilo	thread
hinchazón	swelling (n)
historia	history
hola	hello
Holanda	Netherlands
hombre	man

hombres	men
hombros	shoulder
homosexual	gay
honesto[a]	honest
hongos en los pies	athlete's foot
hora	hour
horario	timetable
horas de apertura	opening hours
horno	oven
horrible	horrible
hoy	today
húmedo	muggy
humo	smoke

I

ida y vuelta	roundtrip
ida, de	one way (ticket)
iglesia	church
imperdible	safety pin
impermeable	raincoat
importado	imported
importante	important
imposible	impossible
Impresionista	Impressionist
imprimir	print
impuesto	tax
incluido	included
inconsciente	unconscious
increíble	incredible
independiente	independent
indigestión	indigestion
industria	industry
infección	infection
infección urinaria	urinary infection

inflamación	inflammation
información	information
ingeniero	engineer
inglés	English
inmediatamente	immediately
inocente	innocent
insecto	insect
insolación	sunstroke
instante	instant
inteligente	intelligent
interesante	interesting
interior	inside
intermitente	turn signal
intersección	intersection
intestinos	intestines
invierno	winter
invitación	invitation
invitado[a]	guest
ir	go
Irlanda	Ireland
isla	island
Italia	Italy
izquierda	left (direction)

J

jabón	soap
jaqueca	migraine
jardín	garden
jardineria	gardening
jefe	boss
joven	young; teenager
jóvenes	youths
joyas	jewelry
joyería	jewelry shop
jubilado[a]	retired
judío[a]	Jewish
juego	game

jueves	Thursday
jugar	play (v)
juguete	toy
juguetería	toy store
julio	July
junio	June
juntos	together
justo	fair (just)
juventude	youth

K

kiosco	newsstand

L

la tarde	evening
la tercera edad	seniors
labio	lip
ladrón	thief
lago	lake
lana	wool
lápiz	pencil
lápiz de ojos	eyeliner
lástima, que	it's a pity
latón	brass
lavabo	sink
lavadora	washer
lavandería	launderette
lavar	wash
laxativo	laxative
leche	milk, baby formula
lejos	far
lenguaje	language
lentillas	contact lenses
libre	vacant
libre de impuestos	duty free
librería	book shop
libro	book

limpiadora de cara	face cleanser
limpiaparabrisas	windshield wipers
limpio[a]	clean (adj)
línea aérea	airline
lino	linen
linterna	flashlight
liquido de insectos	insect repellant
líquido de transmisión	transmission fluid
lista	list
listo[a]	ready
litera	berth (train); bunk beds
litro	liter
llamada gratuita	toll-free
llave	key
llegadas	arrivals
llegar	arrive
llevar	carry
llevar, para	take out (food)
llorar	cry (v)
lluvia	rain (n)
lo siento	sorry; excuse me
local	local
luces de atrás	tail lights
lujoso[a]	charming
luna	moon
luna de miel	honeymoon
lunar	moleskin
lunes	Monday
luz	light (n)
luz del sol	sunshine

M

macho	macho
madera	wood
madre	mother
maduro	ripe
magnífico[a]	great
malentendido	misunderstanding
maleta	suitcase
malo[a]	bad
mamá	mom
mañana	morning; tomorrow
mañana, pasado	day after tomorrow
mandíbula	jaw
mangas	sleeves
mano	hand
mano, equipaje de	carry-on luggage
manta	blanket
manzana	apple; block (street)
mapa	map
maquillaje	makeup
maquinilla de afeitar	razor
mar	sea
marido	husband
marihuana	marijuana
marisco	seafood
mármol	marble (material)
marrón	brown
Marruecos	Morocco
martes	Tuesday
marzo	March
más	more
más tarde	later
máscara	mascara

masculino	male
matar	kill
máximo	maximum
mayo	May
mecánico[a]	mechanic
mediano	medium
medianoche	midnight
medias	nylons (panty hose)
medicina	medicine
medicina para el resfriado	cold medicine
medicina para la diarrea	diarrhea medicine
Medieval	medieval
mediodía	noon
mejor	best
menstruación	menstruation
menstruación, dolor de la	menstrual cramps
mentiras	lies
menú	menu
mercado	market
mercado municipal	open-air market
mes	month
mesa	table
metal	metal
metro	subway
mezquita	mosque
mi	my
miedoso[a]	afraid
miércoles	Wednesday
mínimo	minimum
minusvalido[a]	handicapped
minutos	minutes
mirar	look
misa	mass

mismo	same
mixto	mix (n)
mochila	backpack
moda	fashion
modem	modem
Modernista	Art Nouveau
moderno	modern
mojado	wet
molestar	disturb
momento	moment
monasterio	monastery
monedas	coins
montaña	mountain
montar a caballo	horse riding
monumento	monument
morado	purple
morir	die
Moriscos	Moors
Moros	Moorish
morriña	homesick
mosca	fly (n); bug
moto	motorcycle
motocicleta	motor scooter
móvil, teléfono	cell phone
mozárabe	Christian under Moorish rule (Mozarab)
mucho	much; many
Mudéjar	Gothic-Islamic (post-Reconquest Moorish)
muebles	furniture
muelas, dolor de	toothache
muerto[a]	dead
mujer	woman
mujeres	women
multitud	crowd (n)
mundo	world
muñeca	wrist; doll

músculo	muscle
museo	museum
música	music
muslo	thigh
musulmán[a]	Muslim
muy	very

N

nacionalidad	nationality
nada	nothing
nadar	swim
naipe	cards (deck)
nalgas	buttocks
naranja	orange (color or fruit)
nariz	nose
natural	natural
naturaleza	nature
náusea	nausea
Navidad	Christmas
necesario	necessary
necesitar	need
negocio	business
negro	black
nervioso[a]	nervous
nieble	fog
nieta	granddaughter
nieto	grandson
nilón	nylon (material)
niñera	babysitter
niño[a]	child
niños	children
no	no; not
no fumadores	non-smoking
noche	night
noche, esta	tonight
Nolotil	non-aspirin substitute

nombre	name
normal	normal
norte	north
nosotros	we; us
noviembre	November
nuboso	cloudy
nuevo	new
número clave	PIN code
nunca	never

O

o	or
océano	ocean
octubre	October
ocupado	occupied
odiar	hate
oeste	west
oficina	office
oficio	occupation
oído, dolor de	earache
oír	hear
ojo	eye
Olimpíada	Olympics
olla	kettle
olor	smell (n)
olvidar	forget
ópera	opera
óptico	optician
oreja	ear
órgano	organ
original	original
oro	gold
oscuro	dark
otoño	autumn
otra vez	again
otro	other; another

P

padre	father
padres	parents
pagar	pay
página	page
página de la red	Web site
país	country
pájaro	bird
palabra	word
palacio	palace
palillo	toothpick
pan	bread
panadería	bakery
pañal	diaper
pantalones	pants
pantalones cortos	shorts
pañuelos (de papel)	facial tissue
papá	dad
Papá Noel	Santa Claus
papel	paper
papel higiénico	toilet paper
papelería	office supplies store
paquete	package
para	for
para llevar	take out (food)
parada	stop (n)
parada de autobús	bus stop
paraguas	umbrella
parar	stop (v)
pared fortificada	fortified wall
parque	park (garden)
parque para niños	playpen
pasado	past

pasado mañana	day after tomorrow	**periódico**	newspaper
		período	period (of time)
pasajero[a]	passenger	**pero**	but
pasaporte	passport	**perro**	dog
pasatiempo	hobby	**persona**	person
Pascua	Easter	**pesado**	heavy
pasillo	aisle	**pescado**	fish (n)
pasta de dientes	toothpaste	**pescar**	fish (v)
pastelería	pastry shop	**peso**	weight
patinaje	skating	**picnic**	picnic
patines	roller skates	**pie**	foot
paz	peace	**piel**	skin
peage	toll	**pierna**	leg
peatón	pedestrian	**pijamas**	pajamas
pecho	chest; breast	**píldora**	pill
pecho, dolor de	chest pains	**píldora**	birth control pill
pedazo	piece	**anticonceptiva**	
pedir prestado	borrow	**pincho**	snack
peine	comb (n)	**pintura**	painting
pelea	fight (n)	**pinzas**	clothes pins
película	movie	**pinzas**	tweezers
peligro	danger	**piscina**	swimming pool
peligroso	dangerous	**pistola**	gun
pelo	hair	**planta**	plant; story (floor)
pelota	ball	**plástico**	plastic
peltre	pewter	**plata**	silver
peluquería	beauty salon	**Plateresco**	Plateresque (frilly late Gothic)
pendientes	earrings		
pene	penis	**plato**	plate
pensar	think	**plato hondo**	bowl
peor	worst	**playa**	beach
pequeño	little	**plaza**	square (town)
pequeño[a]	small	**plaza del toros**	bullring
percha	coat hanger	**pobre**	poor
perdido[a]	lost	**poco**	few
perezoso[a]	lazy	**poder**	can (v); power
perfecto	perfect (adj)	**poderoso[a]**	powerful

podrido	rotten
policía	police
poliester	polyester
políticos	politicians
pollo	chicken
polución	pollution
polvos de talco	talcum powder
polvos para la cara	face powder
por favor	please
por qué	why
porcelana	porcelain
porciento	percent
porque	because
porro	joint (marijuana)
poseer	own (v)
posible	possible
postre	dessert
práctico[a]	practical
precio	price
pregunta	question (n)
preguntar	ask
prescripción	prescription
preservativo	condom
prestar	lend
primavera	spring (n)
primera clase	first class
primero	first
primeros auxilios	first aid
primo[a]	cousin
principal	main
privado	private
probar	taste (try)
problema	problem
problemas de corazón	heart condition

profesión	profession
profesor	teacher
prohibido	forbidden
pronto	soon
pronunciacion	pronunciation
prosperar	prosper
protección de sol	sunscreen
protestante	Protestant
próximo[a]	next
prueba de embarazo	pregnancy test
público	public
pueblo	town
puente	bridge
puerta	door
puerto	harbor
puesta de sol	sunset
pulga	flea
pulmones	lungs
pulmonía	pneumonia
púlpito	pulpit
pulso	pulse
punto	dot (computer)
puntual	on time

Q

qué	what
que lástima	it's a pity
qué, por	why
quejarse	complain
quemadura	burn (n); sunburn
querer	want
queso	cheese
quién	who
quiosco	newsstand
quitaesmaltes	nail polish remover

R

rabo	tail
racismo	racism
radiador	radiator
rastro	flea market
rayos x	X-ray
rebajas	sale
recado	message
recambio	refill (n)
recepcionista	receptionist
receta	recipe
recibir	receive
recibo	receipt
reclamar el equipaje	baggage claim
recomendar	recommend
recordar	remember
recto	rectum
reembolso	refund (n)
refugiados	refugees
regalo	gift
regla	rule; period (woman's)
reina	queen
reír	laugh (v)
relajación	relaxation
relajar	relax
religión	religion
reliquia	relic
reloj	clock; watch (n)
Renacimiento	Renaissance
repente, de	suddenly
República Checa	Czech Republic
resbaladizo	slippery
reserva	reservation
reservar	reserve
resfriado	cold (n)
respetar	respect (v)
respeto	respect (n)
respuesta	answer
retraso	delay (n)
revista	magazine
rey	king
rico[a]	rich
río	river
robado	robbed
robusto	sturdy
roca	rock (n)
rodaja	slice
rodilla	knee
rojo	red
Románico	Romanesque
Romántico	Romantic
romántico[a]	romantic
roncar	snore
ropa	clothes
rosa	pink
roto	broken
rozaduras	blisters
rubio[a]	blond
rueda	tire (n)
rueda	wheel
ruidoso[a]	loud
ruinas	ruins
Rusia	Russia

S

sábado	Saturday
sábana	sheet
saber	know
sabor	flavor (n)
sacacorchos	corkscrew
sacerdote	priest

DICTIONARY

Spanish / English

saco de dormir	sleeping bag
sala	hall (big room)
sala de espera	waiting room
salida	exit
salida de emergencia	emergency exit
salida de metro	subway exit
salidas	departures
salir	leave
saltar	jump
salud	health
¡Salud!	Cheers!
salvaje	wild
sandalias	sandals
sangrar	bleeding
sangre	blood
sano	healthy
santo[a]	saint
sdelicioso	delicious
secadora	dryer
secar	dry (v)
seco	dry (adj)
secreto	secret
seda	silk
seda dental	dental floss
sediento[a]	thirsty
segunda clase	second class
segundo	second
seguro	insurance
seguro médico	health insurance
seguro[a]	safe
sello	stamp
semáforo	stoplight
semana	week
señal	sign
sencillo	simple

Señor	Mr.
señor	sir
Señora	Mrs.
señoras	ladies
Señorita	Miss
separado	separate
septiembre	September
serio	serious
servicio	service
servicio	service
servicio de canguro	babysitting service
servicios	toilet
servilleta	napkin
sexo	sex
sexy	sexy
si	if
sí	yes
SIDA	AIDS
siempre	always
siglo	century
siguiente	next
silencio	silence
silla	chair
silla para niños	highchair
similar	similar
sin	without
sin empleo	unemployed
sinagoga	synagogue
sintético	synthetic
sinusitis	sinus problems
sobre	on; envelope
sobrina	niece
sobrino	nephew
sol	sun
sol, tomar el	sunbathe
soleado	sunny

sólo	only	tarjeta	card
solo[a]	alone	tarjeta de crédito	credit card
soltero[a]	single	tarjeta de visita	business card
sombra	shade	tarjeta telefónica	telephone card
sombra de ojos	eye shadow		
sombrero	hat	taxímetro	taxi meter
soñar	dream (v)	taza	cup
soñoliento[a]	sleepy	teatro	theater
sonrisa	smile (n)	techo	roof
sorpresa	surprise (n)	tejido	cloth
sortija	ring (n)	telefonista	operator
sótano	basement	teléfono	telephone
subraya	underscore (_)	teléfono móvil	cell phone
sucio	dirty	telivisión	television
sudar	sweat (v)	temer	fear (v)
sueño	dream (n)	temperatura	temperature
suerte	luck	templado	lukewarm
suéter	sweater	temprano	early
suficiente	enough	tenedor	fork
sufrir	suffer	tener	have
Suiza	Switzerland	tenis	tennis
sujetador	bra	tensión alta	high blood pressure
supermercado	grocery store		
suplemento	supplement	tercera edad	seniors
sur	south	terciopelo	velvet
surfista	surfer	terminado	over (finished)
		terminar	finish (v)
T		termómetro	thermometer
tabla de surf	surfboard	terrible	terrible
tal vez	maybe	terroristas	terrorists
talla	size	tesoro	treasury
tampones	tampons	testículos	testicles
tapón	sink stopper	tía	aunt
tapón de oidos	earplugs	tiempo	weather
tarde	late; afternoon	tienda	shop (n)
tarde, la	evening	tienda de campaña	tent
tarde, más	later	tienda de dulces	sweets shop

tienda de fotos	camera shop
tienda de ropa	clothing boutique
tienda de souvenirs	souvenir shop
tienda de teléfonos móviles	cell phone shop
tienda de vinos	wine shop
tierno	tender
tierra	earth
tijeras	scissors
tímido[a]	shy
tío	uncle
tirador	handle (n)
tirar	pull; throw
tirita	band-aid
toalla	towel
toallitas para la cara	facial tissue
tobillo	ankle
todo	every; everything
tomar	take; eat (v); drink (v)
tomar el sol	sunbathe
tormenta	storm
toro	bull
toros, corrida de	bullfight
toros, plaza del	bullring
torre	tower
tos	cough (n)
toser	cough (v)
total	total
trabajar	work (v)
trabajo	job; work (n)
tradicional	traditional
traducir	translate
tráfico	traffic
tragar	swallow (v)
traje de baño	swim suit
tranquilo[a]	quiet
transbordador	ferry
transbordo	transfer (n)
través, a	through
tren	train
trípode	tripod
triste	sad
tú	you (informal)
tubo de respiración	snorkel
túnel	tunnel
turista	tourist
Turquía	Turkey

U

último[a]	last
uña	fingernail
una vez	once
universidad	university
uretra	urethra
urgencias	emergency room
urgente	urgent
usar	use (v)
usted	you (formal)
útero	uterus

V

vaca	cow
vacaciones	vacation
vacío	empty
vagón	train car
validar	validate
válido	valid
valle	valley
vaqueros	jeans
vaselina	Vaseline

vaso	glass	**vista**	view
vegetariano[a]	vegetarian	**vitaminas**	vitamins
vegija	bladder	**viuda**	widow
velocidad	speed	**viudo**	widower
venda	bandage	**vivir**	live (v)
vendaje de apoyo	support bandage	**volar**	fly (v)
		vomitar	vomit
vender	sell	**voz**	voice
venir	come	**vuelo**	flight
ventana	window	**vuelta, ida y**	roundtrip
ventoso	windy		
ver	see	**Y**	
verano	summer	**y**	and
verde	green	**ya**	already
vértigo	dizziness	**yo**	I
vestido	dress (n)	**yodo**	iodine
vez	time (occurrence)		
vez de, en	instead	**Z**	
vez, otra	again	**zapatillas**	slippers
vez, una	once	**zapatillas de tenis**	tennis shoes
vía	track (train)		
viajante	traveler	**zapatos**	shoes
viajar	travel (v)	**zumo**	juice
viaje	trip; tour		
vida	life		
vídeo	video		
viejo[a]	old		
viento	wind		
viernes	Friday		
vigilar	watch (v)		
viñedo	vineyard		
vino	wine		
violación	rape (n)		
violencia	violence		
visita	visit (n)		
visita con guía	guided tour		
visitar	visit (v)		

English/Spanish

You'll see some of the words in the dictionary listed like this: *agresivo[a]*. Use the *a* ending (pronounced "ah") if you're talking about a female.

A

abortion	aborto	aisle	pasillo
above	encima	alarm clock	despertador
abstract	Abstracto	alcohol	alcohol
abuse (v)	abusar	allergic	alérgico[a]
accident	accidente	allergies	alergias
accountant	contador	alone	solo[a]
adapter, electrical	adaptador eléctrico	already	ya
address	dirección	altar	altar
address, e-mail	dirección de correo electrónico	always	siempre
		ambulance	ambulancia
adult	adulto	ancestor	antepasado[a]
afraid	miedoso[a]	ancient	antiguo
Africa	Africa	and	y
after	después	angry	enfadado[a]
afternoon	tarde	animal	animal
afterwards	después	ankle	tobillo
again	otra vez	another	otro
age	edad	answer	respuesta
aggressive	agresivo[a]	antacid	antiácido
agnostic	agnóstico[a]	antibiotic	antibiótico
agree	de acuerdo	antiques	antigüedades
AIDS	SIDA	antiques shop	anticuarios
air	aire	apartment	apartamento
air mail	correo aéreo	apology	disculpa
air-conditioned	aire acondicionado	appetizers	aperitivos
		appointment	cita
airline	línea aérea	approximately	aproximada-mente
airport	aeropuerto	April	abril

arm	brazo
arrivals	llegadas
arrive	llegar
art	arte
art gallery	galería de arte
Art Nouveau	Modernista
arthritis	artritis
artificial	artificial
artist	artista
ashtray	cenicero
ask	preguntar
aspirin	aspirina
asthma	asma
at	a
at sign (@)	arroba
atheist	ateo[a]
athlete	atleta
athlete's foot	hongos en los pies
attractive	atractivo[a]
audioguide	audioguía
August	agosto
aunt	tía
autumn	otoño

B

baby	bebé, niño[a]
baby booster seat	asiento alto
baby car seat	asiento para el coche
baby food	comida para bebé
baby formula	leche
babysitter	niñera
babysitting service	servicio de canguro
back	espalda
backpack	mochila

bad	malo[a]
bag	bolsa
bag, plastic	bolsa de plástica
bag, zip-lock	bolsa de cremallera
baggage	equipaje
baggage check	facturar el equipaje
baggage claim	reclamar el equipaje
bakery	panadería
balcony	balcón
ball	pelota
bandage	venda
bandage, support	vendaje de apoyo
band-aid	tirita
bank	banco
barber	barbero
barber shop	barbería
Baroque, Spanish	Churrigueresco
baseball	béisbol
basement	sótano
basket	canasta
basketball	baloncesto
bath	baño
bathrobe	albornoz
bathroom	baño
bathtub	bañera
battery	batería
beach	playa
beard	barba
beautiful	bonito[a]
beauty salon	peluquería
because	porque
bed	cama
bedroom	habitación

bedsheet	sábana	bomb	bomba
beef	carne de vaca	book	libro
beer	cerveza	book shop	librería
before	antes	booster seat	asiento alto
begin	comenzar	boots	botas
behind	detrás	border	frontera
Belgium	Bélgica	borrow	pedir prestado
bells	campanas	boss	jefe
below	abajo	bottle	botella
belt	cinturón	bottom	fondo
berth (train)	litera	boutique,	tienda de ropa
best	mejor	clothing	
bib	babero	bowl	plato hondo
bicycle	bicicleta	box	caja
big	grande	boy	chico
bill (payment)	cuenta	bra	sujetador
bird	pájaro	bracelet	brazalete
birth	píldora	brakes	frenos
control pills	anticonceptiva	brass	latón
birthday	cumpleaños	bread	pan
black	negro	breakfast	desayuno
bladder	vegija	breast	pecho
blanket	manta	breath	aliento
bleeding	sangrar	bridge	puente
blisters	rozaduras	Britain	Gran Bretaña
block (street)	manzana	broken	roto
blond	rubio[a]	bronze	bronce
blood	sangre	brooch	broche
blood	tensión alta	brother	hermano
pressure, high		brown	marrón
blouse	camisa	bucket	cubo
blue	azul	bugs	moscas
blue tile (Moorish)	azulejo	building	edificio
blush (makeup)	brocha	bulb	bombilla
boat	barco	bulb, light	bombilla
body	cuerpo	bull	toro
boiled	cocido	bull run	encierro

bullfight	corrida de toros
bullring	plaza del toros
bunk beds	litera
burn (n)	quemadura
bus station	estación de autobuses
bus stop	parada de autobús
bus, city	autobús
bus, long-distance	autocar
business	negocio
business card	tarjeta de visita
but	pero
buttocks	nalgas
button	botón
by (via)	en

C

calendar	calendario
calorie	caloría
camera	cámara
camera shop	tienda de fotos
camper	caravana
camping	camping
campsite	camping
can (n)	bote
can (v)	poder
can opener	abridor de latas
Canada	Canadá
canal	canal
cancel	cancelar
candle	candela
candy	caramelo
canoe	canoa
cap	gorro
captain	capitán
car	coche
car (train)	vagón, coche

car seat (baby)	asiento para el coche
car, dining (train)	coche comedor
car, sleeper (train)	coche cama
carafe	garrafa
card	tarjeta
card, telephone	tarjeta telefónica
cards (deck)	naipe
careful	cuidadoso
carpet	alfombra
carry	llevar
carry-on luggage	equipaje de mano
cash	efectivo
cash machine	cajero automático
cashier	cajera
cassette	cinta; casete
castle	castillo
castle (Moorish)	alcazaba
cat	gato
catch (v)	coger
cathedral	catedral
Catholic	católico[a]
cave	cueva
cell phone	teléfono móvil
cell phone shop	tienda de teléfonos móviles
cellar	bodega
center	centro
century	siglo
ceramic	cerámica
chair	silla
championship	campeonato
change (n)	cambio

English	Spanish
change (v)	cambiar
chapel	capilla
charming	lujoso[a]
cheap	barato
check	cheque
Cheers!	¡Salud!
cheese	queso
chest	pecho
chest pains	dolor de pecho
chicken	pollo
child	niño[a]
children	niños
chills	escalofríos
Chinese (adj)	chino
chocolate	chocolate
choir	coro
Christian	cristiano[a]
Christian under Moorish rule (Mozarab)	mozárabe
Christmas	Navidad
church	iglesia
church service	misa, servicio
cigarette	cigarrillo
cinema	cine
city	ciudad
class	clase
class, first	primera clase
class, second	segunda clase
classical	Clásico
clean (adj)	limpio[a]
clear	claro
cliff	acantilado
clinic, medical	clínica
clock	reloj
clock, alarm	despertador
cloister	claustro

English	Spanish
closed	cerrado
cloth	tejido
clothes	ropa
clothes pins	pinzas
clothesline	cordón para ropa
clothing boutique	tienda de ropa
cloudy	nuboso
coast	costa
coat hanger	percha
cockroach	cucaracha
coffee	café
coffee shop	cafetería
coins	monedas
cold (adj)	frío
cold (n)	resfriado
cold medicine	medicina para el resfriado
colors	colores
comb (n)	peine
come	venir
comfortable	cómodo[a]
compact disc	compact disc
complain	quejarse
complicated	complicado
computer	computadora
concert	concierto
conditioner (hair)	acondicionador
condom	preservativo
conductor	conductor
confirm	confirmar
congestion (sinus)	congestión
congratulations	felicidades
connection (train)	enlace

constipation	estreñimiento	cup	taza
construction	construcción	customs	aduana
contact lenses	lentillas	Czech Republic	República Checa
contagious	contagioso		
contraceptives	anticonceptivos	**D**	
cook (v)	cocinar		
cool	fresco	dad	papá
copper	cobre	dance (v)	bailar
copy	copia	danger	peligro
copy shop	fotocopias	dangerous	peligroso
cork	corcho	dark	oscuro
corkscrew	sacacorchos	dash (-)	guión
corner	esquina	daughter	hija
corridor	pasillo	day	día
corruption	corrupción	day after tomorrow	pasado mañana
cost	precio		
cot	catre	dead	muerto[a]
cotton	algodón	December	diciembre
cough (n)	tos	declare (customs)	declarar
cough (v)	toser	decongestant	descongestinante
cough drops	gotas para la tos		
country	país	delay (n)	retraso
countryside	campo	delete	borrar
cousin	primo[a]	delicatessen	charcutería
cow	vaca	delicious	delicioso
cozy	cómodo	democracy	democracia
crafts	artesanía	dental floss	seda dental
cramps	calambres	dentist	dentista
cramps, menstrual	dolor de la menstruación	deodorant	desodarante
		depart	salir
cream, first-aid	crema de primera ayuda	department store	grandes almacenes
credit card	tarjeta de crédito	departures	salidas
cross	cruz	deposit	depósito
crowd (n)	multitud	dessert	postre
cry (v)	llorar	detergent	detergente
crypt	cripta	detour	desvío

diabetes	diabetes
diabetic	diabético[a]
diamond	diamante
diaper	pañal
diaper rash	escozor del pañal
diaphragm (birth control)	diafragma
diarrhea	diarrea
diarrhea medicine	medicina para la diarrea
dictionary	diccionario
die	morir
difficult	difícil
dining car (train)	coche comedor
dinner	cena
direct	directo
direction	dirección
dirty	sucio
discount	descuento
disease	enfermedad
disease, venereal	enfermedad venérea
disinfectant	desinfectante
disturb	molestar
divorced	divorciado[a]
dizziness	vértigo
doctor	doctor[a]
dog	perro
doll	muñeca
dome	cúpula
donkey	burro
door	puerta
dormitory	dormitorio
dot (computer)	punto
double	doble
down	abajo

download	bajar
downtown	centro
dozen	docena
dream (n)	sueño
dream (v)	soñar
dress (n)	vestido
drink (n)	bebida
drink (v)	beber, tomar
drive (v)	conducir
driver	conductor
drunk	borracho[a]
dry (adj)	seco
dry (v)	secar
dryer	secadora
dungeon	calabozo
duty free	libre de impuestos

E

each	cada
ear	oreja
earache	dolor de oído
early	temprano
earplugs	tapón de oidos
earrings	pendientes
earth	tierra
east	este
Easter	Pascua
easy	fácil
eat	comer, tomar
education	educación
elbow	codo
electrical adapter	adaptador eléctrico
elevator	ascensor
e-mail	correo electrónico
e-mail address	dirección de correo electrónico

embarrassing	embarazoso
embassy	embajada
emergency	emergencia
emergency exit	salida de emergencia
emergency room	urgencias
empty	vacío
engineer	ingeniero
English	inglés
enjoy	disfrutar
enough	suficiente
entrance	entrada
entrance (road)	entrada
envelope	sobre
epilepsy	epilepsia
eraser	borrador
Europe	Europa
evening	la tarde
every	todo
everything	todo
exactly	exactamente
example	ejemplo
excellent	excelente
except	excepto
exchange (n)	cambio
excuse me	lo siento
exhausted	agotado[a]
exit	salida
exit, emergency	salida de emergencia
expensive	caro
explain	explicar
eye	ojo
eye shadow	sombra de ojos
eyeliner	lápiz de ojos

F

face	cara
face cleanser	limpiadora de cara
face powder	polvos para la cara
facial tissue	pañuelos (de papel), toallitas para la cara
factory	fábrica
fair (just)	justo
fall (v)	caer
false	falso
family	familia
famous	famoso[a]
fan belt	correa del ventilador
fantastic	fantástico[a]
far	lejos
farm	granja
farmer	granjero[a]
fashion	moda
fat (adj)	gordo[a]
fat (n)	grasa
father	padre
faucet	grifo
fax	fax
fear (v)	temer
February	febrero
female	femenino
ferry	transbordador
festival	festival
fever	fiebre
few	poco
field	campo
fight (n)	pelea
fight (v)	discutir
fine (good)	bueno

finger	dedo
fingernail	uña
finish (v)	terminar
fire	fuego
fireworks	fuegos artificiales
first	primero
first aid	primeros auxilios
first class	primera clase
first-aid cream	crema de primera ayuda
fish (n)	pescado
fish (v)	pescar
fix (v)	arreglar
fizzy	gaseoso
flag	bandera
flash (camera)	flash
flashlight	linterna
flavor (n)	sabor
flea	pulga
flea market	rastro
flight	vuelo
flip-flops	chanquetas
floss, dental	seda dental
flower	flor
flower market	floristería
flu	gripe
fly (n)	mosca
fly (v)	volar
fog	nieble
food	comida
food poisoning	envenenamiento de comida
foot	pie
football (soccer)	fútbol
football, American	fútbol americano
for	para

forbidden	prohibido
foreign	extranjero[a]
forget	olvidar
fork	tenedor
formula (for baby)	leche
fortress (Moorish)	alcazar
foundation (makeup)	base para la cara
fountain	fuente
fragile	frágil
France	Francia
free (no cost)	gratis
fresh	fresco
Friday	viernes
friend	amigo[a]
friendship	amistad
Frisbee	frisbee
from	de
fruit	fruta
fun	diversión
funeral	funeral
funny	divertido[a]
furniture	muebles
fuses	fusibles
future	futuro

G

gallery	galería
game	juego
garage	garaje
garden	jardín
gardening	jardineria
gas	gas
gas station	gasolinera
gauze	gasa
gay	homosexual
generous	generoso[a]

gentleman	caballero
genuine	auténtico
Germany	Alemania
gift	regalo
girl	chica
give	dar
glass	vaso
glasses (eye)	gafas
gloves	guantes
go	ir
go through	atravesar
God	Dios
gold	oro
golf	golf
good	bueno
good day	buenos días
goodbye	adiós
Gothic	Gótico
Gothic-Islamic	Mudéjar
(post-Reconquest	
Moorish)	
grammar	gramática
granddaughter	nieta
grandfather	abuelo
grandmother	abuela
grandson	nieto
gray	gris
greasy	grasiento
great	magnífico[a]
Great Britain	Gran Bretaña
Greece	Grecia
green	verde
grocery store	supermercado
guarantee	garantía
guest	invitado[a]
guide	guía
guidebook	guía

guided tour	visita con guía
guilty	culpable
guitar	guitarra
gum	chicle
gun	pistola
gymnastics	gimnasia
gynecologist	ginecólogo[a]

H

hair	pelo
hairbrush	cepillo del pelo
haircut	corte de pelo
hall (big room)	sala
hall (passage)	pasillo
hand	mano
hand lotion	crema de manos
handicapped	minusvalido[a]
handicrafts	artesanía
handle (n)	tirador
handsome	guapo[a]
happiness	alegría
happy	feliz, contento[a]
harbor	puerto
hard	difícil
hardware store	ferretería
hash (drug)	hachís
hat	sombrero
hate	odiar
have	tener
hay fever	fiebre del heno
he	él
head	cabeza
headache	dolor de cabeza
headlights	faros
health	salud
health insurance	seguro médico

healthy	sano
hear	oír
heart	corazón
heart condition	problemas de corazón
heat (n)	calor
heaven	cielo
heavy	pesado
hello	hola
help (n)	ayuda
help (v)	ayudar
helpful	amable
hemorrhoids	hemorroides
here	aquí
hi	hola
high	alto
high blood pressure	tensión alta
highchair	silla para niños
highway	autopista
hill	colina
history	historia
hitchhike	hacer auto-stop
hobby	pasatiempo
hockey	hockey
hole	agujero
holiday	festivo
homemade	hecho en casa
homesick	morriña
honest	honesto[a]
honeymoon	luna de miel
hope	esperanza
horrible	horrible
horse	caballo
horse riding	montar a caballo
hospital	hospital
hot	calor

hotel	hotel
hour	hora
house	casa
how	cómo
how many	cuánto
how much ($)	cuánto cuesta
hungry	hambriento[a]
hurry (v)	apresurarse
husband	marido
hydrofoil	hidroplano
hyphen (-)	guión

I

I	yo
ice	hielo
ice cream	helado
if	si
ill	enfermo[a]
immediately	inmediatamente
important	importante
imported	importado
impossible	imposible
Impressionist	Impresionista
in	en
included	incluido
incredible	increíble
independent	independiente
indigestion	indigestión
industry	industria
infection	infección
infection, urinary	infección urinaria
inflammation	inflamación
information	información
injured	herido[a]
innocent	inocente
insect	insecto

insect repellant	liquido de insectos
inside	interior
instant	instante
instead	en vez de
insurance	seguro
insurance, health	seguro médico
insured	asegurado[a]
intelligent	inteligente
interesting	interesante
Internet	Internet
Internet access	acceso a Internet
Internet café	café de Internet
intersection	intersección
intestines	intestinos
invitation	invitación
iodine	yodo
Ireland	Irlanda
is	es
island	isla
Italy	Italia
itch (n)	comezón

J

jacket	chaqueta
January	enero
jaw	mandíbula
jeans	vaqueros
jewelry	joyas
jewelry shop	joyería
Jewish	judío[a]
job	trabajo
jogging	footing
joint (marijuana)	porro
joke (n)	chiste

journey	viaje
juice	zumo
July	julio
jump	saltar
June	junio

K

keep (v)	guardar
kettle	olla
key	llave
kill	matar
kind	amable
king	rey
kiss (n)	beso
kitchen	cocina
kitchenette	cocina
knee	rodilla
knife	cuchillo
knights	caballería
know	saber

L

lace	encaje
ladder	escalera de mano
ladies	señoras
lake	lago
lamb	cordero
language	lenguaje
large	grande
last	último[a]
late	tarde
later	más tarde
laugh (v)	reír
launderette	lavandería
laundry soap	detergente
lawyer	abogado[a]
laxative	laxativo

lazy	perezoso[a]
learn	aprender
leather	cuero
leave	salir
left (direction)	izquierda
leg	pierna
lend	prestar
lenses, contact	lentillas
letter	carta
library	biblioteca
lies	mentiras
life	vida
light (n)	luz
light bulb	bombilla
lighter (n)	encendedor
like (v)	gustar
linen	lino
lip	labio
lip salve	cacao de labios
lipstick	barra de labios
list	lista
listen	escuchar
liter	litro
little	pequeño
live (v)	vivir
local	local
lock (n)	cerradura
lock (v)	cerrar
lockers	casilleros
look	mirar
lost	perdido[a]
lotion, hand	crema de manos
loud	ruidoso[a]
love (n)	amor
love (v)	amar
lover	amante
low	bajo

luck	suerte
luggage	equipaje
luggage, carry-on	equipaje de mano
lukewarm	templado
lungs	pulmones

M

macho	macho
mad	enfadado[a]
magazine	revista
mail (n)	correo
main	principal
make (v)	hacer
makeup	maquillaje
male	masculino
mall (shopping)	centro comercial
man	hombre
manager	director
many	mucho
map	mapa
marble (material)	mármol
March	marzo
marijuana	marihuana
market	mercado
market, flea	rastro
market, flower	floristería
market, open-air	mercado municipal
married	casado[a]
mascara	máscara
mass	misa
matches	cerillas
maximum	máximo
May	mayo
maybe	tal vez

meat	carne	moment	momento
mechanic	mecánico[a]	monastery	monasterio
medicine	medicina	Monday	lunes
medicine, cold	medicina para el resfriado	money	dinero
		month	mes
medicine, non-aspirin substitute	Nolotil	monument	monumento
		moon	luna
medieval	Medieval	Moorish	Moros
medium	mediano	Moorish blue tile	azulejo
men	hombres	Moorish castle	alcazaba
menstrual cramps	dolor de la menstruación	Moorish fortress / palace	alcazar
menstruation	menstruación	Moors	Moriscos
menu	menú	more	más
message	recado	morning	mañana
metal	metal	Morocco	Marruecos
meter, taxi	taxímetro	mosque	mezquita
midnight	medianoche	mosquito	mosquito
migraine	jaqueca	mother	madre
military	ejército	motor scooter	motocicleta
mineral water	agua mineral	motorcycle	moto
minimum	mínimo	mountain	montaña
minutes	minutos	moustache	bigote
mirror	espejo	mouth	boca
miscarriage	aborto espontáneo	movie	película
		Mr.	Señor
Miss	Señorita	Mrs.	Señora
mistake	error	much	mucho
misunderstanding	malentendido	muggy	húmedo
		muscle	músculo
mix (n)	mixto	museum	museo
moat	foso	music	música
modem	modem	Muslim	musulmán[a]
modern	moderno	my	mi
moisturizer	hidratante		
moleskin	lunar		
mom	mamá		

N

nail (finger)	uña
nail clipper	corta uñas
nail polish	esmalte de uñas
nail polish remover	quitaesmaltes
naked	desnudo[a]
name	nombre
napkin	servilleta
narrow	estrecho
nationality	nacionalidad
natural	natural
nature	naturaleza
nausea	náusea
near	cerca
necessary	necesario
neck	cuello
necklace	collar
need	necesitar
needle	aguja
nephew	sobrino
nervous	nervioso[a]
Netherlands	Holanda
never	nunca
new	nuevo
newspaper	periódico
newsstand	kiosco
next	siguiente; próximo[a]
nice	amable
nickname	apodo
niece	sobrina
night	noche
nightgown	camisón
no	no
no vacancy	completo
noisy	ruidoso[a]
non-aspirin substitute	Nolotil
non-smoking	no fumadores
noon	mediodía
normal	normal
north	norte
nose	nariz
not	no
notebook	cuaderno
nothing	nada
November	noviembre
now	ahora
nurse	enfermero[a]
nylon (material)	nilón
nylons (panty hose)	medias

O

O.K.	O.K.
occupation	oficio
occupied	ocupado
ocean	océano
October	octubre
of	de
office	oficina
office supplies store	papelería
oil (n)	aceite
old	viejo[a]
Olympics	Olimpíada
on	sobre
on time	puntual
once	una vez
one way (street)	dirección única
one way (ticket)	de ida
only	sólo
open (adj)	abierto

open (v)	abrir
open-air market	mercado municipal
opening hours	horas de apertura
opera	ópera
operator	telefonista
optician	óptico
or	o
orange (color or fruit)	naranja
organ	órgano
original	original
other	otro
oven	horno
over (finished)	terminado
own (v)	poseer
owner	dueño[a]

P

pacifier	chupete
package	paquete
paddleboat	barca de pedales
page	página
pail	cubo
pain	dolor
pain killer	analgésico
pains, chest	dolor de pecho
painting	pintura
pajamas	pijamas
palace	palacio
palace (Moorish)	alcazar
panties	bragas
pants	pantalones
paper	papel
paper clip	clip
parents	padres
park (garden)	parque

park (v)	aparcar
parking lot	aparcamiento
party	fiesta
passenger	pasajero[a]
passport	pasaporte
past	pasado
pastry shop	pastelería
pay	pagar
peace	paz
pedestrian	peatón
pen	bolígrafo
pencil	lápiz
penis	pene
people	gente
percent	porciento
perfect (adj)	perfecto
perfume	perfume
period (of time)	período
period (woman's)	regla
person	persona
pet (n)	animal de casa
pewter	peltre
pharmacy	farmacia
phone (n)	teléfono
phone booth	cabina telefónica
phone, mobile	teléfono móvil
photo	foto
photocopy	fotocopia
photocopy shop	fotocopias
pickpocket	carterista
picnic	picnic
piece	pedazo
pig	cerdo
pill	píldora
pill, birth control	píldora anticonceptiva
pillow	almohada

pin	alfiler
PIN code	código, número clave
pink	rosa
pity, it's a	que lástima
pizza	pizza
plain	al natural
plane	avión
plant	planta
plastic	plástico
plastic bag	bolsa de plástica
plate	plato
Plateresque (frilly late Gothic)	Plataresco
platform (train)	andén
play (v)	jugar
playground	área para jugar
playpen	parque para niños
please	por favor
pliers	alicates
pneumonia	pulmonía
pocket	bolsillo
point (v)	apuntar
police	policía
politicians	políticos
pollution	polución
polyester	poliester
poor	pobre
porcelain	porcelana
pork	cerdo
Portugal	Portugal
possible	posible
postcard	carta postal
poster	cartel
power	poder
powerful	poderoso[a]
practical	práctico[a]
pregnancy	embarazo

pregnancy test	prueba de embarazo
pregnant	embarazada
prescription	prescripción
present (gift)	regalo
pretty	bonito[a]
price	precio
priest	sacerdote
print	imprimir
private	privado
problem	problema
profession	profesión
prohibited	prohibido
pronunciation	pronunciacion
prosper	prosperar
Protestant	protestante
public	público
pull	tirar
pulpit	púlpito
pulse	pulso
pump (n)	bomba de aire
punctual	puntual
purple	morado
purse	bolsa
push	empujar

Q

quality	calidad
quarter (1/4)	cuarta parte
queen	reina
question (n)	pregunta
quiet	tranquilo[a]

R

R.V.	caravana
rabbit	conejo
racism	racismo

radiator	radiador	**rich**	rico[a]
radio	radio	**right (correct)**	correcto[a]
raft	balsa	**right (direction)**	derecha
railway	ferrocarril	**ring (n)**	sortija
rain (n)	lluvia	**ripe**	maduro
rainbow	arco iris	**river**	río
raincoat	impermeable	**robbed**	robado
rape (n)	violación	**rock (n)**	roca
rash	erupción	**roller skates**	patines
rash, diaper	escozor del pañal	**Romanesque**	Románico
raw	crudo	**romantic**	romántico[a]
razor	Gilete, maquinilla	**Romantic**	Romántico
	de afeitar	**roof**	techo
ready	listo[a]	**room**	habitación
receipt	recibo	**rope**	cuerda
receive	recibir	**rotten**	podrido
receptionist	recepcionista	**roundabout**	glorieta
recipe	receta	**roundtrip**	ida y vuelta
recommend	recomendar	**rowboat**	bote
rectum	recto	**rucksack**	mochila
red	rojo	**rug**	alfombra
refill (n)	recambio	**ruins**	ruinas
refugees	refugiados	**run (v)**	correr
refund (n)	reembolso	**Russia**	Rusia
relax	relajar		
relaxation	relajación	**S**	
relic	reliquia	**sad**	triste
religion	religión	**safe**	seguro[a]
remember	recordar	**safety pin**	imperdible
Renaissance	Renacimiento	**sailboat**	barco de vela
rent (v)	alquilar	**saint**	santo[a]
repair	arreglar	**sale**	rebajas
reservation	reserva	**same**	mismo
reserve	reservar	**sandals**	sandalias
respect (n)	respeto	**sandwich**	bocadillo
respect (v)	respetar	**sanitary napkins**	compresas
retired	jubilado[a]	**Santa Claus**	Papá Noel

English	Spanish
Saturday	sábado
save (computer)	guardar
scandalous	escandaloso
Scandinavia	Escandinavia
scarf	bufanda
school	colegio
science	ciencia
scientist	científico[a]
scissors	tijeras
scotch tape	cinta adhesiva
screwdriver	destornillador
sculptor	escultor[a]
sculpture	escultura
sea	mar
seafood	marisco
seat	asiento
second	segundo
second class	segunda clase
secret	secreto
see	ver
self-service	auto-servicio
sell	vender
send	enviar
seniors	la tercera edad
separate	separado
September	septiembre
serious	serio
service	servicio
service, church	misa, servicio
sex	sexo
sexy	sexy
shade	sombra
shampoo	champú
shaving cream	espuma de afeitar
she	ella
sheet	sábana

English	Spanish
shell	concha
ship (n)	barco
ship (v)	enviar
shirt	camisa
shoelaces	cordones
shoes	zapatos
shoes, tennis	zapatillas de tenis
shop (n)	tienda
shop, antique	anticuarios
shop, barber	barbería
shop, camera	tienda de fotos
shop, cell phone	tienda de teléfonos móviles
shop, coffee	cafetería
shop, jewelry	joyería
shop, pastry	pastelería
shop, photocopy	fotocopias
shop, souvenir	tienda de souvenirs
shop, sweets	tienda de dulces
shop, wine	tienda de vinos
shopping	compras
shopping mall	centro comercial
short	corto[a]
shorts	pantalones cortos
shoulder	hombros
show (n)	espectáculo
show (v)	enseñar
shower	ducha
shy	tímido[a]
sick	enfermo[a]
sign	señal
signature	firma
silence	silencio
silk	seda

silver	plata	snore	roncar
similar	similar	snorkel	tubo de respiración
simple	sencillo	soap	jabón
sing	cantar	soap, laundry	detergente
singer	cantante	soccer	fútbol
single	soltero[a]	socks	calcetines
sink	lavabo	some	algo
sink stopper	tapón	something	alguna cosa
sinus problems	sinusitis	son	hijo
sir	señor	song	canción
sister	hermana	soon	pronto
size	talla	sore throat	dolor de garganta
skating	patinaje	sorry	lo siento
ski (v)	esquiar	sour	agrio
skiing	esquí	south	sur
skin	piel	souvenir	tienda de
skinny	delgado[a]	shop	souvenirs
skirt	falda	Spain	España
sky	cielo	sparkplugs	bujías
sleep (v)	dormir	speak	hablar
sleeper (train)	coche cama	specialty	especialidad
sleeping bag	saco de dormir	speed	velocidad
sleepy	soñoliento[a]	spend	gastar
sleeves	mangas	spider	araña
slice	rodaja	spoon	cuchara
slide (photo)	diapositiva	sport	deporte
slip	calzoncillo	spring (n)	primavera
slippers	zapatillas	square (town)	plaza
slippery	resbaladizo	stairs	escaleras
slow	despacio[a]	stamp	sello
small	pequeño[a]	stapler	grapadora
smell (n)	olor	star (in sky)	estrella
smile (n)	sonrisa	state	estado
smoke	humo	station	estación
smoking	fumadores	stomach	estomago
snack	pincho	stomachache	dolor de
sneeze (n)	estornudo		estómago

stoned	colocado[a]	sun	sol
stop (n)	parada	sunbathe	tomar el sol
stop (v)	parar	sunburn	quemadura
stoplight	semáforo	Sunday	domingo
stopper, sink	tapón	sunglasses	gafas de sol
store	tienda	sunny	soleado
store, department	grandes almacenes	sunrise	amanecer
store, hardware	ferretería	sunscreen	protección de sol
store, office supplies	papelería	sunset	puesta de sol
store, toy	juguetería	sunshine	luz del sol
storm	tormenta	sunstroke	insolación
story (floor)	planta	suntan (n)	bronceado
straight	derecho	supplement	suplemento
strange	extraño[a]	surfboard	tabla de surf
stream (n)	arroyo	surfer	surfista
street	calle	surprise (n)	sorpresa
string	cordón	swallow (v)	tragar
stroller	carrecoche	sweat (v)	sudar
strong	fuerte	sweater	suéter
stuck	atascado	sweet	dulce
student	estudiante	sweets shop	tienda de dulces
stupid	estúpido[a]	swelling (n)	hinchazón
sturdy	robusto	swim	nadar
style	estilo	swim suit	traje de baño
subway	metro	swim trunks	bañador
subway entrance	entrada al metro	swimming pool	piscina
		Switzerland	Suiza
subway exit	salida de metro	synagogue	sinagoga
subway map	mapa	synthetic	sintético
subway station	estación de metro		

T

subway stop	parada	table	mesa
suddenly	de repente	tail	rabo
suffer	sufrir	tail lights	luces de atrás
suitcase	maleta	take	tomar
summer	verano	take out (food)	para llevar
		talcum powder	polvos de talco

talk	hablar
tall	alto[a]
tampons	tampones
tanning lotion	bronceador
tap water	agua del grifo
tape (adhesive)	cinta adhesiva
tape (cassette)	cinta; casete
taste (n)	sabor
taste (try)	probar
tax	impuesto
taxi meter	taxímetro
teacher	profesor
team	equipo
teenager	joven
teeth	dientes
teething (baby)	dentición
telephone	teléfono
telephone card	tarjeta telefónica
television	telivisión
temperature	temperatura
tender	tierno
tennis	tenis
tennis shoes	zapatillas de tenis
tent	tienda de campaña
tent pegs	estacas de tienda
terrible	terrible
terrorists	terroristas
testicles	testículos
thanks	gracias
theater	teatro
thermometer	termómetro
they	ellos
thick	grueso
thief	ladrón
thigh	muslo

thin	delgado[a]
thing	cosa
think	pensar
thirsty	sediento[a]
thread	hilo
throat	garganta
through	a través
throw	tirar
Thursday	jueves
ticket	billete
tight	apretado
tile, blue (Moorish)	azulejo
time, on	puntual
timetable	horario
tire (n)	rueda
tired	cansado[a]
tissue, facial	pañuelos (de papel), toallitas para la cara
to	a
today	hoy
toe	dedo del pie
together	juntos
toilet	servicios
toilet paper	papel higiénico
token	ficha
toll	peage
toll-free	llamada gratuita
tomorrow	mañana
tomorrow, day after	pasado mañana
tonight	esta noche
too (much)	demasiado
tooth	diente
toothache	dolor dc muelas
toothbrush	cepillo de dientes
toothpaste	pasta de dientes
toothpick	palillo

total	total
tour	viaje
tour, guided	visita con guía
tourist	turista
tow truck	grúa
towel	toalla
tower	torre
town	pueblo
toy	juguete
toy store	juguetería
track (train)	vía
traditional	tradicional
traffic	tráfico
train	tren
train car	vagón, coche
transfer (n)	transbordo
transfer (v)	cambiar
translate	traducir
transmission fluid	líquido de transmisión
travel (v)	viajar
travel agency	agencia de viajes
traveler	viajante
traveler's check	cheque de viajero
treasury	tesoro
tree	árbol
trip	viaje
tripod	trípode
trouble	dificultad
T-shirt	camiseta
Tuesday	martes
tunnel	túnel
Turkey	Turquía
turn signal	intermitente
tweezers	pinzas
twins	gemelos

U

ugly	feo[a]
umbrella	paraguas
uncle	tío
unconscious	inconsciente
under	debajo
underpants	calzoncillos
underscore (_)	subraya
understand	entender
unemployed	sin empleo
unfortunate	desafortunado
United States	Estados Unidos
university	universidad
up	arriba
upstairs	de arriba
urethra	uretra
urgent	urgente
urinary infection	infección urinaria
us	nosotros
use (v)	usar
uterus	útero

V

vacancy sign	habitaciónes
vacancy, no	completo
vacant	libre
vacation	vacaciones
vagina	vagina
valid	válido
validate	validar
valley	valle
Vaseline	vaselina
vegetarian	vegetariano[a]
velvet	terciopelo
venereal	enfermedad

disease	venérea	waterskiing	esquí acuático
very	muy	we	nosotros
vest	chaleco	weather	tiempo
video	vídeo	Web site	página de la red
video camera	cámara de vídeo	wedding	boda
view	vista	Wednesday	miércoles
village	aldea	week	semana
vineyard	viñedo	weight	peso
violence	violencia	welcome	bienvenido
virus	virus	west	oeste
visit (n)	visita	wet	mojado
visit (v)	visitar	what	qué
vitamins	vitaminas	wheel	rueda
voice	voz	wheelchair-accessible	acceso de silla de ruedas
vomit	vomitar	when	cuándo
		where	dónde

W

waist	cintura	white	blanco
wait (v)	esperar	who	quién
waiter	camarero	why	por qué
waiting room	sala de espera	widow	viuda
waitress	camarera	widower	viudo
wake up	despertarse	wife	esposa
walk (v)	andar	wild	salvaje
wall, fortified	pared fortificada	wind	viento
wallet	cartera	window	ventana
want	querer	windshield wipers	limpiaparabrisas
war	guerra		
warm (adj)	caliente	windsurfing	windsurfing
wash	lavar	windy	ventoso
washer	lavadora	wine	vino
watch (n)	reloj	wine shop	tienda de vinos
watch (v)	vigilar	wing	ala
water	agua	winter	invierno
water, drinkable	agua potable	wish (v)	desear
water, tap	agua del grifo	with	con
waterfall	cascada	without	sin

DICTIONARY

English / Spanish

woman	mujer
women	mujeres
wood	madera
wool	lana
word	palabra
work (n)	trabajo
work (v)	trabajar
world	mundo
worst	peor
wrap (v)	envolver
wrist	muñeca
write	escribir

X

| X-ray | rayos x |

Y

year	año
yellow	amarillo
yes	sí
yesterday	ayer
you (formal)	usted
you (informal)	tú
young	joven
youth	juventude
youth hostel	albergue de juventud
youths	jóvenes

Z

zero	cero
zip code	código postal
zip-lock bag	bolsa de cremallera
zipper	cremallera
zoo	zoo

TIPS FOR HURDLING
THE LANGUAGE BARRIER

Don't Be Afraid to Communicate

Don't be afraid to communicate. Even the best phrase book won't satisfy your needs in every situation. To really hurdle the language barrier, you need to leap beyond the printed page and dive into contact with the locals. Never allow your lack of foreign language skills to isolate you from the people and cultures you traveled halfway around the world to experience. Remember that in every country you visit, you're surrounded by expert, native-speaking tutors. Spend bus and train rides letting them teach you.

Start conversations by asking politely in the local language, "Do you speak English?" When you speak English with someone from another country, talk slowly, clearly, and with carefully chosen words. Use what the Voice of America calls "simple English." You're talking to people who are wishing it was written down, hoping to see each letter as it tumbles out of your mouth. Pronounce each letter, avoiding all contractions and slang. For bad examples, listen to other tourists.

Keep things caveman-simple. Make single nouns work as entire sentences ("Photo?"). Use internationally-understood words ("Self-service" works in Madrid). Butcher the language if you must. The important thing is to make the effort. To get air mail stamps, you can flap your wings and say "tweet, tweet." If you want milk, moo and pull two imaginary udders. Risk looking like a fool.

If you're short on words, make your picnic a potluck. Pull out a map and point out your journey. Draw what you mean. Bring photos from home and introduce your family. Play cards or toss a Frisbee. Fold an origami bird for kids or dazzle 'em with sleight-of-hand magic.

Go ahead and make educated guesses. Many situations are easy-to-fake multiple choice questions. Practice. Read timetables, concert posters, and newspaper headlines. Listen to each language on a multilingual tour. Be melodramatic. Exaggerate the local accent. Self-consciousness is the deadliest communication-killer.

Choose multilingual people to communicate with, such as students, business people, urbanites, young well-dressed people, or anyone in the tourist trade. Use a small note pad to jot down handy phrases and to help you communicate more clearly with the locals by scribbling down numbers, maps, and so on. Some travelers carry important messages written on a small card: "Allergic to nuts," "Strict vegetarian," "Your finest ice cream."

International Words

As our world shrinks, more and more words hop across their linguistic boundaries and become international. Savvy travelers develop a knack for choosing words most likely to be universally understood ("auto" instead of "car," "kaput" instead of "broken," "photo" not "picture"). Internationalize your pronunciation . "University," if you play around with its sound (oo-nee-vehr-see-tay), will be understood anywhere. The average American is a real flunky in this area. Be creative.

Here are a few internationally understood words. Remember, cut out the Yankee accent and give each word a pan-European sound.

Amigo	Communist	Mañana	Restaurant
Attila	Computer	McDonald's	Rock 'n' roll
(mean, crude)	Disco	Michael Jackson	Self-service
Auto	Disneyland	Michelangelo	Sex / Sexy
Autobus	(wonderland)	(artistic)	Sport
("booos")	Elephant	Moment	Stop
Bank	(big clod)	No	Super
Beer	English	No problem	Taxi
Bill Gates	("Engleesh")	Nuclear	Tea
Bon voyage	Europa	OK	Telephone
Bye-bye	Fascist	Oo la la	Toilet
Camping	Hello	Pardon	Tourist
Casanova	Hercules	Passport	U.S. profanity
(romantic)	(strong)	Photo	University
Central	Hotel	Photocopy	Vino
Chocolate	Information	Picnic	Yankee,
Ciao	Internet	Police	Americano
Coffee	Kaput	Post	
Coke, Coca-Cola	Mama mia	Rambo	

Spanish Verbs

These conjugated verbs will help you construct a caveman sentence in a pinch.

Spanish has two different verbs that correspond to the English "to be"—*ser* and *estar*. Generally speaking, *ser* is used to describe a condition that is permanent or longer-lasting, and *estar* is used for something that is temporary. Which verb you use can determine the meaning of the sentence. For example, *"Ricardo es contento,"* using *ser*, means that Ricardo is a happy, content person (as a permanent personality trait). *"Ricardo está contento,"* using *estar*, means that Ricardo is currently happy (temporarily in a good mood).

TO GO	*IR*	eer
I go	*yo voy*	yoh boy
you go (formal)	*usted va*	oo-**stehd** bah
you go (informal)	*tú vas*	too bahs
he / she goes	*él / ella va*	ehl / **ay**-yah bah
we go	*nosotros vamos*	noh-**soh**-trohs **bah**-mohs
you go (plural formal)	*ustedes van*	oo-**stehd**-ays bahn
they (m / f) go	*ellos / ellas van*	**ay**-yohs / **ay**-yahs bahn

TO BE (permanent)	*SER*	sehr
I am	*yo soy*	yoh soy
you are (formal)	*usted es*	oo-**stehd** ays
you are (informal)	*tú eres*	too **ay**-rays
he / she is	*él / ella es*	ehl / **ay**-yah ays
we are	*nosotros somos*	noh-**soh**-trohs **soh**-mohs
you are (plural formal)	*ustedes son*	oo-**stehd**-ays sohn
they (m / f) are	*ellos / ellas son*	**ay**-yohs / **ay**-yahs sohn

TO BE (temporary)	*ESTAR*	ay-**star**
I am	*yo estoy*	yoh ay-**stoy**
you are (formal)	*usted está*	oo-**stehd** ay-**sta**
you are (informal)	*tú estás*	too ay-**stahs**
he / she is	*él / ella está*	ehl / **ay**-yah ay-**sta**
we are	*nosotros estamos*	noh-**soh**-trohs ay-**stah**-mohs
you are (plural formal)	*ustedes están*	oo-**stehd**-ays ay-**stahn**
they (m / f) are	*ellos / ellas están*	**ay**-yohs / **ay**-yahs ay-**stahn**

TO DO, TO MAKE	*HACER*	ah-**thehr**
I do	*yo hago*	yoh **ah**-goh
you do (formal)	*usted hace*	oo-**stehd ah**-thay
you do (informal)	*tú haces*	too **ah**-thays
he / she does	*él / ella hace*	ehl / **ay**-yah **ah**-thay
we do	*nosotros hacemos*	noh-**soh**-trohs ah-**thay**-mohs
you do (plural formal)	*ustedes hacen*	oo-**stehd**-ays **ah**-thayn
they (m / f) do	*ellos / ellas hacen*	**ay**-yohs / **ay**-yahs **ah**-thayn

TO HAVE	*TENER*	tay-**nehr**
I have	*yo tengo*	yoh **tayn**-goh
you have (formal)	*usted tiene*	oo-**stehd** tee-**ehn**-ay
you have (informal)	*tú tienes*	too tee-**ehn**-ays
he / she has	*él / ella tiene*	ehl / **ay**-yah tee-**ehn**-ay
we have	*nosotros tenemos*	noh-**soh**-trohs tay-**nay**-mohs
you have (plural formal)	*ustedes tienen*	oo-**stehd**-ays tee-**ehn**-ehn
they (m / f) have	*ellos / ellas tienen*	**ay**-yohs / **ay**-yahs tee-**ehn**-ehn

TO SEE	*VER*	behr
I see	*yo veo*	yoh **bay**-oh
you see (formal)	*usted ve*	oo-**stehd** bay
you see (informal)	*tú ves*	too bays
he / she sees	*él / ella ve*	ehl / **ay**-yah bay
we see	*nostros vemos*	noh-**soh**-trohs **bay**-mohs
you see (plural formal)	*ustedes ven*	oo-**stehd**-ays bayn
they (m / f) see	*ellos / ellas ven*	**ay**-yohs / **ay**-yahs bayn

TO SPEAK	*HABLAR*	ah-**blar**
I speak	*yo hablo*	yoh **ah**-bloh
you speak (formal)	*usted habla*	oo-**stehd ah**-blah
you speak (informal)	*tú hablas*	too **ah**-blahs
he / she speaks	*él /ella habla*	ehl / **ay**-yah **ah**-blah
we speak	*nosotros hablamos*	noh-**soh**-trohs ah-**blah**-mohs
you speak (plural formal)	*ustedes hablan*	oo-**stehd**-ays ah-**blahn**
they (m / f) speak	*ellos / ellas hablan*	**ay**-yohs / **ay**-yahs **ah**-blahn

TO LIKE	*GUSTAR*	goo-**star**
I like	*me gusta*	may **goo**-stah
you like (formal)	*le gusta*	lay **goo**-stah
you like (informal)	*te gusta*	tay **goo**-stah
he / she likes	*le gusta*	lay **goo**-stah
we like	*nos gusta*	nohs **goo**-stah
you like (plural formal)	*les gusta*	lays **goo**-stah
they like	*les gusta*	lays **goo**-stah

TO WANT (literally "would like")	*GUSTARÍA*	goo-stah-**ree**-ah
I would like	*me gustaría*	may goo-stah-**ree**-ah
you would like (formal)	*le gustaría*	lay goo-stah-**ree**-ah
you would like (informal)	*te gustaría*	tay goo-stah-**ree**-ah
he / she would like	*le gustaría*	lay goo-stah-**ree**-ah
we would like	*nos gustaría*	nohs goo-stah-**ree**-ah
you would like (plural formal)	*les gustaría*	lays goo-stah-**ree**-ah
they would like	*les gustaría*	lays goo-stah-**ree**-ah

TO WANT	*QUERER*	kay-**rehr**
I want	*yo quiero*	yoh kee-**ehr**-oh
you want (formal)	*usted quiere*	oo-**stehd** kee-**ehr**-eh
you want (informal)	*tú quieres*	too kee-**ehr**-ehs
he / she wants	*él / ella quiere*	ehl / **ay**-yah kee-**ehr**-eh
we want	*nosotros queremos*	noh-**soh**-trohs kay-**ray**-mohs
you want (plural formal)	*ustedes quieren*	oo-**stehd**-ays kee-**ehr**-ehn
they (m / f) want	*ellos / ellas quieren*	**ay**-yohs / **ay**-yahs kee-**ehr**-ehn
TO NEED	*NECESITAR*	nay-thay-see-**tar**
I need	*yo necesito*	yoh nay-thay-**see**-toh
you need (formal)	*usted necesita*	oo-**stehd** nay-thay-**see**-tah
you need (informal)	*tú necesitas*	too nay-thay-**see**-tahs
he / she needs	*él / ella necesita*	ehl / **ay**-yah nay-thay-**see**-tah
we need	*nostros necesitamos*	noh-**soh**-trohs nay-thay-see-**tah**-mohs
you need (plural formal)	*ustedes necesitan*	oo-**stehd**-ays nay-thay-**see**-tahn
they (m / f) need	*ellos / ellas necesitan*	**ay**-yohs / **ay**-yahs nay-thay-**see**-tahn
TO HAVE TO	*TENER (QUE)*	tay-**nehr** (kay)
I have to	*yo tengo (que)*	yoh **tayn**-goh (kay)
you have to (formal)	*usted tiene (que)*	oo-**stehd** tee-**ehn**-ay (kay)
you have to (informal)	*tú tienes (que)*	too tee-**ehn**-ays (kay)
he / she has to	*él / ella tiene (que)*	ehl / **ay**-yah tee-**ehn**-ay (kay)
we have to	*nosotros tenemos (que)*	noh-**soh**-trohs tay-**nay**-mohs (kay)
you have to (plural formal)	*ustedes tienen (que)*	oo-**stehd**-ays tee-**ehn**-ehn (kay)
they (m / f) have to	*ellos / ellas tienen (que)*	**ay**-yohs / **ay**-yahs tee-**ehn**-ehn (kay)

Spanish Tongue Twisters

Tongue twisters are a great way to practice a language and break the ice with locals. Here are a few Spanish tongue twisters that are sure to challenge you and amuse your hosts.

Pablito clavó un clavito.
¿Qué clavito clavó Pablito?

Paul stuck in a stick.
What stick did Paul stick in?

Un tigre, dos tigres, tres tigres
comían trigo en un trigal.
Un tigre, dos tigres, tres tigres.

One tiger, two tigers, three tigers
ate wheat in a wheatfield.
One tiger, two tigers, three tigers.

El cielo está enladrillado.
¿Quién lo desenladrillará?
El desenladrillador que lo
desenladrille un buen
desenladrillador será.

The sky is bricked up.
Who will unbrick it?
He who unbricks it,
what a fine unbricker
he will be.

English Tongue Twisters

After your Spanish friends have laughed at you, let them try these tongue twisters in English.

If neither he sells seashells,
nor she sells seashells,
who shall sell seashells?
Shall seashells be sold?

Peter Piper picked a peck
of pickled peppers.

Rugged rubber baby
buggy bumpers.

The sixth sick sheik's
sixth sheep's sick.

Red bug's blood and
black bug's blood.

Soldiers' shoulders.

Thieves seize skis.

I'm a pleasant mother pheasant plucker. I pluck mother pheasants. I'm the most pleasant mother pheasant plucker that ever plucked a mother pheasant.

Spanish Song

Try connecting with locals by singing a song together. Most of the Spanish-language songs familiar to Americans originated in Latin America (such as *La Cucaracha*), but here is a romantic pop song that came from Spain in the 1970s and enjoyed modest success in the United States. If you haven't heard it, get a local to teach you the tune.

Eres Tú	**You Are**
—Juan Carlos Calderón	

Como una promesa,	Like a promise,
eres tú, eres tú,	you are, you are,
Como una mañana de verano.	Like a summer morning.
Como una sonrisa,	Like a smile,
eres tú, eres tú.	you are, you are.
Así, así, eres tú.	Like that, like that, you are.
Toda mi esperanza,	All of my hope,
eres tú, eres tú.	you are, you are.
Como lluvia fresca	Like fresh rain
en mis manos,	on my hands,
Como fuerte brisa,	Like a strong breeze,
eres tú, eres tú.	you are, you are.
Así, así, eres tú.	Like that, like that, you are.

(Chorus)

Eres tú como el agua de	You are like the water of my
mi fuente (algo así eres tú).	fountain (something like this, you are).
Eres tú el fuego de mi hogar.	You are the fire of my hearth.
Eres tú como el fuego	You are the fire
de mi hoguera.	of my bonfire.
Eres tú el trigo de mi pan.	You are the wheat of my bread.

(End Chorus)

Como mi poema,	Like my poem,
eres tú, eres tú.	you are, you are.
Como una guitarra	Like a guitar
en la noche,	in the night,
Todo mi horizonte	All my horizon
eres tú, eres tú.	you are, you are.
Así, así, eres tú.	Like that, like that, you are.

(Repeat Chorus)

Numbers and Stumblers

- Europeans write a few of their numbers differently than we do. 1 = 1 , 4 = 4 , 7 = 7 .
- Europeans write the date in this order: day/month/year. Christmas is 25-12-04, not 12-25-04.
- Commas are decimal points and decimals are commas. A dollar and a half is 1,50 and there are 5.280 feet in a mile.
- The European "first floor" isn't the ground floor, but the first floor up.
- When counting with your fingers, start with your thumb. If you hold up only your first finger, you'll probably get two of something.

APPENDIX

Let's Talk Telephones

Making Calls within a European Country: About half of all European countries use area codes (like we do); the other half uses a direct-dial system without area codes.

To make calls within a country that uses a direct-dial system (Belgium, Czech Republic, Denmark, France, Italy, Portugal, Norway, Spain, and Switzerland), you dial the same number whether you're calling across the country or across the street.

In countries that use area codes (such as Austria, Britain, Finland, Germany, Ireland, the Netherlands, and Sweden), you dial the local number when calling within a city, and you add the area code if calling long-distance within the country.

Making International Calls: You always start with the international access code (011 if you're calling from America or Canada, or 00 from Europe), then dial the country code of the country you're calling (see codes below).

What you dial next depends on the phone system of the country you're calling. If the country uses area codes, drop the initial zero of the area code, then dial the rest of the number.

Countries that use direct-dial systems (no area codes) vary in how they're accessed internationally by phone. You always start by dialing the international access code, followed by the country code. Then, if you're calling the Czech Republic, Denmark, Italy, Norway, Portugal, or Spain, simply dial the phone number in its entirety. But if you're calling Belgium, France, or Switzerland, drop the initial zero of the phone number.

Country Codes

After you've dialed the international access code, dial the code of the country you're calling.

Austria—43	Belgium—32
Britain—44	Canada—1
Czech Rep.—420	Denmark—45
Estonia—372	Finland—358
France—33	Germany—49
Gibraltar—350	Greece—30
Ireland—353	Italy—39
Morocco—212	Netherlands—31
Norway—47	Portugal—351
Spain—34	Sweden—46
Switzerland—41	United States—1

Directory Assistance

Dial 1004 for local numbers and 025 for international numbers (expensive). (Note: A 608 or 609 area code indicates a mobile phone.)

Embassies

American Embassy
- Tel. 915-872-240 or 915-872-200
- Serrano 75, **Madrid,** Spain
- www.embusa.es/cons/services.html

Canadian Embassy
- Tel. 914-233-250
- Núñez de Balboa 35, **Madrid,** Spain
- www.canada-es.org

Tear-Out Cheat Sheet

Tear out this sheet of Spanish survival phrases and keep it in your pocket to use in case you're caught without your phrasebook.

Hello.	Hola.	**oh**-lah
Do you speak English?	¿Habla usted inglés?	**ah**-blah oo-**stehd** een-**glays**
Yes. / No.	Sí. / No.	see / noh
I don't understand.	No comprendo.	noh kohm-**prehn**-doh
Please.	Por favor.	por fah-**bor**
Thank you.	Gracias.	**grah**-thee-ahs
You're welcome.	De nada.	day **nah**-dah
I'm sorry.	Lo siento.	loh see-**ehn**-toh
Excuse me (to get attention).	Perdone.	pehr-**doh**-nay
Excuse me (to pass).	Discúlpeme.	dee-**skool**-pay-may
It's (not) a problem.	(No) hay problema.	(noh) ī proh-**blay**-mah
Good.	Bueno.	**bway**-noh
Goodbye.	Adiós.	ah-dee-**ohs**
How much is it?	¿Cuánto cuesta?	**kwahn**-toh **kway**-stah
Write it?	¿Me lo escribe?	may loh ay-**skree**-bay
euro (€)	euro	**yoo**-roh
one / two	uno / dos	**oo**-noh / dohs
three / four	tres / cuatro	trays / **kwah**-troh
five / six	cinco / seis	**theen**-koh / says
seven / eight	siete / ocho	see-**eh**-tay / **oh**-choh
nine / ten	nueve / diez	**nway**-bay / dee-**ayth**
20	veinte	**bayn**-tay
30	treinta	**trayn**-tah
40	cuarenta	kwah-**rehn**-tah
50	cincuenta	theen-**kwehn**-tah
60	sesenta	say-**sehn**-tah
70	setenta	say-**tehn**-tah
80	ochenta	oh-**chehn**-tah
90	noventa	noh-**behn**-tah
100	cien	thee-**ehn**

English	Spanish	Pronunciation
I / We would like...	Me / Nos gustaría...	may / nohs goo-stah-**ree**-ah
...this.	...esto.	**ay**-stoh
...more.	...más.	mahs
...a ticket.	...un billete.	oon bee-**yeh**-tay
...a room.	...una habitación.	**oo**-nah ah-bee-tah-thee-**ohn**
...the bill.	...la cuenta.	lah **kwayn**-tah
Is it possible?	¿Es posible?	ays poh-**see**-blay
Where are the toilets?	¿Dónde están los servicios?	**dohn**-day ay-**stahn** lohs sehr-**bee**-thee-ohs
men	hombres, caballeros	**ohm**-brays, kah-bah-**yay**-rohs
women	mujeres, damas	moo-**hehr**-ays, **dah**-mahs
entrance / exit	entrada / salida	ayn-**trah**-dah / sah-**lee**-dah
no entry	sin salida	seen sah-**lee**-dah
open / closed	abierto / cerrado	ah-bee-**yehr**-toh / thehr-**rah**-doh
What time does this open / close?	¿A qué hora abren / cierran?	ah kay **oh**-rah **ah**-brehn / thee-**ay**-rahn
Just a moment.	Un momento.	oon moh-**mehn**-toh
Now.	Ahora.	ah-**oh**-rah
Soon.	Pronto.	**prohn**-toh
Later.	Más tarde.	mahs **tar**-day
Today.	Hoy.	oy
Tomorrow.	Mañana.	mahn-**yah**-nah
Monday	lunes	**loo**-nays
Tuesday	martes	**mar**-tays
Wednesday	miércoles	mee-**ehr**-koh-lays
Thursday	jueves	**h**way-bays
Friday	viernes	bee-**ehr**-nays
Saturday	sábado	**sah**-bah-doh
Sunday	domingo	doh-**meen**-goh

MAKING YOUR HOTEL RESERVATION

Most hotel managers know basic "hotel English." E-mailing or faxing are the preferred methods for reserving a room. They're clearer and more foolproof than telephoning. Photocopy and enlarge this form, or find it online at www.ricksteves.com/reservation.

One-Page Fax

To: _____ @ _____
　　　　　　　hotel　　　　　　　　　　　　　　　　　fax

From: _____ @ _____
　　　　　　　name　　　　　　　　　　　　　　　　　fax

Today's date: _____/_____/_____
　　　　　　　　　day　　month　　year

Dear Hotel_____

Please make this reservation for me:

Name: _____

Total # of people: _____ # of rooms: _____ # of nights: _____

Arriving: _____/_____/_____　　Arrival time: (24-hr clock):_____
　　　　　day　　month　　year　　　　　(I will telephone if I will be late)

Departing: _____/_____/_____
　　　　　　day　　month　　year

Room(s): Single____ Double____ Twin____ Triple____ Quad ___ Quint ____

With: Toilet____ Shower____ Bathtub____ Sink only____

Special needs: View____ Quiet ____ Cheapest____ Ground floor ____

Credit card: Visa____ Mastercard____ American Express____

Card #: _____

Expiration date: _____

Name on card: _____

If a deposit is necessary, you may charge me for the first night. Please e-mail, fax, or mail me confirmation of my reservation, along with the type of room reserved, the price, and whether the price includes breakfast. Please also inform me of your cancellation policy. Thank you.

Signature _____

Name _____

Address _____

City_____ State ____ Zip Code _____ Country_____

E-mail address _____

The perfect complement
to your phrase book

Travel with Rick Steves' candid, up-to-date advice
on the best places to eat and sleep, the must-see
sights, getting off the beaten path—and getting
the most out of every mile, minute, and dollar
while you're in Europe.

Take a trip to ricksteves.com

Our website is bursting with free information to boost your Travel I.Q. and liven up your European adventure. Here's a sampling of what you'll find…

▼ The latest from Rick on where he's been and what's hot in Europe.

▼ Excerpts from Rick's books, including self-guided tours.

▼ Rick's comprehensive **Guide to European Railpasses**, complete with maps.

▼ Frequently asked travel questions and years of archived newsletter articles.

▼ Streaming video previews from the all-new season of **Rick Steves' Europe**.

▼ Full itineraries and seat availability for our free-spirited tours.

▼ A directory of the best travel websites.

▼ Our **Rick Steves Travel Store** features fast, secure, user-friendly online ordering for all your favorite travel bags, accessories, books and videos— with frequent money-saving specials.

Free, fresh travel tips, all year long.

Visit **www.ricksteves.com**
to get Rick's free
64-page newsletter... and more!